Resisting Linguistic Imperialism in English Teaching

A. Suresh Canagarajah

Oxford University Press

OXFORD
UNIVERSITY PRESS

Great Clarendon Street, Oxford OX2 6DP

Oxford University Press is a department of the University of Oxford.
It furthers the University's objective of excellence in research, scholarship,
and education by publishing worldwide in

Oxford New York

Auckland Cape Town Dar es Salaam Hong Kong Karachi
Kuala Lumpur Madrid Melbourne Mexico City Nairobi
New Delhi Shanghai Taipei Toronto

With offices in

Argentina Austria Brazil Chile Czech Republic France Greece
Guatemala Hungary Italy Japan Poland Portugal Singapore
South Korea Switzerland Thailand Turkey Ukraine Vietnam

OXFORD and OXFORD ENGLISH are registered trade marks of
Oxford University Press in the UK and in certain other countries

© Oxford University Press 1999

The moral rights of the author have been asserted

Database right Oxford University Press (maker)

First published 1999
2009 2008 2007 2006 2005
10 9 8 7 6 5 4

ISBN-13: 978 0 19 442154 6
ISBN-10: 0 19 442154 6

Typeset by Oxford University Press

Printed in China

Contents

Acknowledgments iv

Preface vi

Introduction 1

1 Adopting a critical perspective on pedagogy 9

2 Challenges in researching resistance 39

3 Resistance to English in historical perspective 57

4 Conflicting curricula: interrogating student opposition 79

5 Competing pedagogies: understanding teacher opposition 103

6 Clashing codes: negotiating classroom interaction 125

7 Contrasting literacies: appropriating academic texts 147

8 The politics and pedagogy of appropriating discourses 173

Bibliography 199

Index 212

Acknowledgments

The authors and publisher are grateful to those who have given permission to reproduce the following extracts and adaptations of copyright material:

pp1, 57, 79, 173 Excerpts from 'A Far Cry from Africa', 'North and South', 'The Schooner Flight', 'The Season of Phantasmal Peace' from *The Collected Poems* 1948-1984 by Derek Walcott, published by Faber and Faber Ltd. Copyright © 1986 by Derek Walcott. Reprinted by permission of Farrar, Straus & Giroux, Inc. and Faber and Faber Limited.

p39 Excerpt from 'On African Writing' from *Chameleons and Gods* by Jack Mapanje. Reprinted by permission of Heinemann Educational Publishers, a division of Reed Educational & Professional Publishing Ltd.

p103 Excerpt from 'Song of Lawino' from *Song of Lawino and Song of Ocol* by Okot p'Bitek, published by East African Educational Publishers Ltd. Reprinted by permission of East African Educational Publishers Ltd.

p125 Excerpt from 'An Introduction' from *Summer in Calcutta* by Kamala Das. Reprinted by permission of the author.

To Nanthini, Lavannya, and Nivedhana

Preface

It is anachronistic to observe the conventions of textual ownership, such as copyright and author identification, when most authors know that their text is a collective product, representing many voices. Even if I were to leave aside such abstract forms of influence as my native community, and its history of struggle, I owe a debt of gratitude to far more people than I can acknowledge here.

While students and research subjects often contribute to books written by their teachers, that support tends to be passed over. So I must begin by thanking my students at the University of Jaffna (UJ), who turned out to be my teachers of pedagogy and politics. When I returned to my home town in 1984, as one more 'generic' English graduate nurtured on Elizabethan sonnets and romantic odes in the capital, Colombo, I discovered a student community that was spearheading a movement for social change. In very large classes conducted under mango trees during humid afternoons, with ears alert to catch any movement of trigger-happy military patrols, the students posed questions about the meaning and purpose of English in our community. They were in the middle of a grand project of national liberation, facing the harsh reality of earning a few more rupees for their families in difficult times of economic embargo. Yet many agreed to let me interview them, and to complete questionnaires, in what must have seemed an ivory tower preoccupation with pedantic research.

My colleagues at UJ also contributed much to my thinking, not least by manifesting a healthy suspicion towards my scholarship, when I returned from the USA in 1990 with a doctorate, flaunting my mastery of faddish post-modernist/post-structuralist discourses. When we weren't running to the underground bunker from our vulnerable third-floor office during air raids, we somehow found time to navigate our way through local and Western thinking on education and society. In a teaching community unused to formal research, my colleagues also suffered the discomfort of letting me sit at the back of their classes as they taught, and offered their after-class hours for interviews. I am especially indebted to A. J. Canagaratne—a veteran English instructor, and my mentor—who had started to think about the politics of ELT, and had even published in local circles, long before the subject became fashionable. The fact that Canagaratne's thinking has still not received a transnational audience may be a reflection of how the political economy of publishing and scholarship works against many periphery scholars.

My opportunity to indulge in academic publishing from within war-torn Jaffna was made possible by many people. My brothers Sudarshan, Nishan, and Jehan—who were graduate students (in unrelated fields) in England and the USA at that time—kept me in touch with developments in my discipline. They photocopied every article I wanted, bought me expensive books as they were printed, tracked down my manuscripts when they were lost in the post, and liaised my revisions with editors. Imagine the lengths they had to go to, to get Phillipson's *Linguistic Imperialism*, the inspiration for this book. After purchasing the book in England, they mailed it to a mutual friend in the capital, who found someone who was traveling to Jaffna and was prepared to carry it for me. The traveler was a student I did not know, who somehow brought the book (and a box of essential medicines only available in Colombo) across a heavily mined 'no man's land' in Omanthai, avoiding skirmishes between the militia at Vavuniya, and through a swamp at Elephant Pass. I no longer remember this person's name, nor the names of many others who kept the traffic of knowledge and information open in a community where making such sacrifices is taken for granted.

There are others at this end (in the West) who made my research work possible. Sandra Silberstein initiated me into the world of publishing, after finding some value in a manuscript sent to *TESOL Quarterly* from an unknown Sri Lankan town, in frayed recycled paper, typed on a worn-out ribbon, and clumsily edited with ink, accompanied by photocopies that were too smudged to be decipherable. As soon as the paper had been recommended for publication by the referees, she had it composed electronically for revision, mailed her correspondence multiple times to multiple addresses, so that communication was not broken, and somehow lived with the inordinate delays associated with sending revisions backwards and forwards across a battle zone. Few editors would have been so sensitive to the difficulties of periphery scholars. She then directed my sights higher, by being the first to suggest that I might develop my research work with a view to publishing a book with Oxford University Press.

The Press could not have engaged a better pair of readers for my manuscript than Henry Widdowson and Alastair Pennycook. While Widdowson checked for signs of pedagogical naiveté, Pennycook questioned any display of ideological shallowness. Both were rigorous but sympathetic reviewers, who motivated me to pursue my ideas with greater balance and discipline. Cristina Whitecross, my Editor and Publishing Manager at OUP, has advised me patiently over the five years this book was being developed. Her scrupulous editing has contributed a lot towards getting a coherent text. My friends Brian Morgan (University of Toronto) and John Flowerdew (City University of Hong Kong) have also commented on the draft. While thanking all of those mentioned above, I must take responsibility for any of the unavoidable choices taken here that may be seen as limitations.

Here in my new academic home at the City University of New York, the faculty at Baruch College have been generous in making it possible for me to complete the manuscript, while the reduction in my teaching load in each academic year has given me the time to engage in multiple revisions. I would also like to thank the department Chair, John Todd, and the Dean of the Weissman School of Arts and Sciences, Lexa Logue, for considering this project to be worthy of their support.

My wife, Nanthini, and our daughters, Lavannya and Nivedhana, have always been supportive of my endeavors. When I make eccentric decisions—such as abandoning peaceful Austin to teach in battle-scarred Jaffna immediately after obtaining my doctorate—they have made the necessary changes in lifestyle to accommodate my 'calling'. As my daughters cross cultural and linguistic borders again, entering elementary school in New Jersey, the daily challenges they experience in negotiating conflicting identities and values confirm to me that the events, experiences, and ideas discussed in this book are of more than academic concern.

Introduction

I who am poisoned with the blood of both,
Where shall I turn, divided to the vein?
I who have cursed
The drunken officer of British rule, how choose
Between this Africa and the English tongue I love?
Betray them both, or give back what they give?

Derek Walcott, *A Far Cry from Africa*

The conflict Walcott expresses is an everyday experience for millions of people in post-colonial communities. They find themselves torn between the claims of Western values and their indigenous cultures, between English and the vernacular. Ironically, however, with the passing of time, the possibility of choosing one or the other may no longer be open to them: the English language has become too deeply rooted in their soil, and in their consciousness, to be considered 'alien'.

In parts of the Third World, what is biologically true for Walcott—that two traditions mingle in his blood, and flow through his veins—is culturally true for entire populations. Some have chosen convenient, self-serving resolutions to this conflict, by understating the complex interconnection between the two linguistic traditions. History is replete with examples of colonized subjects who have 'betrayed' the claims of the vernacular for the advantages of English, and who now feel they are in some sense outsiders in both Western and local communities. Others, especially in the period since decolonization, have rejected English lock, stock, and barrel, in order to be faithful to indigenous traditions—a choice which has deprived many of them of enriching interactions with multicultural communities and traditions through the English language.

The alternative suggested by Walcott—to 'give back what they give' and respond favorably to both languages—can take many different forms. Instead of maintaining both languages separately, one can appropriate the second language, and absorb parts of it into the vernacular. The creative tension between the languages can also bring forth new discourses, as Walcott, who has referred to himself as 'the mulatto of style', so eloquently exemplifies in his own writing. The fact that such productive interactions are possible demonstrates that our consciousness is able to accommodate more than one language or culture, just as our languages can accommodate alien grammars and discourses. So it would appear that there are ways of transcending this painful linguistic conflict, and even of turning it to our advantage.

Achieving this transcendence, however, is not easy. It cannot be achieved by desiring a universal, race-less, culture-free identity. Such an ideal is only possible in our dreams—never in social reality, where we are fated to occupy one identity or the other, however much we might wish otherwise. The very fact that we are for ever rooted in the primary community of socialization is what enables us to negotiate or appropriate other languages (and cultures) more effectively. Research in language acquisition and cognitive development confirms that a thorough grounding in one's first language and culture enhances the ability to acquire other languages, literacies, and knowledge.[1] The achievement of new identities and discourses none the less involves a painful process of conflicting ideologies and interests. If we are to appropriate the language for our purposes, the oppressive history and hegemonic values associated with English have to be kept very much in mind, and engaged judiciously.

The negative or positive responses to the vernacular and English—leading either to the 'betrayal' of one language, or to the 'giving back' of both—are largely influenced by underlying differences in perspectives on power. A decision to reject English in order to be true to the vernacular (or vice versa) constitutes a specific ideological orientation. The assumptions made by proponents of this position are that subjects are passive, and lack agency to manage linguistic and ideological conflicts to their best advantage; languages are seen as monolithic, abstract structures that come with a homogeneous set of ideologies, and function to spread and sustain the interests of dominant groups. I will term such a deterministic perspective on power—which has had considerable influence in linguistics, discourse analysis, social sciences, and education—the *reproduction orientation*. The alternative response, of engaging favorably with both languages, calls for a different set of assumptions, in which subjects have the agency to think critically and work out ideological alternatives that favor their own empowerment. It recognizes that while language may have a repressive effect, it also has the liberatory potential of facilitating critical thinking, and enabling subjects to rise above domination: each language is sufficiently heterogeneous for marginalized groups to make it serve their own purposes. This is the *resistance perspective* alluded to in the title of this book. It provides for the possibility that, in everyday life, the powerless in post-colonial communities may find ways to negotiate, alter, and oppose political structures, and reconstruct their languages, cultures, and identities to their advantage. The intention is not to *reject* English, but to *reconstitute* it in more inclusive, ethical, and democratic terms, and so bring about the creative resolutions to their linguistic conflicts sought by Walcott and others in the periphery.

This book takes the discussion on the post-colonial status of English beyond the stereotypical positions (for or against English; for or against the vernacular) adopted thus far. I want to reflect on the diverse interests and motivations of individuals while investigating the strategies they employ, with varying levels of success, in order to negotiate their linguistic conflicts in community and classroom contexts. I consider these issues as they relate to the activity of English language teaching (ELT). Applied linguistics and ELT have hitherto been influenced (perhaps unwittingly) by the dichotomizing perspectives referred to above. A debilitating monolingual/monocultural bias has revealed itself in the insistence on 'standard' English as the norm, the refusal to grant an active role to the students' first language in the learning and acquisition of English, the marginalization of 'non-native' English teachers, and the insensitive negativity shown by the pedagogies and discourses towards the indigenous cultural traditions. All such assumptions ignore the creative processes of linguistic mediation, interaction, and fusion that take place in social life.

To pursue these concerns is to adopt a socially-situated orientation to pedagogy, in which learning is considered as a value-free, pragmatic, egalitarian enterprise, and where the acquisition of a new language or discourse should not give rise to undue inner conflict among students. But, in the post-modern world, education has lost its innocence. The realization that education may involve the propagation of knowledges and ideologies held by dominant social groups has inspired a critical orientation to pedagogical paradigms. This book is informed by such a critical orientation to pedagogy and schooling, and explores the ideological and discursive conflicts experienced by learners of English in post-colonial communities.

Although teaching English worldwide has become a controversial activity, few ELT professionals have considered the political complexity of their enterprise. Does English offer Third World countries a resource that will help them in their development, as Western governments and development agencies would claim? Or is it a Trojan horse, whose effect is to perpetuate their dependence? In his major study of the politics of ELT, Phillipson (1992) conducts a scathing attack on English for functioning as a tool for imperialist relations and values. However, his reproductionist orientation is responsible for some of the limitations as well as the strengths of his book. There is inadequate sensitivity to the conflicting demands and desires experienced by Walcott and others like him. The overly global approach to the subject is not conducive to exploring the day-by-day struggles and negotiations with the language that take place in Third World communities. More importantly, the subtle forms of resistance to English and the productive processes of appropriation inspired by local needs, are not sufficiently represented. It is time, therefore, to take the exploration of this subject further.

The framework

This book explores the challenges and possibilities facing ELT in the context of the relationships between the *center* and the *periphery*. 'Center' refers to the technologically advanced communities of the West which, at least in part, sustain their material dominance by keeping less developed communities in periphery status.[2] Significant among the center nations are the traditionally 'native English' communities of North America, Britain, Australia, and New Zealand, and for the purposes of analyzing ELT in this book I will use 'center' in a restricted sense to refer to these communities (overlooking non-English-speaking center communities such as France and Germany). Because many less developed communities are former colonies of Britain, I will use the term 'periphery' here for such communities where English is of post-colonial currency, such as Barbados, India, Malaysia, and Nigeria. Also included under this label are many communities which formerly belonged to other imperial powers, such as Belgium, France, or Spain, but have now come under the neo-imperialist thrusts of English-speaking center communities. They include Indonesia, Mexico, South Korea, Tunisia, and Vietnam. The latter group of communities, in which English has acquired a somewhat limited and recent currency, is called the 'expanding circle' by Kachru (1986) to distinguish it from the British colonies listed earlier, which he calls the 'outer circle'. However, in this book I am using the label 'periphery' to accommodate both sets of communities. Although *post-colonial* is another label that can be employed to refer to these communities, I am primarily reserving this term to describe perspectives generated by periphery communities themselves.

The center/periphery terminology also helps us to represent another distinction crucial for this book: that of *native* English communities and *non-native* communities. Considerable rethinking is taking place on this linguistic categorization (Y. Kachru 1994, Sridhar 1994). Note that many speakers in the periphery use English as the first or dominant language; others may use it as a language that was simultaneously acquired with one or more local languages, and may display equal or native proficiency in them all. Add to this the argument that many of the periphery communities have developed their own localized forms of English, and might consider themselves to be native speakers of these new 'Englishes' (Kachru 1986). Since the native/non-native distinction loses its force in this context, I will stretch the center/periphery terminology to accommodate the linguistic distinction between the traditionally English-speaking center communities (which claim ownership over the language) and those periphery communities which have recently appropriated the language. The variants of these two communities will be referred to as *center Englishes* and *periphery Englishes*, respectively.

The organization

This book is primarily an investigation of classrooms from a critical pedagogical perspective. In the first chapter I argue that traditional understanding of education needs to be reconceived along the lines of a more critical pedagogy, and outline the philosophical changes that motivate the development of liberatory pedagogies. I then discuss the manner in which the life and thinking of periphery subjects relate to some of the Western academic discourses that influence both traditional *and* critical pedagogies as they are currently understood in the center. This is in tune with the aim of the book to develop *grounded theory*, in other words, a thinking on language, culture, and pedagogy that is motivated by the lived reality and everyday experience of periphery subjects.

A methodological approach suitable for this purpose is afforded by ethnography, which in attempting to understand the values and assumptions that motivate the behavior of people in their everyday contexts, provides a useful challenge to theories and pedagogies that are produced from the ivory towers of academia. Using an ethnographic perspective to understand the attitudes of teachers and students in the periphery, I will develop constructs that better reflect the challenges they face in ELT. However, it is important for an ethnographic orientation to be clearly defined and contextually circumscribed. This book focuses therefore on the Tamil community in the northern peninsula of Sri Lanka to illustrate some of the challenges facing post-colonial communities today. Choosing a small community in an already small island-state obviously limits the generalizations that can be made, but the interpretive depth deriving from careful observation of the everyday life of a community provides ethnographic validity.

A perspective generated from the periphery community by an insider to that community is badly needed in applied linguistic circles today. At a time when multiculturalism and diversity are fashionable movements in the center, knowledge construction in ELT, as in other academic fields, is still dominated by Western scholars. Realities of periphery communities and center influences are often discussed by center scholars, which accounts for some of their limitations (Phillipson 1992, Holliday 1994, Pennycook 1994a). The location of these scholars prevents their well-intentioned books from representing adequately the interests and aspirations of periphery communities. On the other hand, the fact that periphery scholars enjoy membership of these communities does not automatically make them authorities on the cultures and conditions they describe. Their intimacy also brings with it certain methodological and perspectival problems, as we shall see in Chapter 2.

The observations emerging from the Sri Lankan Tamil community will be compared to findings of scholars in other periphery communities. This will help us to theorize the pedagogical challenges for post-colonial communities. Since this book is not limited to periphery concerns, I will relate the pedagogical observations developed here to the dominant constructs in applied linguistics and ELT. It is the argument of many post-colonial thinkers that their insights challenge the legitimized knowledge of the center and its governing assumptions (hooks 1990, Said 1993).

The focus of this book is on the classroom life of periphery teachers and students. Many of the publications on center/periphery relations in ELT have approached the subject from a macroscopic theoretical perspective (Phillipson 1992, Pennycook 1994a), paying less attention to the micro-social level of linguistic and cultural life. For this reason, much of this book is given over to the narration of everyday life, and to the interactions of periphery communities. Whatever theoretical constructs are developed here will emerge through the narratives. But first, if we are to understand how reproduction and resistance are played out at the micro-social level, it is important to situate the classrooms in the larger historical and social contexts of the community. For this reason, in Chapter 3, before discussing classrooms, I will provide a bird's-eye view of the linguistic and other cultural developments in the Tamil community, seen in the light of post-colonial experiences elsewhere.

While the three introductory chapters contextualize the relevant theoretical, methodological, and historical background, the next four chapters analyze several specific areas in the ELT enterprise. The main questions we will ask are:

- What discourses do local students and teachers confront in teaching materials produced by center agencies? What effects do such discourses have on the language acquisition process? How do the agendas of the center textbooks conflict with the personal agendas local students bring to the classroom? How do students cope with the tensions that characterize their encounter with center-based teaching materials and hidden curricula?
- Which discourses inform the teaching methods promoted by the mainstream professional circles? How do these methods relate to the pedagogical traditions of periphery communities familiar to local teachers and students? What effects do center-based methods have on the language acquisition process in periphery communities? What are the challenges for periphery teachers in implementing these methods?
- How do teachers and students negotiate the challenges posed to their identity, community membership, and values, by the vernacular and English? How do they negotiate these tensions in their classroom discourse and interactions? What implications does such classroom discourse have for the development of communicative competence?
- What assumptions motivate the dominant pedagogical approaches for developing literacy skills in English? How do they relate to the traditions of literacy in periphery communities? What strategies do periphery students employ to deal with the discursive challenges they confront in practicing academic reading and writing in English?

This description of periphery classrooms and communities will prepare the ground, for proposals in the final chapter on how marginalized communities can acquire and use English language for their empowerment.

Notes

1 For a review of the relevant research in this area, see Hamers and Blanc 1989: 187–212.
2 Although there is a significant tradition of work in developing the center/ periphery perspective, dating from economist Frank (1969), the model that enjoys special currency these days is the *world systems perspective* outlined by social theorist Wallerstein (1974, 1991). While Wallerstein develops his model primarily in terms of economic relations, Giddens's (1990) multi-faceted model includes the nation-state system (i.e. a political dimension), world military order (a military dimension), and the international division of labor (a production dimension), in addition to economy. But even this analysis fails to do justice to the diverse domains that participate in constructing the world system. Galtung develops a multidimensional model that posits equal influence for multiple channels of center influence (Galtung 1971, 1980). In an interlocking, cyclical process, politico-economic dominance sustains mass media, technology, popular culture, education, transport, and other domains of center superiority. But Appadurai (1994) has recently argued that the geopolitical relationship is 'messy', with many ironies and paradoxes. For example, the periphery today displays a drive for technology and industrial production that surpasses the center. Appadurai therefore constructs a dynamic model which assumes disjuncture as a constitutive principle, and adopts a 'radically context-dependent' approach.

1 Adopting a critical perspective on pedagogy

The students crowded around the thatched classrooms on the university campus, warily eyeing the military helicopter circling overhead. Some suggested it was on the lookout for rebel troops, which could lead to another rocket attack on the nearby town; others said it was just a routine flight, taking supplies to the army base. As a majority began to favor the first explanation, the students started to look for an excuse to stay away from the English class, which was due to start shortly. Ravi could not make up his mind whether to go home early to join his family, or to stay ...

As Mrs Kandiah came into view, carrying her teaching material, and walking briskly towards the classroom, the students saw that she was determined to hold the class. Ravi and some of the others quickly made their way into the dilapidated study block, where they could hear the droning sound of the power generator through the classroom wall. This told them that Ravi's friends from secondary school, who had recently joined the resistance movement, were busy making fresh stocks of weapons and ammunition. Ravi always felt guilty when he heard them working, since before the university reopened he had said he wanted to join them. Where should he really be now—in the arms factory, or the classroom?

Mrs Kandiah—known to all as 'Mrs K.'—marched up to the podium and greeted them in her rather stilted British accent: 'Good morning, students.' For her students, Mrs K. represented order and discipline in the midst of the chaos and violence outside. She believed that education, and the English language in particular, could provide meaning and hope in an otherwise desperate environment. English could give her students employment, opportunities to get on in life, and access to the cultural and material privileges of more developed countries. Ravi's feelings about the language were more mixed: sometimes English represented a world that was remote and threatening, and far removed from his family and friends; at others, he was tempted by the images of sensual pleasure and material wealth endlessly promoted in foreign movies, magazines, and music.

One of the foreign cultural agencies based in the capital had recently sent the university several sets of ELT textbooks. From one of these books Mrs K. had picked out a particular activity she was sure her students would find interesting. In spite of all the difficulties, she prided herself on being well informed about the latest teaching methods and materials, and was currently championing a combination of process-oriented, collaborative, and task-based teaching methods. As usual, having no access to a photocopier or cassette player, she would be reading the text to the class herself. She explained that they should take notes on the short article, which was about a student living in Britain. After the students had heard the passage she would be asking them to practice the simple present, which they had studied in the previous class, as a group activity. Worried that they might be distracted by the noise and confusion outside, and not be able to focus all their attention on the text, she advised them to listen carefully for the main themes, and to look out for the grammatical structures she'd taught them in a recent lesson inductively.

Mrs K. began the first passage: 'Peter is in his final year at the University of Reading, where he is studying Chemistry. He hopes to obtain first class honors in his final examinations so that he can continue with postgraduate work in photochemistry.'

These words set Ravi thinking about his own situation. He had been worried for some time about whether he would ever be able to sit for his own degree. The civil war meant that some graduates had taken up to eight years to complete what was supposed to be a three-year course. Even if he managed to get his degree, he didn't know what he would do after that. The fighting had left more than half the local people without jobs; many had lost their homes as well. Worst of all, Ravi's father and several other local farmers had been arrested earlier in the year, on suspicion of helping the rebel forces, and no one had any idea when they might be freed. If Ravi was to have any hope of finding paid work to support his family, he would almost certainly have to leave his mother with his younger brother and sister, and move to the capital, or even to another country.

'Peter is very well organized, and usually manages a reasonable balance between work and study. Since he has exams this term, he tends to spend about two hours reading in the library after school, and another hour or so at home ...'

At the sound of a small explosion, Mrs K. paused momentarily in her reading. There was a scream from outside, and several students took cover beside their desks, but the blast had been some distance away. Mrs K. decided that this was hardly sufficient cause for dismissing the class, and carried on with the narration. She didn't consider this distraction to be life threatening—not yet.

'Peter doesn't spend all his time working. He also belongs to the photography club, which he helped to start up last year. He likes sailing, and goes surfing whenever he can in the summer term; in the winter he plays in the university rugby team.'

In the previous year, when the university was closed, Ravi had tried to keep up with his studies by day while training with the local militia by night, but it hadn't worked out too well. The training exercises and political classes took up too much of his time and energy, and meant he couldn't help his mother with their smallholding.

'*At weekends he spends some time relaxing with friends.*'

Ravi spent much of his time working on the family farm. He watered the plants, manured the soil, and helped his mother take their produce to the Monday market. Seeds and fertilizers were very expensive, but they couldn't afford not to cultivate their small plot of land. Even though the recent harvest had been very poor, the family depended on the rice they grew, and the baskets his mother made.

'*On Saturday nights he usually goes to a party or a disco with his girlfriend, Susan, but sometimes they borrow his parents' car and go to a disco or a play in London.*'

This passage provoked mild excitement in the class. Giggles could be heard coming from the far end of the classroom, where the girls had barricaded themselves behind some empty desks, at a safe distance from the boys. Ravi felt tempted to join his friends, who were teasing the girls. Rajan was calling out to them: 'It's party time!', 'How about it?', 'Who's gonna dance with me?' As an avid watcher of pirated American videos, Rajan's colloquial English was particularly fluent—and as a diligent student, he already felt happier talking about science in English than in his first language.

Mrs K. pretended not to hear anything, and divided the class into separate groups of boys and girls. She asked them to draw a chart showing how Peter organized his time. Ravi had been too preoccupied with his own thoughts to remember what Peter did or didn't do, and with the exception of Rajan, the rest of his group hadn't paid much attention to the discussion either. The noise of another helicopter in the distance took their minds away from the work they had been doing in the class, and set them talking in their own language about the latest fighting, and the rumors they'd heard of another military operation. They knew that Mrs K. would go over the passage again at the end, and provide them with the correct answers. After all, that's what she was supposed to do—she was the teacher.

Ravi sat across the aisle from Rajan, who never seemed to have trouble with his English exercises. Apart from that, they had a lot in common; in particular, both detested the poverty, chaos, and corruption that surrounded them, and longed for the sort of full and purposeful life enjoyed by Peter in the story. However, only Rajan believed Mrs K. when she said that English could give him that sort of life—an opportunity to go abroad to study or work. That's why he liked English classes best of all.[1]

In the West, there is a rose-tinted, but not entirely false image of university life in which classrooms are equipped with the latest audio-visual and computer technology, and students go quietly about their work in a setting of green lawns and ancient quadrangles. This is far from being the full picture, but conditions are certainly much better than those found in most periphery communities, where the perennial questions about the purposes, attitudes, motivations, and consequences of learning, and the costs and benefits of schooling, have to be weighed with immense care. Education has many implications for a student's identity and relationships, which might extend, as in the case of Ravi and Rajan, to making choices between an involvement in community struggles, and the prospect of looking for a safer and more prosperous life elsewhere. These conflicts naturally affect students' attitudes towards learning English—including the goals and means of ELT—and show how far attitudes to ELT can be informed, shaped, and challenged by the larger social and political forces outside the classroom.

This book will bring a sharper orientation to such questions as they inform ELT in the periphery. The inquiry is controversial because contemporary education as a whole (not only ELT) is considerably influenced by the knowledge produced, disseminated, and defined by the materially-developed center communities (Scheurich and Young 1997). It is well known that Western centers of education, research, and publishing—whether funded by state or non-governmental agencies—provide financial backing, donate textbooks, share expertise, train teachers and scholars, and sometimes even run ELT enterprises in the periphery.

Western involvement in the ELT enterprise is also expressed through other channels. Many of the structures and practices of schooling in the modern world are built on educational philosophies and pedagogical traditions which can be traced back to the colonial mission of spreading Enlightenment values for civilizing purposes. As the foregoing passage seeks to show, the English language itself can embody ideological and cultural values alien to these communities. What happens in the sort of classroom context familiar to teachers such as Mrs K., therefore, raises questions about the relevance and appropriateness of the teaching material, curriculum, and pedagogies developed by the Anglo-American communities for periphery contexts. The contrast between Peter's well-organized, goal-directed life and the mental and social chaos surrounding Ravi could scarcely be more marked. The fact that their learning opportunities are poles apart increases the dissonance between the values represented in Mrs K.'s imported reading material and the culture of her students. As a result, the more she depends on faddish pedagogies promoted by Western teaching experts, the more her students are likely to disengage from the learning process. We are left with the most disturbing question, which is how far these many and varied influences may be shaping periphery communities according to the preferred cultural practices, ideologies, and social relations of the center.

Competing pedagogical paradigms

The assumptions motivating dominant pedagogical practices fail to accommodate the type of questions arising in the periphery educational context. If we are to explore these questions in any depth, we shall need to interrogate the available pedagogical paradigms, and adopt necessary changes in our perspective.

Mrs K.'s well-intentioned practices, which have come to be accepted as professional commonsense in ELT, assume that mastering a language is essentially a matter of acquiring its grammatical system. So she presents the simple present tense in a specific textual context, and facilitates the students' understanding by showing how grammar functions in actual communication. She also seeks to satisfy the affective and imaginative dimensions of learning through the narrative about Peter's life, and contextualizes the lesson in an attempt to evoke the students' interest, and help them to relate to it more directly. However, her approach is based on the assumption that learning is primarily a cognitive activity: she emphasizes that students should acquire the grammar inductively by observing its use in texts; the tasks she provides at the end of the reading provide ample opportunities for discovery and practice. By encouraging students to focus all their attention on activities inside the classroom, she gives them the impression that *outside* events are distractions from effective learning.

For Mrs K., therefore, learning is implicitly defined as something that results from the isolated activity of the mind, unaffected by environmental influences. In addition, her interest in borrowing from the latest Western pedagogical developments suggests a belief that cognitive strategies are universal—that learning styles found to be effective for students from one community may be assumed to be equally effective for students from others. If we were to ask her for a definition of ELT, Mrs K. would probably describe it as an essentially innocent pragmatic activity of facilitating the transmission of linguistic rules and communicative skills, accompanied by the beneficial side-effects of ennobling the mind and enabling social mobility.

Whilst much of this could be said to make good pedagogical sense, it is important to consider how students respond to the classroom experience. Ravi's tendency to let his thoughts roam away from the business in hand suggests that much more than grammar or language skills is being transmitted here. He and his fellow students are confronting a range of controversial values deriving from the association of English with liberal Western culture and all that it represents, including science and technology, access to power and wealth, and a generally stigmatized place in colonial history. Other values emerge from the reading material. Ravi is very conscious of, and to some extent demoralized by, the contrast between Peter's happy, privileged life and his own. The fact that these socio-cultural differences interfere with Ravi's comprehension of the passage remind us of the critical role played by such cultural frames in the understanding of language and texts. Ravi's personal experiences and background lead him to read messages into the text which disturb him in a way its authors, and his teacher, could never have anticipated. His reactions suggest that it would be wrong to assume that learning is always autonomous, and never hindered or contaminated by contextual forces. Socio-cultural conditions always influence our cognitive activity, mediating how we perceive and interpret the world around us.

Contextual influences of the sort described are intrinsic to learning, and not the optional extras Mrs K. takes them to be in her limited attempts to accommodate affective features in her teaching. Her pedagogical approach also poses cultural problems for students. Many teachers in the periphery use the task-based, process-oriented, student-centered pedagogy because it comes stamped with the authority of center professional circles. But from the attitudes and motivation of the students Mrs K. is teaching, it seems likely that they would prefer a more formal, product-oriented, teacher-centered pedagogy, of the sort now denigrated by center professional circles. If this were indeed the case, the assumption that learning strategies are common across cultures would also come under question, since it could result in teachers influencing students to adopt inappropriate cognitive and interactive styles; they might also be conveying cultural messages and images which could adversely affect their attitude to the course. We have seen how images of Western affluence and development have motivated Rajan to take his English studies seriously, while they have the opposite effect on Ravi, who is so rooted in his community that he feels alienated by them. This polarity suggests that learning has far-reaching implications for students' values, identity, and community solidarity, and that students will always make connections between classroom proceedings and the outside world.

What all this implies is that, knowingly or not, while Mrs K. follows an explicit curriculum of grammar and communication skills, she is also teaching a 'hidden curriculum' of values, ideologies, and thinking which can mold alternate identities and community allegiance among the students. In contrast to the usual image of the teacher in control of the classroom, this narrative suggests that there are powerful socio-cultural forces that influence learning in a subtly pervasive manner. Granted that this is the case, language learning cannot be considered an entirely innocent activity, since it raises the possibility of ideological domination and social conflict. Teachers should therefore attempt to critically interrogate the hidden curricula of their courses, relate learning to the larger socio-political realities, and encourage students to make pedagogical choices that offer sounder alternatives to their living conditions.

The pedagogical conflicts illustrated above call for a radically different orientation to instruction. We need to reconceptualize such important constructs as knowledge and learning, and indeed, some rethinking has already begun. The new realizations informing our pedagogical practice are coalescing under the broad label of *critical pedagogy* (hereafter CP). Its assumptions and practices differ from those promoted by what we might term the *pedagogy of the mainstream* (hereafter MP).[2] We can delineate the evolving choices in pedagogical orientation as follows:

- *learning as a detached cognitive activity vs. learning as personal*

  MP assumes that learning involves the mind solely (or primarily) in analysis, comprehension, and interpretation. The more reason is allowed to work by itself, the 'truer' the knowledge produced. Emotions, imagination, and intuition are to be suppressed, since they could distort the objectivity required in learning. By contrast, CP would say that it is unwise, if not impossible, to remain uninvolved in the learning process. Just as the personal background of the learner influences how something is learned, what is learned shapes the person: our consciousness, identity, and relationships are implicated in the educational experience. We should therefore consciously engage the influences, consequences, and implications of the personal in the learning process.

- *learning as transcendental vs. learning as situated*

  Traditionally, the learner is supposed to rise above everything in the environment (i.e. society, culture, ideology) in order to be impartial and neutral in the acquisition of knowledge. CP posits that the learner is located in the environment, conditioned by the influences of his or her own context. It follows that the knowledge people produce or acquire will also be grounded in their social practice and material context. Similarly, schooling has been traditionally defined a neutral site—conducted in isolation from the other messy social realities. But CP realizes that schooling is deeply influenced by the larger social and political contexts in which it is situated. The rules, regulations, curricula, pedagogies, and interactions in schooling shape, and are shaped by, socio-political realities. Schooling is so implicated in the needs, interests, and imperatives of the dominant institutions and social groups that it is often difficult to see the full effect of their influence in the classroom.

- *learning processes as universal vs. learning as cultural*

  Modes of learning and thinking have typically been considered to be common for all people. CP considers that they vary according to the social practices and cultural traditions of different communities. Hence the new thinking on the methods and techniques of teaching. For MP, these are value-free instruments motivated by efficiency to conduct instruction in the most effective way possible. CP holds that the established methods embody the preferred ways of learning and thinking of the dominant communities—and that this bias can create conflicts for learners from other pedagogical traditions. Similarly, MP believes that what is learned is factual, impartial, and, therefore, correct for everyone. Knowledge is considered to provide the one universally true view of reality. Since CP holds that knowledge is socially constructed, what is considered reality, fact, or truth by the different communities is understood in relation to their social practice. This is why the different traditions of knowing found in diverse communities have to be negotiated in the learning process.

- *knowledge as value-free vs. knowledge as ideological*

  MP treats knowledge as devoid of values of any moral, cultural, or ethical character. CP holds that everything is value-laden. The institutionalized forms of knowledge embody assumptions and perspectives of the dominant social groups, which introduce other communities to the same value system in order to legitimize the dominance of the élite groups. Subordinate groups may have their own philosophical traditions, and competing versions of reality that favor their own interests. Since everything that is taught already comes with values and ideologies that have implications for students' social and ethical lives, teaching is always problematic. It is part of a teacher's responsibility to help students interrogate the hidden assumptions and values that accompany knowledge.

- *knowledge as preconstructed vs. knowledge as negotiated*

  MP assumes that teaching is a process whereby established facts, information, and rules are simply to be handed over to the students. CP posits that knowledge results from constant negotiation between communities in terms of their values, beliefs, and prior knowledge. Knowledge is itself a changing construct, shaped by the social and cultural practices of those who produce it. It is therefore important to negotiate knowledge more consciously, and to involve the teachers as well as the students in the learning process. Collaboration between the two groups, as they aim to reach consensus through debate, simulates the social process of knowledge construction.

- *learning as instrumental vs. learning as political*

  Given CP's realizations, it is understandable that schooling is considered to be implicated in the exercise of power and domination in society. If learning is value-ridden, and shaped by the imperatives of the dominant social groups, what is learned orientates the learner to the world view and to ideologies of the status quo. In the same way, it is not surprising that key aspects of education, such as curriculum, pedagogy, and instructional policies, are defined by the groups and institutions that control society. Learning, therefore, is a highly contested, conflict-ridden enterprise where the competing knowledge, values, and practices of diverse communities struggle for dominance. Since mainstream pedagogues assume that learning is value-free, pragmatic, and autonomous, they can practice teaching as an innocent and practical activity of passing on correct facts, truths, and skills to students. Even if a teacher does not sympathize with the 'facts', he or she could function as the uninvolved intermediary, and transmit them to students. For CP, however, teachers have the ethical responsibility of negotiating the hidden values and interests behind knowledge, and are expected to help students to adopt a critical orientation to learning.

The context of critical pedagogy

It would be unwise to argue for CP in universal and absolute terms, without reference to the contexts and purposes of teaching. It is impossible to make a disinterested case on behalf of any position, and I can only argue why CP provides a better pedagogical framework by pointing to the relevant location and interests that motivate this work.

Given the social and material context of marginalized communities, CP offers perspectives that serve their challenges, aspirations, and interests more effectively. It is also necessary to understand that ideological and socio-cultural concerns have gained importance in the pedagogical domain as a result of the larger philosophical changes that have taken place in recent history. So the best apology one can make for CP is to situate it in its historical and social context.

Before considering CP in the light of these positions, I must observe a simple difference between the two pedagogies. CP conceives pedagogical practice in terms of an expanded notion of context. Both the strengths and limitations of MP derive from working with a more restricted or focused context for the learning activity. Since the classroom is separated from larger historical and social conditions, and learning is perceived primarily as a cognitive activity, teachers in this tradition can conduct more controlled observation of the learning activity, within more manageable variables. The targets and stages of learning are also made narrower and clearer, thus providing a convenient means of measuring pedagogical progress. But CP practitioners would charge that the pedagogical activity is over-simplified, and that in the process results are somewhat distorted. CP adopts a more holistic approach to learning, situating it amidst the diverse influences, and giving it complexity.

From a philosophical perspective, we must realize that the mainstream pedagogical tradition is identified with such intellectual movements as Enlightenment, rationalism, science, and modernism, which share many ideological and chronological similarities.[3] These movements had a radical beginning. They championed the thinking, observation, and experience of the individual against the dogmas of the state, aristocracy, and Church. These developments went hand in hand with the emergence in Europe, around the 16th and 17th centuries, of the pragmatic middle classes, of individualism, and the Renaissance. In the new dispensation, the valued mode of thought was *inductive*. This encouraged an attitude of observing things without any presuppositions, feelings, or biases, and letting the facts speak for themselves to form valid generalizations. According to its most extreme versions, only those things that could be apprehended by the senses were defined as real. It was this *empirical* approach to phenomena that was supposed to provide a complete understanding of the laws which governed life and promised human and material progress. According to this *positivistic* philosophy, we were considered to inhabit a closed world which possessed the complete answers to its laws of operation. The mind had the power to distinguish fact from myth, apprehend the laws of nature, and channel them for human progress.

Much of this thinking has been debunked of late, by both philosophers of science and practicing scientists, as an exaggeration of intellectual activity.[4] We recognize now that it is impossible for us to understand and interpret things without the mediation (and even active help) of tradition, shared values, personal predispositions, and creative imagination. In fact, knowledge constitutes a body of interpretive grids (or explanatory paradigms) that interpret reality, and is periodically revised according to the interests and experiences of the specific community.

Knowledge, therefore, is intrinsically social, and constructed through interaction between community members. The question as to which community's knowledge paradigm becomes the operating explanation of things is settled by an exercise of power. The knowledge of the dominant groups is imposed through the institutions at their disposal, including the school. This knowledge in turn serves to justify the status quo. It is from this perspective that the post-Enlightenment and post-modern orientation understands educational activity as political.

There is a reason why periphery communities may nurse a grudge against the Enlightenment movement, which helped, enhanced, and/or initiated parallel socio-political movements in the West, such as industrialism, capitalism, and colonialism. These led to the domination of the periphery (Lunn 1982, Giddens 1990, Larsen 1990, Hess 1995), since the West's technological superiority provided it with the military power and resources to colonize the Asian, African, and Latin American communities. The West believed that it was the 'white man's burden' to spread its message of Enlightenment and scientific advancement throughout the world. But behind this avowedly altruistic mission was the West's need to find more raw materials for its industry, and more markets to sell its products. The result was that colonialism boosted capitalist industry and economy, as all communities became integrated into a vast network of capitalist market economies and industrial production, and the scientific vision gained global approval. This development led to the configuration of center/periphery geopolitical relations. Although science claimed to be apolitical, therefore, it actually complemented and benefited from a favorable set of socio-political conditions. Periphery scholars such as Nandy (1988) demonstrate how, even today, scientific and technological activities continue to victimize non-Western communities.

The Enlightenment also led to the suppression of the knowledge systems of the periphery. Science was defined as a universally applicable project, rather than a cultural product of the West—one based on a Judeo-Christian/Renaissance belief in dominion over nature, a teleological view of history, and the celebration of individualism and reason (Huff 1993, Hess 1995). The many different forms of knowing and learning represented by minority communities, which were suppressed under the universalistic claims and globalizing trend of science, have acquired a measure of prominence in the post-colonial climate. The claim that knowledge and pedagogy are value-free and acontextual has only led to the legitimation of the Western intellectual tradition. A partial corrective to this view has come from emergent post-colonial thinking and periphery knowledge, and has inspired contemporary Western communities to develop a critical attitude towards their modernist intellectual tradition (Said 1993: 239–61).

The shift from Enlightenment to anti-Enlightenment philosophies, from modernist to post-modernist thinking, and from colonial hegemony to post-colonial resistance, explains why the assumptions and practices of mainstream pedagogies are questioned today. Loaded with its own brand of interests and values, MP represents no less an ideology than CP. The difference is that while MP is informed by the ideologies of the dominant communities, CP has the potential to interrogate this hegemony. The fact that the politico-cultural implications of teaching English to other communities are being questioned today is due to such philosophical changes. It is important for language teachers to recognize the ways in which these philosophical developments redefine their work in classrooms. Given that there is no such thing as value-free, disinterested, or acontextual teaching, teachers are faced with a stark choice between adopting undemocratic interests (perhaps as a result of not being sufficiently aware of their pedagogical ideologies) or quite openly undertaking a pedagogy for resistance.

Academic reception of critical pedagogies

The notions constituting a critical pedagogy are currently gaining attention in many fields. Adult literacy (Freire 1970), college composition (Bizzell 1982), literature (hooks 1989), social sciences (Marcus and Fischer 1986), feminist studies (Lather 1991), cultural studies (Grossberg 1994), and, of course, education (Giroux 1992) are just some of the fields where a critical perspective on teaching is proving to be popular. This orientation is called by different names in different circles, including pedagogies of resistance (Aronowitz and Giroux 1985), liberatory teaching (Shor 1987), radical pedagogy (hooks 1989), post-modern pedagogy (Giroux 1992), border pedagogy (Giroux and McLaren 1994), and pedagogies of possibility (Simon 1987). However, contemporary appropriations of CP by the Western academy bring with them certain simplifications and distortions.

It can be argued that some of the earliest developments towards such a pedagogy were made by peasant and marginalized communities, especially in the periphery, for whom learning was always a contested and controversial activity. Social workers, clergy, and community leaders all practiced versions of CP long before it was 'discovered' by Western academics. Perhaps the best known example of a periphery practitioner is Paolo Freire (1970; 1985). The Brazilian educator's *Pedagogy of the Oppressed*, which formulates the principles that guided his teaching of literacy for peasants, became sanctified scripture for Western academics in the 1980s, having served as a little-known handbook for social workers and church-based literacy organizations in the periphery for more than a decade. I will later make subtler distinctions within the CP movement to bring into relief other aspects of periphery thinking and practices.

CP has become fashionable in some of the disciplinary fields mentioned above, but in ELT and language-teaching circles generally it has evoked much hostility. There are many reasons why ideological concerns are often ignored or suppressed in language teaching. Phillipson (1992) and Pennycook (1994a) have argued that the formative discourses and practices in ELT are influenced by its roots in the colonial period. It suited ELT to define language and teaching as a value-free cognitive activity, since in that way its material and ideological interests in spreading English globally could be conveniently ignored. The dominant Enlightenment tradition in the West has also helped by providing a scientistic and positivistic cast to ELT, and by encouraging its perception as an apolitical, technocratic, and utilitarian enterprise.

Besides this basic ideological conflict, ELT practitioners have other minor quarrels with CP. These are eloquently reflected in a letter to me from a British colleague, in which he expresses some of the concerns felt by language teachers, and reflects on a set of exchanges on CP where I was a participant:

> [These exchanges in *TESOL Quarterly* 28/4: 609–23] highlight for me how 'Comments' pages are turning into a kind of academic Punch and Judy show, each party bashing the other over the head with 'isms'—grand theoretical constructs, bearing imposing names, and perhaps like Star Wars technology, each calibrated to target the Achilles heel of a specific adversary. Mainstream perceptions of ideologies tend to be as obsessions of marginal groups, threatening stability and a rational order; liberal humanists tend to feel insulted at theories which widen the net of those who should take responsibility for perpetuating oppressive practices— whether in education or elsewhere ... Too often we see wholesale labeling

or pigeonholing passing for academic discussion ... We stitch on labels, and stitch the world up in them, too.
(Personal communication, Nigel Bruce, 24.11.94)

Note that in describing the opponents of critical approaches as belonging to the 'mainstream', my colleague is consigning CP to the margins of the discipline. The fact that the assumptions and scholarship of CP appear incomprehensible to non-initiates undoubtedly accounts for much of the opposition it attracts. Symptomatic of its difficulty is the specialized jargon deriving from the 'isms'—the grand theoretical constructs, and imposing names. CP is also perceived to be too judgmental and condescending towards other practitioners, 'who should take responsibility for perpetuating oppressive practices'. It is therefore considered to posit certain 'politically correct' (the much abhorred 'PC') ways of thinking. A third reason is that CP is considered to be too reductive, in narrowing down all issues of teaching to matters of ideology, thereby 'stitching the world up in labels'. In reading politics into everything, CP is 'widening its net' and imposing its 'obsessions'. Finally, it is considered to be too confrontational, disturbing, and perhaps cynical, to the extent of 'threatening stability and a rational order'.

Many critical pedagogues have responded to these sorts of charges, for instance by explaining that their neologisms are required by the new perspectives they are trying to develop. The old language derives from assumptions that are rejected by the new theoretical orientation. Giroux (1992: 151) argues in more strident terms:

> We're pointing to a theory that examines how you view the very realities you engage. When people say that we write in a language that isn't as clear as it could be, while that might be true, they're also responding to the unfamiliarity of a paradigm that generates questions suppressed in the dominant culture.

The language of CP therefore involves a fundamental and far-reaching paradigm shift. This might be compared to changing one pair of colored spectacles for another for a different view of the world. It is to be expected that the new pair of spectacles will show *everything* in a different light. Such is the nature of paradigms, of whatever brand, whether traditional or new. Since CP is radical in the root sense of that term, it is to be expected that its perspective will strike outsiders as being too judgmental and disturbing.

To appreciate the significance of CP, therefore, an effort must be made to understand its underlying premises and assumptions, a point made by my British colleague:

> [those critics of CP] indicate to me at the very highest level of abstraction and the deepest level of socio-political belief, a lack of the kind of reflexivity which might permit them to appreciate the deeper political points being made—or their validity. [They don't] seem to me to have a

profound—or 'grounded'—sense of the implications of the attribute 'critical' when attached to pedagogy—certainly not grounded in any broader empathetic political philosophy.
(Personal communication, Nigel Bruce, 24.11.94)

In order to understand the project of CP, therefore, ELT practitioners need to orientate themselves to the post-Enlightenment ways of looking at pedagogical issues. Lack of rigorous reading and imaginative understanding cannot be used as an excuse for opposing a pedagogical paradigm. For their part, critical pedagogues must give heed to the charge that they are sometimes reductive and jargon-ridden, and seek to provide a clear and balanced view of their assumptions.

Competing models of critical pedagogy

CP must not be taken as a settled body of thought, with a uniform set of pedagogical practices and assumptions. There are different ways of orientating to power and inequality within the critical pedagogical paradigm. We will mainly distinguish here between models of reproduction and resistance. These models derive from social philosophies that explicitly or implicitly theorize the nature of education and schooling. In brief, while *reproduction theories* are based on somewhat deterministic brands of structuralist and Marxist thinking that developed around the 1970s, *resistance theories* are more open-ended post-structuralist perspectives. Reproduction models explain how students are conditioned mentally and behaviorally by the practices of schooling to serve the dominant social institutions and groups; resistance theories explain how there are sufficient contradictions within institutions to help subjects gain agency, conduct critical thinking, and initiate change. CP has itself accommodated these competing perspectives at different periods under its umbrella.[5] The distinction between the models, introduced in this section, will be debated as a subtext to the ethnographic narratives in the later chapters. Examining these competing perspectives can help us develop a sounder research orientation, and a balanced pedagogy for ELT.

To orientate ourselves to the main perspectives and questions generated by each model, it is useful to return to the opening narrative. In admiring Peter's culture and lifestyle, Rajan shows greater receptivity to the values embodied in the text. Peter represents the values of urban, professional, middle-class groups through his drive for success, goal orientation, personal discipline, routinized lifestyle, and delayed gratification. These are the typical values of a society based on competition and individualism. The other features of Mrs K.'s classroom practice—such as learning to orientate to the lesson by ignoring the distractions outside the classroom, obeying the teacher, unquestioningly respecting her authority, and sticking to the order and routine in the class—also have ideological implications. They can influence Rajan to undertake alienating mechanical labor while suppressing other expressive and spiritual concerns, accept hierarchical social arrangements, accommodate the demands of authority figures, and prioritize self-interest.

The partisan nature of these practices become evident when we consider the alternative set of values the lesson chooses not to present—particularly the traditional rural values based on collective living and a relatively slow pace of life. In presenting the former set of values through its curriculum and pedagogy, the school is making a statement on the communities and cultures it considers as normative. It aligns itself with the dominant culture (based in this instance on urban, technocratic, middle-class values) and disassociates itself from others. Since the school claims to deal only with value-free facts and practices, students like Rajan may not suspect the biased nature of these values. Their legitimacy and superiority would therefore seem entirely 'natural' to students—they are, after all, the course's hidden curriculum, presented under the guise of teaching the simple present tense. Students would actually compete with each other to absorb these values, without any compulsion from outside, since falling into line with these pedagogies and curricula defines educational success. However, the longer-term social consequences of absorbing such values may be imagined. Rajan, certainly, will have greater chances of joining the urban, professional, middle classes. Holding the values of the system, he will be a faithful citizen and a productive worker. He will endorse the social system whose values he holds and profits by. In short, we can see a cyclical process: the dominant social arrangement passes on its values to the school; the school (through its curriculum and pedagogy) passes on those values to students; the students uphold the status quo.

The fact that Ravi is somewhat detached from these values does not mean that he is free from domination. His attitudes, being based on a rural lifestyle and values, would lead to his subjection in a more indirect and paradoxical way. To the extent that he is torn between mental and physical labor, curricular and extra-curricular activities, and individual and collective claims (with a bias towards the second set of values), we may suspect that he will not be successful in a curriculum that happens to favor the former set of values. Furthermore, his opposition to some of the messages from the lesson, and his lack of motivation, suggest that educational failure could thrust him into a farming life—which he comes from, and seems to prefer anyway. This would help rather than upset the functioning of the social system, since farmers are in any case needed to produce food for urban professionals. The school would be able to send Ravi to his chosen vocation without being blamed for his failure. Instead, he would blame himself, and accept his return to a lowly position in life as the natural outcome of his poor academic performance. He would not consider his status and educational achievement to have been determined by an unfair educational system, based on partisan values that favored one social group over the other. Rather than questioning why Peter's (and Rajan's) values should account for success, Ravi would simply blame himself for failing to acquire the required values and dispositions—thereby confirming their legitimacy. So the school is able to reward students unequally, and to preserve the division of labor and status hierarchy in a way that is equally acceptable to the powerful and the powerless. It therefore plays an important function in enforcing these social distinctions and legitimizing inequalities. On the other hand, if Ravi is to become a professional like Rajan, he will have to start by becoming educationally successful, and acquiring the required set of values—which means he will have to grow out of his peasant culture and dispositions. In short, through the different rewards for Ravi and Rajan the school reproduces the dominant ideologies and status quo.

This is a simplified explanation of reproduction theory, but we must remember that each society displays different types of stratification, and therefore gives a different priority to its values. The ways in which the school may serve different social systems have to be studied in context. We can in fact stretch this vignette further to consider geopolitical relations in education, inquiring how schooling can influence subjects from the periphery to serve the interests of the center. Apart from the goal-oriented lifestyle and pragmatic values represented by Peter (which Tawney 1964 would associate with the Protestant work ethic and capitalism), certain aspects of the classroom relations are also built on Western technocratic values that are very different from the indigenous educational traditions. The task-based, student-centered approach, coupled with the impersonal relations between students and the teacher, are different from the teacher-centered but more personalized pedagogical relations practiced in the indigenous tradition. Being attracted to urban technocratic values, Rajan also indirectly accepts the logic of that social system. In fact, he detests the local culture and society. Clearly, his aim is to emigrate to the West and to enjoy the sophisticated lifestyle and material comforts on offer there. Rajan's assumption that his community is underdeveloped also implies an acceptance of the Western definition of social development and progress (based on technological and material criteria). In addition to the learning environment, the English language would also play a part in internalizing the values of the liberal, individualistic, technocratic culture with which it is predominantly associated. Even if he doesn't emigrate, Rajan will work to realize similar values and institutions in his own community. He will join the periphery élite that depends on and supports the center—thus helping to reproduce its values and institutions.

A reproductionist perspective provides many important insights into processes of schooling and pedagogy. Reproduction models show how pervasively and subtly socio-political forces may shape the learning process. So through its hidden curricula, schooling serves the status quo very effectively. The ways in which educational processes may make the dominant ideologies appear natural and legitimate, thereby making subordinate groups internalize such values, are perceptively unraveled by this theory. Such a perspective alerts us to interrogate all aspects of the learning process— curriculum, pedagogy, classroom interactions, school regulations, and educational policies—with a critical eye.

The model does, however, appear to overstate the case somewhat, by developing a deterministic and impersonal perspective. It has been pointed out, for example, that domination is never wholesale or inexorable. The processes of domination and reproduction are even more complex, and always involve multifaceted forces, responses, and implications. A closer look at the vignette raises some complicating questions, and evidence that reproduction may not be fully achieved. The conflict Ravi experiences throughout the lesson, for example, should not be ignored. He is clearly uncomfortable with the disparity between what is going on inside and outside the classroom. This unease can be used for reproductive purposes by the status quo (as I have mentioned earlier); it also holds the possibility of motivating oppositional responses. Ravi's friends, too, display displeasure with the process-oriented and collaborative teaching strategies, preferring their own culturally-motivated learning styles. Their lack of interest can motivate opposition to the ideologies implicit in the lesson and the pedagogy; their tensions may in turn generate critical thinking that will help them to rise above domination. Such evidence leads us to the conclusion that students come with a relatively independent consciousness that can display signs of opposition to domination; that the cultures they bring with them can clash with the alien ideologies to resist domination; that human experience is of sufficient complexity and indeterminacy to override what impersonal institutions may predicate; and that students enjoy some agency to challenge reproductive forces.

There are other complexities that we need to consider. The culture, ideologies, and discourses of the dominant groups are not monolithic; they are multiple, and even contradictory. So just as the textbook presents ideologies of the work ethic, it also contains messages on the need for leisure, warm relationships, and an expressive lifestyle (reflected in the way Peter spends his weekends). By tapping these counter-cultural elements in the dominant ideology, subordinate groups can resist reproduction. Similarly, the cultures of subordinate people contain diverse conflicting characteristics. They may display traces of domination, but may also embody potential for resistance. It is wrong to assume that the cultures of the subordinate groups are always passive and accommodative. They have a long history of struggle and resistance against the dominant cultures, and members of these communities can tap the resources in their cultures to oppose the thrusts of alien ideologies. Ravi's Tamil culture, for instance, has a long history, spanning two centuries, of interaction with colonial nations and ideologies.

Local discourses, cultural practices, and literary artifacts embody this conflictual interaction. In fact, in Ravi's contemporary society there is a thriving linguistic nationalism that opposes the learning and use of English. Students draw from these resources to produce forms of resistance to the alien curricula and pedagogies. Even the local classroom should not be conceived in monolithic terms, because it cannot be fully controlled by the social and political forces from outside its walls. There are complex layers of culture in the classroom itself which will mediate the alien pedagogies and ideologies. The local classroom contains many other forms of culture—indigenous values, students' peer-group cultures, and teachers' professional values—which will interact with the dominant ideologies in complex ways. The school may also be sufficiently detached from other social institutions and structures to enjoy a measure of autonomy. The classroom may be at tension with other institutions, generating conflict and friction with the dominant ideologies of the status quo—thereby preserving a space for resistance. In this way, the classroom can nurture some of the oppositional attitudes and cultures students bring with them.

By granting more complexity to the subjects, the classroom, and the culture, we will find that domination is not guaranteed. The influence of the socio-political forces on classrooms and students can take different trajectories and outcomes. This is why Ravi's experience of discomfort in the classroom is significant, and merits further exploration: this affirms the relative independence of consciousness, the possibility of a critical perspective, and the potential for opposition. Resistance theorists will say that it is the responsibility of teachers to channel Ravi's dissatisfactions and conflicts along a more constructive and ideologically-informed direction. How can Ravi's partial insights be developed and informed by theoretical clarity so that he may challenge and perhaps help transform the sources of domination he confronts? This is the burden of resistance theories.

Although this book is in sympathy with theories of resistance for offering possibilities of empowerment for periphery communities, the insights of reproduction theorists cannot be ignored. It has been pointed out that if reproductive models of schooling provide 'a language of critique' to deconstruct dominant schooling processes, resistance models offer 'a language of possibility' for reconstructing suitable alternatives (Aronowitz and Giroux 1993: 103). These two models, then, generate questions that will be explored further in the following chapters. In what forms does center ideological influence penetrate into periphery ELT classrooms? What does the everyday life of teachers and students in the periphery suggest about how they confront, cope with, and negotiate forces of reproduction from the center? What tensions in periphery classrooms (in terms of the instructional cultures, interactions, and policies) offer space for resistance? How do the languages, discourses, and cultures of periphery communities offer resources to encourage opposition?

Theoretical backdrop to studying resistance

In order to understand the assumptions motivating the emergent paradigm of pedagogical resistance we need to step back briefly from the pedagogical scene. We must also realize that the paradigm encapsulates theoretical controversies that have taken place for at least a half century between many schools of thought. We need to survey, if briefly, how these debates have helped redefine familiar constructs such as discourse, subjectivity, culture, and power.

The philosophical movements of Marxism and structuralism which influence reproduction models have challenged Enlightenment belief in the autonomy of the human mind, purity of knowledge, and the ability to attain a correct, undistorted, objective understanding of reality. The Marxist perspective sees material life (especially economy) as the primary shaping influence on other domains, including education, culture, and even consciousness. The material dimension is considered to be the *base* and the latter set, including education, the *superstructure* of social life. Some early interpretations of Marxist thinking posited that the economic relations of the base unilaterally shaped the superstructure (see, for a critique, Williams 1977: 75–82). It thus follows that schooling and knowledge are determined by the material necessities of a particular society. What are called *economic reproduction models* show a direct influence from Marxism in theorizing this connection.[6]

For structuralism, the subject is a construct of the social symbol system. Although structuralism gives more importance to mental life than Marxism, consciousness is coded in symbols that are socially constructed. Contradicting the humanist perspective that granted independence and autonomy for the subject, structuralism views the subject as dominated by linguistic and symbol systems. These symbol systems are ideological, and provide a partisan orientation to reality and social institutions for subjects. Institutions such as the school are perceived as helping to internalize these discourses among students. Influenced by structuralist thinking, *ideological reproduction models* view classrooms as determined by the dominant discourses of society, and shaping the perspectives of the students accordingly.[7] Thinkers such as Althusser reconcile their Marxism by suggesting that although the economic realm is the important driving force, it does not have full control of the superstructure. It is what he terms the *ideological state apparatus* (of which the school is a part) that performs the mediating function of reproducing society.

Less deterministic than the above are the *cultural reproduction models* which theorize the mediating role of culture in achieving social reproduction.[8] These models are influenced by the theoretical insights of cultural politics developed by Raymond Williams, Bourdieu and Passeron, and the like. While economic reproduction theorists consider the relationship between

material requirements and school to be more or less direct, cultural reproduction theorists perceive reproduction to be the result of an interesting
correspondence between the values upheld by the school and those of the
dominant social groups. The school shapes the consciousness and behavior
of the students by distributing the cultural practices of the dominant groups
as the norm. Students who acquired this linguistic and cultural capital would
grow to justify and serve the interests of the dominant groups. Because of the
perceived neutrality of the school, the subordinate groups imbibe the school
culture without recognizing its biased and partisan nature, and, thus,
participate in their own domination. So for cultural reproduction theorists,
the school does not have to mirror the economic and political conditions
outside its walls. Its practices and agenda may only indirectly suit the
reproductive needs of the dominant institutions. This notion of the school's
relative autonomy from the economic and political institutions provides
greater complexity to the reproductive process. But the culturalist models fail
to exploit this detachment of the school to consider how it may function as
an oppositional site to help change social institutions.

The common point of departure for the various resistance theories from
the reproductive orientation of structuralism and Marxism can be explained
in the following way. When Marxism's material grounding of consciousness
and institutions is disturbed by linguistic mediation, the superstructure
acquires a relative independence and fluidity to initiate change. Although
structuralism helped to remove the stifling hold of the material base in just
such a manner, it posited that there was a uniform set of codes that governed
the functioning of subjects and institutions. These socially-constructed codes
were treated as beyond individual control or production. But if these codes
are heterogeneous and conflictual, defying the construction of rigid systems
(as post-structuralist notions of language define), domination cannot be
guaranteed. Post-structuralist thinking thus unravels the inherent
contradictions within subjects and institutions that may defy the reproductive
thrusts of material or ideological structures. The project of the different
models of resistance is to critique centeredness, binding, uniformity,
cohesion, generalization, abstraction, globalism, and determinism in favor of
decentering, unboundedness, diversity, splintering, concreteness, specificity,
localism, and indeterminateness.

The redefinition of constructs such as subjecthood, culture, power, and
knowledge by resistance theories has enabled us to conceptualize the
potential for teachers and students to negotiate power. The movements
influencing resistant thinking, such as post-structuralism, post-modernism,
post-colonialism, neo-Marxism, and feminism, do not fall into neat
compartments.[9] In fact, they borrow from each other quite fluidly. But there
are also ongoing (sometimes vehement) arguments and debates between and
within these schools. We will only explore here how these theoretical schools
converge to develop a perspective on resistance. If we are to appreciate the

discourses of resistance we must understand how the following basic constructs have been contested and redefined, and will therefore begin with the medium which is considered to lie at the heart of these redefinitions.

Language

Over the years we have been taught to perceive language as an abstract and neutral entity that does not embody values or ideologies. Such a transparent medium was thought to reveal to the transcendental human mind a reality without distortions. It was this orientation that gave the Enlightenment the confidence to use the passive tool of language to penetrate the veil of nature, and to master its laws. Structuralist linguistics, through the foundational work of Saussure (1959), challenged this perspective. Structuralism considers language to be a socially constructed symbol system that reflects, embodies, and constitutes the values of the speech community.[10] Besides being value-laden, language is a much more independent and dynamic agent. It is viewed as constructing or socializing our consciousness. It is also through the symbol system of language that we make sense of the world and conduct thought. As such, language serves to represent, interpret, and constitute the reality available to subjects. If ideologically-loaded language serves to define our sense of reality and subjectivity, we can understand how hegemonical language can be. It internalizes the dominant values and ideologies in a pervasive and deep-rooted manner. These notions add up to politicize language and explain its powerful reproductive function. However, constructs such as discourse, ideology, texts, and social system are treated as isomorphic by structuralism. Language thus enjoys little space to resist the imposition of ideology. Subjects, too, are totally governed by the dominant discourses.[11]

Post-structuralist perspectives challenge the deterministic aspects of the structuralist legacy, opening avenues for the development of a resistance linguistics. While Saussure posited that linguistic signs have no positive content, but define each other in relation to the total system by being unlike each other, post-structuralists latch on to this insight to cut off linguistic signs from any control of the system or structure whatsoever. Saussure had restricted the proliferation of meaning by accommodating the signs into a tight, overarching structure. For post-structuralists, the signs were caught in a play of endless oppositions, destabilizing the structure and producing multiple meanings. Meaning thus becomes fluid and dynamic as signs are placed in different contexts. This orientation inspires a critical practice of deconstructing texts to reveal the linguistic contradictions and inconsistencies and, thus, expose the hidden ideologies that control meaning. The exposure of suppressed meanings and discourses is the primary form of resistance for what is labeled the *micro politics* of post-structuralism (Foucault 1980). Because dominant groups sustain economic and political power by manipulating meanings, unpacking this linguistic base is supposed to undermine the whole socio-political edifice.[12]

The definition of *discourse* has gone through parallel changes. While structuralism enabled the perception of language-as-discourse in orientating to the linguistic genres which come with concomitant rules of thinking, communicating, and interacting, it had perceived these genres in monolithic terms. Post-structuralism situates discourse in historical and social context as being periodically redefined according to the conflict of different communities for dominance. The resultant tension within and between each discourse enables subjects to negotiate their status and, in the process, to reconstruct discourses according to their interests and changing orientations. Furthermore, the relations between notions such as ideology, discourse, and text have been more complexly reconceptualized. While ideology finds its clearest manifestation in language, the connection between language and ideology depends on the category of discourse. The defined and delimited set of statements that constitute a discourse are themselves expressive of and organized by a specific ideology. Ideology and discourse are considered to be aspects of the same phenomenon, regarded from two different standpoints. *Discourse* is the linguistic realization of the social construct *ideology*. Furthermore, text and discourse are distinguished by the fact that the abstract paradigms of *discourse* are linguistically manifested in *texts*. It is now possible for critical linguists to posit that within one text there could be a manifestation to two or more discourses. Theorizing ideology, discourse, texts, and language as distinct constructs, while being interconnected and mutually influential, suggests the various levels of mediation involved, and opens up the tensions that enable resistance.

The post-structuralist orientation to language, then, frees subjects to reclaim their agency, negotiate the different subjectivities and ideologies offered by competing discourses, and adopt a subject position favorable to their empowerment. This linguistic orientation has encouraged some schools of socio- and ethno-linguistics to reorient to linguistic conflict at the micro-social and interpersonal level, and explicate how language is implicated in the creative ways subjects negotiate identities, roles, and statuses in everyday life. Critical linguists interpret how speech genres and texts may serve the ideological interests of the powerful. More pertinent to this project, researchers of post-colonial communities reveal how subjects alternate the vernacular and English in a contextually advantageous manner to challenge the unequal distribution of symbolic and material rewards.[13]

Subjectivity

Many implications for subjectivity derive from the above linguistic redefinitions. The heterogeneous and conflictual nature of discourses provides the possibility that one may enjoy a range of *subject positions* according to the different discourses available, and that subjectivity is always fluid and negotiable (Smith 1988). This provides subjects with the possibility of forming new identities and gaining a critical consciousness by resisting dominant discourses. Much of this thinking has centered around gaining one's *voice*, that is, being able to articulate one's interests and aspirations by negotiating a space through the competing discourses (Mohanty 1990, Walsh 1991). The specific strategy of gaining voice is contrapuntal, i.e. it is not achieved by escaping from discourse or by conforming to one, but by working against the available discourses. Resistance theories have thus been able to develop the agency of the subject to resist domination against the overdetermined control of social and ideological discourses theorized by structuralism. By arguing that subjecthood is constructed by a unitary system of language and discourse, structuralist thinking had effaced the agency, individuality, and integrity of the 'person'. Although Enlightenment thinking placed the human subject as transcendental and autonomous, rising above influences from the material environment, with an inner core of consciousness that provided each with a unique identity, this was too idealistic. While resistance thinking acknowledges the power of dominant discourses to constitute subjectivity and confer marginalized identities for some, it enables a critical negotiation with the dominant discourses as an important step in resisting power structures.

Culture

Resistance theories have also opened up culture to show its inner creative tensions. While reproduction models insightfully politicized culture by noting the manner in which it performs ideological and hegemonical functions, they adopt a monolithic orientation that posits only unilateral influence. For example, the cultures of the subaltern groups are homogeneously defined, and considered to mediate on behalf of forces of domination, rather than to enable resistance. But post-structuralist theories assume that each community's culture is made up of a conglomeration of diverse strands which embody hybrid traditions of domination and resistance. The multiple symbols, discourses, artifacts, texts, and practices that constitute a culture in a particular community are always at tension (Hassan 1987, Hutcheon 1989). Endeavors to homogeneously define a culture and impose labels such as high or low (as in the Enlightenment tradition) are attempts from the perspective of the dominant groups to limit the complexity of the cultural formation in their favor. The notion of *hegemony* articulates how the dominant groups are always involved in building consent to their power by influencing the culture and knowledge of subordinate groups (Williams 1977: 108–14). From this perspective, cultural hegemony is an ongoing activity, a process, that can always be met by opposition. This perspective augurs well for developing strategies of resistance. It is possible for subordinate groups to discover the liberatory elements in their own cultures that will enable them to develop a critical consciousness and resist domination, just as dominant groups will negotiate these oppositional strategies with their own acts of appropriation. Such are the lines in which a more complex cultural politics is being developed. Resistance involves deconstructing what passes for culture, discovering the contradictions in the dominant culture, and developing the liberatory traditions of marginalized communities to tap their oppositional potential.

Knowledge

The insights into the multiplicity of codes and voices have been amplified by post-modernists such as Lyotard (1984) who have attacked what they call the grand theories, the meta narratives, and totalities which have shackled the heterogeneity of discourses to impose unitary meanings. Such grand theories are considered totalitarian in imposing the dominant group's world view and intellectual tradition on other communities who have their own local knowledges. Given the non-foundationalist view that one cannot apprehend reality without the mediation of language, and the social constructionist view which assumes the creation of knowledge as shaped by social practice, it is not hard to see how knowledge is partisan and partial to the communities which construct it. The tension between the different knowledge traditions is settled by power, that is, by the imposition of the dominant group's paradigms. Enlightenment reason is one such paradigm— in fact, a totalizing grand theory—that has suppressed the knowledge of other communities. Women and other periphery groups have added to the pluralization of reason by making a powerful case for the recognition of their own preferred forms of knowing (Harding 1986, Mills 1987, Haraway 1989, Harding 1991). In place of the grand theories that strive to throttle the creation of knowledge by subaltern communities, resistance theories value local knowledge. These are the grounded forms of theorization that arise from everyday life and experience in specific domains, leading to the construction of relevant explanatory paradigms. Although reproduction theories also make the knowledge/power connection forcefully, they assume that knowledge is unilaterally owned and disseminated by the dominant groups. Resistance perspectives theorize the possibility that the counter-knowledge of subaltern groups has its own critical insights to demystify the dominant ideologies and empower them to achieve their own interests. This view also assumes that the knowledge/power interconnection is not always pejorative—that there are ethically responsible forms of knowledge for liberatory purposes.

Power

For reproductionist models, power is monolithic and absolute. But the exercise of power always implies the existence of counter-power or counter-discourses. Unilateral force gains only a pyrrhic victory. Power works by absorbing alternate forms of power to further its hegemony. This dialectical—or conflict-oriented—perspective accounts for the possibility of resistance. If power is sustained by controlling the irrepressible interplay of heterogeneous discourses, this provides scope for the creative and critical reinterpretation of those discourses for purposes of resistance. Moreover, while power is perceived in global terms by reproduction theories, resistance theories recognize multiple sources of power. Power is sustained at the micro-level by diverse local networks encompassing personal and collective domains, that is, in relationships, in social institutions, and in community life. But this interlocking system of power provides scope for tension and conflict between the divergent domains to enable opposition and change. Finally, for resistance theories, power in not always a pejorative force—one used solely for domination. Power is also enjoyed by subaltern communities at different local domains, which can be developed by them to resist domination at a larger structural level. These redefinitions give scope for micro-politics, encouraging subjects to negotiate power in specific areas of local life. Hence the sensitivity to the different manifestations of power: notions of identity politics explore how power reaches into the recesses of consciousness and subjectivity; cultural politics interrogates how power takes a cultural expression in our everyday life; the politics of representation shows how it is difficult to perceive or interpret anything without adopting an ideologically-based standpoint. Hence the significance of pedagogical politics in classrooms. All this gives new ramifications to power—it is not something solely exercised by the state or by 'politicians', as had traditionally been understood.

The post-colonial connection

The relationship of post-colonial thinking to the resistance theories outlined above is complex. While these theories are often spoken of in the same breath as belonging to the same critical intellectual tradition, it is fair to say that many strands of periphery thinking have developed indigenously without direct interaction with Western paradigms.[14] At present, there is greater visibility to post-colonial thinking in the center because resistance theories have provided a favorable intellectual climate for their reception. However, I will show below that post-colonial thinking is also critical of certain discourses of resistance peculiar to the Western academy.

In some senses, post-colonial thinking is an example of how suppressed people can see through the dominant knowledge systems, and critically interrogate them for their empowerment. Their many strategies of resistance exemplify the views articulated by post-structuralist theorists above. Consider, for instance, the strategy of appropriating the discourses of the center to develop a critical consciousness and voice for marginalized communities. This is an example of how dominated people can shift positions within an oppressive discourse to reclaim their agency, conduct critical thinking, and demand fair representation. To make the paradox sharper, periphery thinkers may use Western theories to critique the West and, in fact, to celebrate their own cultures and traditions.[15] This is not unlike another strategy they display: that of using English, the colonial language, to speak and write against the Empire.

However, post-colonial thinkers have also redressed some of the limitations of the resistance theories in the center academy. Some tendencies in these fashionable movements may militate against resistance. The splintering and decentering of the subject can be taken to the point of erasing agency altogether. The non-foundationalist world view and the endless play of signs constituting reality may encourage a debilitating relativism. The notion that all discourses are partial and partisan in representing reality can lead to a liberal detachment towards discourses. Such attitudes can prevent someone from taking a position on behalf of a specific discourse or community. The preoccupation with detecting ideologies in language and texts can become an esoteric and escapist activity that may encourage a complacency about structural inequalities. And the denial of larger totalities, to the point of lacking any coherence or rootedness, can encourage a preoccupation with micro-level issues that can be powerless to challenge macro-level structures. The idea that deconstructing language and texts is the ultimate form of liberation has led to ignoring the material context altogether. In fact, material life is treated as if it constituted purely linguistic codes and texts that some of the more recalcitrant elements of power are often overlooked. For periphery subjects who experience multiple forms of oppression and very pressing needs of food, clothing, and shelter, a diet of linguistic guerrilla warfare, textual resistance, and micro-politics will not suffice. Therefore, they have endeavored to connect the interrogation of discourses with larger concerns relating to their traditions, geopolitical realities, and historical conditions. The contribution of post-colonial thinkers has thus served to historicize and materialize resistance thinking.[16]

Post-colonial discourses have not only stimulated knowledge production in the periphery; they have also invigorated the intellectual life of the center. Post-colonial thinkers have claimed that their work from the margins of academic and political life has the potential to deepen and further democratize center discourses (hooks 1989, Said 1993). What enables their critical reading of knowledge and texts is their unique location. Their oppositional subject position, outsider identity, marginalized status and alternate cultural traditions provide a critical interpretive perspective on

Western discourses. The African-American scholar, bell hooks, calls this the *politics of location* (hooks 1989: 177–82). Not surprisingly, she and other minority feminists have criticized Western women for articulating modes of resistance that are insensitive to the many-faceted oppression faced by periphery women, caught in the nexus of race, class, ethnicity, nationality, and gender. Just as center resistance is grounded in the social practice and cultural concerns of center communities, periphery thinking has to be shaped by its own location.

Periphery thinkers are also cautious about over-intellectualizing things. Freire (1970, 1985) argues that intellectuals should not function from outside the community to work for its empowerment, but actively participate in solidarity with the masses. The oppressed should consider developing their own intellectuals (from their ranks) who can critically theorize their experiences from everyday struggle. Such a perspective implies that theory can arise in different social sites—not only in schools or academia. It should arise in a grounded manner, from practical experience and participation in specific contexts of struggle. Thus theory dialectically interacts with practice in an ongoing way, and develops in locally relevant directions. The flexibility deriving from this position is evident in Freire himself. Thinking along Marxist lines, but equally influenced by liberation theology, he has developed a pedagogy that is appropriate to his locale. This attitude checks the possibility all too evident in contemporary academic circles, to do theory for theory's sake in an abstruse and esoteric fashion, especially influenced by post-structuralist and post-modernist discourses.

Conclusion

The theoretical orientations we have surveyed above help us see how even commonplace features of classroom life and everyday experience may be charged with ideological implications. Such aspects as textbooks, knowledge, discourse conventions, and identities of teachers and students are heterogeneously constituted, steeped in conflict, and implicated in the exercise of power. Those wishing to look at classrooms through traditional paradigms miss most of the conflicts taking place in education. In order to orient to certain aspects of reality, therefore, one needs to adopt the appropriate theoretical spectacles or angles of vision. But, as periphery thinkers warn us, these theories have to be negotiated in terms of the material conditions and social practices of one's community. Periphery thinkers may also negotiate fearlessly with other traditions of thinking to borrow useful constructs for their purposes, albeit from a clear location in their community and its interests. Adopting a periphery standpoint does not mean that I have to ignore center traditions of thinking and discourses. I can engage with them from my location as a periphery subject. Throughout this book, therefore, I employ the resistance paradigm reflexively—that is, even as I use it as an interpreting medium, I appraise its usefulness for periphery communities and classrooms, with a readiness to revise its constructs.

Notes

1   This is a reconstruction from the observation notes of a class which took place at the University of Jaffna on December 1st 1990. The description is slightly dramatized in places to throw certain ironies into relief.

2   CP and MP are ideo-typical constructs that are used here for merely expository purposes. MP includes different approaches and methods in ELT that will be critiqued in detail in Chapters 5 and 7.

3   For a perspective on the connections between these movements, see Hampson 1968, Lunn 1982, Kolb 1986, Giddens 1990, Larsen 1990, and Chappell 1992.

4   The work of philosophers Kuhn 1962, Feyarabend 1975, Gadamer 1981, and Law 1993 develops the value-ridden nature of science and Enlightenment reason. The gender bias of science is critiqued by Harding 1986, 1991, and Haraway 1989.

5   We can identify these shifting orientations towards reproduction and resistance in the single scholar Henry Giroux, as we compare his work during the 1970s (Giroux 1979) with his later work (Giroux 1983, 1992).

6   The work of Dreeben (1968), Bowles and Gintis (1977), and Anyon (1980) shows the influence of the economic reproduction models.

7   The work of Althusser (1971) illustrates the position of the ideological reproduction model. For an introduction to structuralist thinking, see Lane (ed.) 1970, de George and de George 1972.

8   The work of Bernstein (1977, 1981), Bourdieu (1977, 1979, 1984), Bourdieu and Passeron (1977), and Willis (1977) illustrates cultural reproduction models. For an excellent critical review of the contributions of these different reproduction models, see Willis 1983 and Aronowitz and Giroux 1993.

9   For an introduction to post-structuralist and post-modernist constructs, see Harland 1987, Hutcheon 1988, 1989, and Jameson 1990. For an orientation to feminist thinking, see de Lauretis 1986, Showalter (ed.) 1989, and Butler 1990. For recent Marxist thinking, see Ryan 1989.

10   Note that the term 'structuralist linguistics,' used here to describe the work of those like Barthes and Kristeva, is different from the brand of American linguistics of the same name practiced by Bloomfield, Chomsky, and others, which borrows Saussurean notions piecemeal. For an interpretation of the radical potential in Saussurean linguistics, see Coward and Ellis 1977, Hodge and Kress 1988.

11   While literary and communication scholars have explored these semiotic implications of power, very few schools in mainstream linguistics have

done so. Even sociolinguistic approaches look at the values in language as not being part of its deep structure, and adopt the egalitarian view that languages are 'different-but-equal'. But towards the end of the 1970s the school of critical linguists approached language as fundamentally an ideological system. Perceiving that language mystifies people as to its underlying ideologies, and leads subjects to a blind acquiescence, critical linguists unravelled these connections. However, they also assumed that there is only a single ideology in social structure, that only one ideology gets recorded in texts, and that there is a one-to-one correspondence between language and ideology (to the extent that each grammatical item carries a concomitant ideology)—see Fowler and Kress 1979. For representative studies, see Kress and Trew 1978, Trew 1979, Fowler, Hodge, Kress, and Trew 1979, and Kress 1983.

12 For an articulation of post-structuralist orientations on language, see Derrida 1972, 1981a, Foucault 1972.

13 For a theoretical argument on the micro-social life of discursive resistance, see Woolard 1985, Gal 1989, and Heller 1992, as they develop it in opposition to the deterministic linguistics of Bourdieu and Bernstein. Specific studies that exemplify the use of language for resistance in the periphery are: Myers-Scotton 1990, 1992, Duranti 1992, Lindstrom 1992, Canagarajah 1995a, 1995b; see also Chapters 3 and 6 for examples of a resistance orientation to interpersonal interactions in communities and classrooms, respectively. Critical linguists have also cast away their deterministic leanings and adopted a post-structuralist orientation of resistance—as exemplified in Kress 1985, Hodge and Kress 1988, and Fairclough 1989.

14 For a discussion of the problems in defining the relation of post-colonial thinking to the Western academic discourses, see Mishra and Hodge 1991, Williams and Chrisman 1994.

15 Some of the contemporary scholars in this field, such as Said (1979, 1993, 1995) and Spivak (1990), have used post-structuralist thinkers (Foucault by the former, and Derrida by the latter) to expose the unfair representation of periphery communities and cultures.

16 For critiques by periphery thinkers of post-structuralist and resistance thinking in the West, see Mohanty 1988, hooks 1989, Minh-ha 1989, and Loomba 1994.

2 Challenges in researching resistance

Why do you imagine they never understand
Things? They too can be alert to all this
Absurdity about what you think they think!

Jack Mapanje, *On African Writing*

The theoretical orientation developed in the last chapter has radical implications for the methodologies one might employ to study the politics of ELT. The questioning of the Enlightenment tradition, with its positivistic orientation to knowledge construction, challenges the research practices taken for granted in the academy. The dichotomizing of the objective and subjective, data and interpretation, description and application, and fact and opinion—with the former in each pair considered as consummately scientific, and the latter admissible only as a secondary or extrinsic concern—now has to be reconceived. It can be argued that the manner in which the research problem is defined, objectives are framed, setting is chosen, and data are sought are influenced by the researcher's values and on-going interpretation of things. Therefore the data may imply and even presuppose an interpretation. These dichotomized constructs can then be shown to be interconnected in subtle ways. Notions about being objective, inductive, empirical, and factual in inquiry now have to be redefined in more qualified terms.

Studying a subject from a resistance perspective also demands certain sound commitments. It assumes a vision of the ideal social or educational conditions one would like to realize through the research. It is informed by a clear ideological and theoretical standpoint, and motivated by the urgency of social action. While these features would violate the attitude that sees research as disinterested intellectual activity, it need not be so for those holding a post-Enlightenment view of knowledge construction. The realization that all knowledge is ideological and interested demands that contemporary researchers be frank about the values and interests that motivate their work. In other words, the question is not *whether* research should be interested, but *which* interests should motivate it.

There is, however, a questionable view in ELT that a critical orientation to research would demand a specific research method or approach among a range of available approaches. The proceedings of the TESOL Research interest section in the 1992 convention, reported in a recent issue of *TESOL Quarterly*, presents the following approaches: analysis of learners' language, verbal reports on learning strategies, text analysis, classroom interaction analysis, ethnography, critical pedagogical approaches in research, and participatory action research (Cumming 1994). These approaches are presented by the editor of this special report under three broad groupings: descriptive, interpretive, and ideological orientations. This mode of structuring still reflects the traditional scientific orientation to scholarship, even though the inclusion of ideological orientations (represented here by critical pedagogical approaches and participatory action research) is remarkably accommodative. The fact is that the three orientations (i.e. description, interpretation, and ideology) are interconnected. Description implies interpretation; interpretation is informed by one's discourses and ideologies. Furthermore, such categorization creates the impression that ideological orientation is a distinct approach to research—with perhaps its own set of techniques and methods. This is confirmed when the report lists 'critical pedagogical approaches in research' (Pennycook 1994b) as one more alternative among many TESOL research approaches, with the worrying implication that being socially or ideologically conscious is optional. We must insist that all research methods be sensitive to issues of power and difference. In fact, some of the other approaches listed in the survey have distinct sub-schools, representing a well-developed tradition of critical inquiry.[1]

Before explaining the methods and approaches employed to explore the concerns of this book, I will analyze what are perhaps the earliest book-length works undertaking a critical orientation to ELT in the periphery, namely, Phillipson's *Linguistic Imperialism* (1992) and Adrian Holliday's *Appropriate Methodology and Social Context* (1994). These publications employ two distinct approaches. Understanding their achievement will help channel my own inquiry along more productive lines.

Two critical approaches to ELT in the periphery

Phillipson's *Linguistic Imperialism* offers a forceful critique of the global spread of English and ELT, beginning from its military imposition by colonial powers and extending to the subtler neo-imperialist activities of Western cultural organizations and aid agencies today.[2] An invaluable contribution of Phillipson's work is the careful documentation of the hidden interests motivating the supposedly altruistic activities of these agencies. Analyzing the historiography of British and American attempts to promote ELT from the middle of this century, Phillipson unearths important documents to show the political and economic functions envisaged for the work of the British Council and United States Information Agency during their inception at the height of the cold war. He quotes amply from the archives in order to show the ulterior motivations behind language promotion in the periphery. As an insider to center educational and cultural establishment, he is able to present less known (confidential?) documents for wider scrutiny.

Central to Phillipson's frame of analysis is his notion of *linguicism*. Analogous to constructs like sexism and racism, Phillipson considers linguicism as effecting inequalities based on the language one speaks. He defines linguicism as 'ideologies, structures, and practices which are used to legitimate, effectuate, and reproduce an unequal division of power and resources (both material and immaterial) between groups which are defined on the basis of language' (1992: 47). He defines English linguistic imperialism as a specific type of linguicism whereby 'the dominance of English is asserted and maintained by the establishment and continuous reconstitution of structural and cultural inequalities between English and other languages' (*ibid.*: 47). Although it is very insightful to see language in this manner as a tool that is involved in the hegemony of developed countries, we should scrutinize the definition for the exact role language plays. According to the first definition, language functions as one possible way of categorizing communities to perpetrate inequalities. What enables this dominance are 'ideologies, structures and practices' that are considered extra-linguistic. In other words, language does not effect this inequality—it is just an arbitrary construct exploited by politico-economic structures to carry out their own agenda of dominance. The second definition, that of English linguistic imperialism, similarly sees the dominance of English as maintained and reconstituted by pre-existing, pre-linguistic, and presumably more fundamental 'structural and cultural inequalities'. In fact, Phillipson eventually declares that language in itself is not good or evil—it is how language is used by power structures that implicates it in evil (*ibid.*: 318). We must note, however, that this perspective fails to probe some of the subtler ways in which language is implicated in imperialism. When language is defined as a semiotic system that encodes ideologies and possesses the power to reproduce politico-economic structures, the connection with imperialism can be perceived in more direct ways. It is now possible to understand how language embodies and sustains the 'ideologies, structures, and practices' to effect inequality. The dominance of English is therefore not only a *result* of politico-economic inequalities between the center and periphery, it is also a *cause* of these inequalities.

Employing a structuralist perspective on linguistic imperialism, Phillipson announces at the beginning that 'ELT needs to be situated in the macro-societal theoretical perspective' (*ibid.*: 2). In considering how social, economic, governmental, and cultural institutions effect inequality, his perspective becomes rather too impersonal and global. What is sorely missed is the individual, the local, the particular. It is important to find out how linguistic hegemony is experienced in the day-to-day life of the people and communities in the periphery. How does English compete for dominance with other languages in the streets, markets, homes, schools, and villages of periphery communities? How does English infiltrate the hearts and minds of the people there? What is missing, then, is a micro-social perspective—the lived culture and everyday experience of periphery communities. These are important considerations that would not only complement Phillipson's perspective but, as I will demonstrate below, help to qualify some of his claims.

A consequence of this macro-societal perspective is that there is little sense of the classroom. In a project claiming to 'unravel some of the links between ELT and imperialism' (*ibid.*: 313), and to contribute mainly to the English language teaching enterprise (rather than to political economy, for example), this is a much needed perspective. However, we do not see how linguistic inequalities are effected, propagated, or played out in instructional contexts in the periphery.[3] Similarly, teachers fail to receive any advice on whether and how English can be taught in the context of imperialism. Phillipson envisages no ways by which English can be learned and then used to empower the local communities, or to further their own cultural, social, and educational interests.

Phillipson's vision of change is also influenced by his macro-social perspective. He argues that the status of English will only be challenged in the event of structural changes in geopolitical relations. He wonders whether the rise of Japan or Germany as economically powerful countries will usher the fall of English and the rise of alternate languages. He also tries to draw an analogy from the disintegration of the USSR and the rise of languages colonized by Russian. Much of this discussion is speculative. However, post-colonial theorists will argue that resistance to English is already taking place in the everyday life of people in the periphery. Such subtle strategies of resistance are more often discursive and behavioral than ambitiously global or overtly structural. So nativized versions of English, novel English discourses in post-colonial literature, and the hybrid mixing of languages in indigenous communities, are quiet ways in which resistance against English is already being displayed. They challenge the ideologies and institutions which undergird the dominance of English. The ESL classroom itself can function as a site of resistance against the values and pedagogical practices from the center. To orientate to such modes of resistance, Phillipson needs not just a semiotic perspective on language, but a different model of socio-political domination. The determinism and impersonality of his analytical models (i.e. Marxism and Galtung's structural theory of imperialism) prevent Phillipson from exploring some of the more complex issues of linguistic domination and resistance raised above.

Phillipson's inability to attend to the micro-societal issues of domination can be related also to his research methodology. His findings are developed from interviews with experts, applied linguists, and cultural officers from the West (specifically, eight in number) and official documents pertaining to the activities of Western cultural agencies. First, the data base is very limited for a complete treatment of some of the themes he explores. Also, the book does not contain the *range* of data sources and research approaches that can help the writer (and readers) cross-check his findings. A more troubling question is, how can one find out about linguistic imperialism in the periphery from the very personnel and agencies from the center who implement this domination? Of course, Phillipson performs a skillful piece of deconstructionist interpretation, reading between the lines to display the hidden motives and functions embodied in the documents and pronouncements of these agencies. But this is a methodology of indirection. He cites brief examples on language planning from Scandinavia and Namibia, but admits 'I have drawn on much of the relevant written evidence accessible to a scholar who is resident in the Centre' (*ibid.*: 313). But to really study how linguistic imperialism is carried out in the periphery and, in particular, how it is complexly experienced in everyday life, one must undertake work in the periphery. Library research in Britain will not suffice. Therefore, Phillipson's contribution suffers as well as gains from being a perspective of and from the center.

Holliday's project, which explores the cultural conflicts that result from center-sponsored ELT pedagogy in the periphery, offers what in many respects is a much-needed corrective to Phillipson's approach. While Phillipson explores the subject from a macro-level orientation, Holliday develops a micro-level perspective emerging from instructional practices. Holliday takes us to specific periphery communities to provide vignettes of teaching experiences there. A consequence of this approach is that while Phillipson suggests the political domination of the periphery through ELT to be somewhat inexorable, Holliday shows the different layers of culture and context in the local teaching situations that complicate unilateral domination. In other words, Holliday's perspective suggests how and why ideological domination by the center is not always guaranteed.

However, Holliday's approach lacks a strong theoretical grounding (comparable to Phillipson's) that would enable him to interpret his data in the light of emerging developments in critical scholarship. This also affects the analytical constructs Holliday employs. His main distinction throughout the book between BANA (standing for Britain, Australasia, and North America) and TESEP ('derived from *ter*tiary, *se*condary, *p*rimary'), to refer respectively to the countries which supply and receive ELT resources, lacks sufficient motivation. There is a mixing of categories here, since the acronym BANA is made up of nations and TESEP refers to different *levels* of education. In contrast, Phillipson's categories *center* and *periphery* tap a long tradition of scholarship in political economy, and situate ELT directly in the global socio-political nexus. Moreover, Holliday (1994: 13, 95, 105) states that education in BANA countries is commercially motivated, while in TESEP it is 'state oriented'. However, not all educational levels and institutions in the periphery are state oriented. Similarly, the center ELT enterprise is not completely commercial. (See Phillipson 1992 for an examination of the intriguing complicity between state, academic, and commercial institutions in the Western ELT enterprise.)

Holliday's approach is also affected by a limited definition of culture. He argues that since culture is so multiple and shifting we should consider broad terms like 'national culture' as unwieldy, and decides not to devote as much attention to them as to classroom and school cultures. But this is hardly an acceptable reason to ignore larger cultural domains, particularly when they are crucial for understanding micro-cultures of the classroom. Furthermore, Holliday separates culture from power in order to discuss pedagogical differences in an uncontroversial and non-political manner. Because of this separation, he misses many of the insights of cultural politics that would have enabled him to explore the more problematic conflicts in transnational pedagogy transfer. In fact, he goes on to atomize the classroom context in such a way that the larger ideological and cultural problems between BANA and TESEP are conveniently obscured. As a result, he ends up arguing that the pedagogical problems are universal across all BANA and TESEP classrooms, and that if there are differences between both instructional sites they are those of degree and not kind (*ibid.*: 168). While Holliday's microscopic focus on classroom life is commendable, this does not mean that one has to lose sight of the larger political context in which the classrooms are located. In this, he displays the reverse limitation of Phillipson's.

There is also a lack of historical depth in Holiday's orientation. The TESEP communities seem as if they only have a present (i.e. the moment Holliday observed the classrooms) and no past. This affects some of the interpretations he offers. For instance, he says that the 'integrationist' (or, pedagogically flexible and process-oriented) methods from BANA are difficult to employ in TESEP because their educational system is 'collectionist'. But one can argue that the rigidly defined curriculum and product-oriented educational system of 'collectionist' TESEP were actually introduced by the West during the colonial period. Some of the indigenous educational traditions have been successful in connecting knowledge and life through non-formal education, and integrating different disciplinary perspectives. But Holliday shows limited awareness of indigenous educational practices and does not attempt to explore them. What Holliday eventually offers us are brief and shifting vignettes from different classrooms in diverse TESEP settings. This lack of a solid grounding in the larger context of community life could lead to the imposition of the researcher's views on other people's cultures.

Although Holliday claims that his study is ethnographic, he gives no indication that a systematic study with pre-designed research objectives was conducted in a well focused setting.[4] Claims based on brief observation notes of classes he had visited as an expatriate teacher and project officer raise many questions. What, for example, gives authority to the researcher to claim that his own interpretation of the teaching problems in an alien society is the valid explanation? Even in the cases where he acknowledges differences of point of view with the locals, would the writer's authorial position provide more legitimacy for *his* version of the story? In what way would his identity affect the study? How would the understanding of an insider on the same issues be different? There are also questions on the validity and reliability of the data—does one vignette in a classroom provide sufficient evidence to generalize about all classes in the periphery?

Holliday goes on to offer a revised version of the communicative approach as the way out for pedagogical imperialism. While many would challenge the ability of communicative approach to be culture-neutral, or to grapple with issues of power (Peirce 1989), it is also unsatisfactory to consider pedagogical correctives without discussing the ideological role of English language. Is the inappropriate application of teaching methods the only cause of opposition to ELT by periphery teachers and students? What about the colonial associations English holds for periphery communities? Would using a 'correct' method help overcome opposition to English language? Can teaching methods enable effective language acquisition irrespective of the attitudes and motivations of students? Phillipson, it must be commended, takes a more holistic approach in considering the politics of English as a language together with the export of methods and textbooks to teach it.

Holliday's failure to empower periphery communities by tapping their own educational and linguistic traditions for ELT purposes raises questions about the purposes and aims of his project. Holliday (1994: 216) states that

> In a sense, the means analysis plays the role of ongoing market research, finding out what form this commodity should take to ensure fair and meaningful exchange. (There is no reason, in these terms, to pretend that the aid donor is not getting anything in return. 'Making friends and influencing people' seems to me perfectly respectable as long as the trade is clear and meaningful.)

Assuming that the 'trade' has to, and will, go on, he is interested in making the 'commodity' more marketable. Holliday therefore seems to address his book primarily to aid donors and cultural officers. It is from this point of view that some of the other ethnographic practices seem to be recommended. Holliday (*ibid.*: 217) says that it is inevitable that a certain amount of 'impression management', 'covert procedure', and 'repression of conflict provoking findings', should be adopted while researching in expatriate settings. Such practices would raise serious ethical questions about center-sponsored educational aid and research in the periphery.

The recent flurry of publications on the challenges facing ELT in the periphery is commendable, but prompts the question: whose interests are served by this scholarly attention? Holliday makes no secret of his intentions—he is interested in improving the center-based commercial enterprise. He therefore educates the aid donors, project managers, and expatriate teachers on the cultural conflicts in methods transfer in order to make the funding, managing, and teaching of ELT in the periphery more efficient. Even Phillipson's critique is center-influenced, since he uses predominantly center-based experts and data to conduct his analysis. For critical pedagogical research on periphery ELT to be initiated and conducted primarily by center-based scholars invites suspicion. Scholars and teachers from the periphery can be expected to be wary of resistance to English being diluted, even appropriated, by the center in order to further its hegemonic thrusts.

Rectifying the imbalances

This comparative discussion of the two strands of work on the geopolitics of ELT suggests some correctives to be adopted in future studies. We must first realize the moral and intellectual necessity of adopting a periphery-based perspective on the subject. The danger of the center appropriating periphery resistance and the over-representation of center-based perspectives in the field, are important reasons for this corrective. The dearth of empirical data on ELT in the periphery, and on the perspectives of periphery students and teachers, is conveyed by none other than the center-based scholars who have published on this subject (Holliday 1994: 10, Phillipson 1992: 308). Furthermore, Phillipson's distanced library research, and Holliday's fleeting images of periphery classrooms, point to the need for grounded knowledge construction on this subject. This book will therefore offer a comprehensive description of periphery instructional contexts, locating the study in a clearly defined setting over an extended period of participant observation in order to develop an insider perspective.

While Phillipson overstates the rigidity of power structures, Holliday underestimates the reproductive power of larger political forces in his atomized cultural sites. The treatment in this book is conscious of the complementary claims of the forces of reproduction and resistance in schooling, and explores this dynamic with greater balance. Similarly, while Phillipson is too macro-social in his treatment, and Holliday is too micro-social, this book will attempt to integrate both perspectives. Although the data employed here come from ethnographic methods which orientate closely to discourse, everyday behavior, and the lived culture of the subjects, the interpretation will be informed by the larger socio-political conditions in the community. While it is important to understand how ideological domination of ELT is manifested in everyday life, the casual happenings in the classroom and the lived culture of the students would make sense only in the larger context of the socio-political structures that govern the life of the community. In fact, it is possible to focus on classroom life, and still see how larger socio-political concerns get dramatized through instructional activities. This approach is made possible by the theoretical perspective on schooling adopted here, which sees classroom and school life as open to forces of political economy.

The type of inquiry outlined above calls for an ethnographic orientation for the collection of data cited in this book. Ethnographic research focuses on culture and discourse as practiced by members of the particular community. It is also well known for considering the behavior and attitudes of community members, as displayed in the local, everyday level of social interactions. It has a tradition of understanding cultural life in naturalistic sites, amidst the diverse social forces that influence it. This approach helps us to understand ELT and English from the perspective of periphery communities, and enables an analysis of the socio-political factors that shape learning in the day-to-day life of community and classroom. The ample scope ethnography provides for interpretation enables the researcher to read complex ideological messages from the localized data. There are, of course, special challenges in using an ethnographic approach for critical pedagogical purposes, which we will now address.

Practicing a critical ethnography

The strength of traditional ethnography lies in its focus on the local, particular, and concrete. However, this microscopic focus on the local has usually influenced ethnography to ignore the larger, macro-level, socio-political forces. In fact, the positivistic tradition in ethnography has made practitioners treat ideological considerations as distorting, if not irrelevant. Furthermore, the somewhat abstract socio-political structures and processes are not always immediately visible in the contexts where ethnographers do their everyday fieldwork. But there is an increasing awareness that the concrete language, symbols, rituals, and behavior of the community make better sense when seen in the light of larger political forces. Similarly, scholars of macro-social structures (such as political scientists) realize that it is important to analyze how everyday discourses influence and are influenced by political processes (Marcus and Fischer 1986). Such merging fields of inquiry augur well for a cultural description sensitive to wider political concerns.

Another limiting practice in traditional ethnography is its ahistorical perspective. Typically, the cultural conditions described are captured in a static state—convenient for description, abstraction, and generalization. In fact, the structuralist tradition in anthropology has made a virtue of such an ahistorical perspective. Usually ethnographers reconcile the problem of time with the notion of the *ethnographic present*—i.e. culture captured in an existential state, true only at the time it was observed by the scholar (Heath 1983: 7–8). But to understand the complexity of the discursive practices of the periphery, we have to situate the communities in their changing historical contexts, and develop an interpretive framework that looks at their linguistic and cultural practices, as shaped (for example) by recent colonial and post-colonial realities. We have to historicize the ethnographic present.

The challenge, however, is not just to connect the local with the global, the concrete with the abstract, and structure with history, but to do so with a critical edge. In other words, the purpose of meshing these domains is to better understand the potential of culture to lead that community towards domination or empowerment. This task is not served by a noncommittal description of culture. Ethnography becomes a personally committed interpretive activity, whereby the researcher attempts to explicate the cultural strands that may facilitate community empowerment and self-determination. Such concerns are difficult to develop from the tradition of *descriptive ethnography* hitherto practiced, which adopts a detached, value-free, egalitarian view of culture. What is needed is a *critical ethnography* that can build an element of ideological critique into cultural description.

The project of critical ethnography has been inspired by the realization that even descriptive ethnography is not, after all, free from ideological biases. An uncritical ethnography has only laid itself open to being used by dominant communities for their political purposes. Asad (1973) and Hymes (1969) explore the manner in which ethnography has served the imperialistic purposes of Western regimes. Colonial administrators have used ethnographic knowledge to understand the culture of periphery communities to make their rule effective, and to expropriate their cultural resources and artifacts. Such revelations have made it important for contemporary ethnographers to be wary of the interests and uses that motivate their work.

There are many challenges to be faced in adopting a critical ethnography, not least the ethnographer's need for more interpretative freedom than would typically be allowed to articulate the meanings of the informants. While traditional ethnography has claimed to treat the words of the informants from the community as sacrosanct, critical ethnography analyzes the words in relation to the larger historical processes and social contradictions, searching for the hidden forces that structure life. While descriptive ethnography would attempt to smooth over the contradictions among informants, critical ethnography considers the explanation of these contra-dictions to be its very quest (Willis 1978: 18). Although this raises the difficult problem of the (often alien) ethnographer claiming to have more knowledge of the community than the community members themselves, others such as Geertz (1983) have explained this as a strength of the disciplined outsider. While everyday cultural life is taken for granted and merely 'lived out' without theorization by the community members, the ethnographer possesses the detachment to rationalize it. However, one must be careful not to read things into the culture arbitrarily—the native perspective and lived experience are still important. Geertz describes the challenge as one of balancing the insider's 'experience near' view of culture with the outsider's 'experience far' perspective (*ibid.*: 55–70).

Apart from such hermeneutic challenges, there are tricky issues of power inherent in the relationship between the researcher and subjects—the observer and observed—which need to be negotiated with sensitivity. When a researcher studies the culture of a community, he or she is necessarily objectifying the subjects. This objectification provides immense power to the ethnographer to read into the community notions which the researcher believes its members cannot articulate. Their intellectual status and knowledge (certified usually by their institutional affiliations and their degrees) can also provide them further means of power over the typically less educated informants. The description of culture under such unequally weighted research contexts can produce skewed findings.[5] Since it is questionable whether power difference can be avoided altogether, researchers should negotiate this power difference in such a way that it would not distort their findings. Researchers and subjects are now collaborating on the design and implementation of the research so that their relative status can be negotiated more directly in the process of conducting the study.

It is not unusual for informants to rebel against the subtle forms of power they sense in the researcher. There are cases where they resist volunteering information, or deliberately mislead the researchers in order to get even with them. This is also a way for informants to reclaim their agency and individuality. As a result, researchers increasingly realize that they are not dealing with the conventional 'naive' native informant. The wider dissemination of knowledge and the spread of literacy mean that informants may be remarkably well informed about studies on their own culture and those of the researcher's community. The 'data' they proffer researchers are therefore informed by such knowledge. During interviews by a researcher on Tamil culture, a villager could first consult previous ethnographic accounts by MacGilvray or Banks (i.e. by American ethnographers) in order to provide a safe, 'textbook' answer. There is complex reflexivity in the contemporary research situation—where informants are aware of what persona researchers expect them to adopt as 'naive' informants, what knowledge researchers can be expected to possess about their culture, and the type of notions stereotypically held by the researcher's community on the informant's culture. The answers elicited from the informant will then be highly mediated by such awareness, and are by no means 'pure' (i.e. spontaneous, innocent, or authentic).

It is also the case that the researcher–informant relationship is guided by certain conventionalized expectations and behavior. Take, for example, the research interview. This has been revealed to be a highly routine speech event with discourse conventions of its own (Milroy 1987: 41–51). We all know, for example, that it is the right of the researcher to ask questions and that of the informant to answer. The researcher initiates the conversation, sets or changes topics, and terminates the conversation. The informant's role is discursively passive. The interviewer possesses ample scope to derive certain answers through the right to frame questions in desired ways. (The discourse conventions of the interview again highlight the power of the researcher.) Interviews conducted under such constraints are more likely to produce the researcher's assumptions on culture than the informant's.

What all this implies is that the researcher cannot stand apart from the events and actions of the community to observe them objectively for scholarly purposes. The researchers are always acting and generating action during their long stay in the community. The mere presence of a non-member is enough to activate certain social dynamics that may alter the everyday life of the community. (This can be more dramatic when the researcher is a foreigner.) The awareness of the outsider's lifestyle and values can influence the community to look at their own values with new eyes, and to alter their behavior in significant ways. It follows that the social and cultural life of the community will never be the same once a researcher enters the scene, and that the context of research has to be actively incorporated in interpreting the data. The post-modernist realization of the mediated nature of knowledge enables us to reconcile ourselves to such contingencies.

If the discourse and subjectivity of the researcher can mediate ethnographic findings in the fieldwork situation, there are other ways in which this can occur in the writing of ethnography. First of all, ethnographic writing follows genre rules of its own. Marcus and Fischer (1986: 23) describe the rules of conventional ethnographic writing, which they call *ethnographic realism*, as 'allud[ing] to a whole by means of parts ... which constantly evoke a social and cultural totality' with 'close attention to detail and redundant demonstrations' to prove 'that the writer shared and experienced this whole other world'. In presenting the research according to these textual conventions, one claims authenticity, accuracy, and empirical validity for one's findings. Since the reams of field notes and audiotapes are never completely available to the readers or the scholarly community, it is always difficult to say to what extent the data has been filtered through the genre conventions of ethnographic writing. The presentation of research is also influenced by the relevant academic discourses and scholarly conventions, such as the previous knowledge on that subject and/or the dominant questions in the field. Back from the fieldwork process of (presumably) looking at the culture from the natives' point of view, the ethnographer will now interpret it from his or her community's point of view for its reception. What comes out as ethnographic text, then, is a highly reconstructed, discursively mediated, product. Between the fieldwork and the textual construction, there are many intermediary discourses and contextual forces that shape the cultural knowledge. (In fact, 'ethno-graph'—the writing of culture—is already in written form as field notes, having already gone through the discursive mediation of researcher's language and cultural perspectives.)

What all this suggests is that the ethnographer's culture is a construct. We must give up the assumption that what the ethnographer presents is a value-free, undistorted, unmediated, complete description of a community's ways and words. What is described is constructed by the ethnographer in a highly selective way in congruence with the discourses and conventions governing research. While descriptive ethnography would feel uncomfortable in the face of such multifaceted issues of discursive mediation, critical ethnography is open to such concerns. It encourages a reflexive attitude towards the presentation of the culture in question.[6]

Recent publications popularizing ethnographic research for practitioners in ELT circles (Watson-Gegeo 1988, Holliday 1994, Hornberger 1994) operate comfortably within the descriptive tradition, and fail to alert readers to the ideological and discursive complexities of doing research in 'alien' communities—especially situations in which predominantly white-skinned teacher/researchers from rich communities visit dilapidated classrooms of brown-skinned vernacular-speaking students in periphery communities. We need to give special attention to the subtle mediation of values in the *process* (i.e. the research practice) and *product* (i.e. the writing) of ethnography as we read cultural descriptions—including the one that follows.

The research context

In order to meet the challenges described above, I foreground the voices and acts of the periphery subjects in their context, and narrate the classroom experiences with some reflexivity, inviting the readers' own interpretive initiative. The grounded data are also used to interrogate theoretical constructs in currency in the ELT profession, to help initiate a dialog between theory and practice. At higher levels of abstraction, I relate the stories here to experiences narrated by other scholars in a variety of periphery communities and classrooms in order to generate useful pedagogical and cultural generalizations. I attempt, therefore, to sustain a creative tension between the *narrative* of the concrete situation and the *argumentation* in terms of published scholarly constructs.

The experiences narrated here derive from my fieldwork in the communities and classrooms in Sri Lanka over a period of four years (from June 1990 to July 1994). The focus is on the Tamil community in the northern peninsula of Jaffna, which is defined by its native language (a 'prestigious' dialect of the Tamil language), culture (identified with Saiva religion and Dravidian traditions, distinct from the majority Sinhalese people and other ethnic groups in the island), geography (inhabiting a peninsula detached from India in the north and the rest of Sri Lanka in the south), and political aspiration (manifested in its struggle for self-determination from the majority Sinhala community, while enjoying a *de facto* separate state during the period of the research).

Although I am a native of this community, having taught English for about ten years at secondary and tertiary educational levels, the data I have used in the book come from the more disciplined period of ethnographic fieldwork (during the four years mentioned above). Although the focus of the study is clearly on classroom practices, it is important to situate these amidst the larger socio-political processes. Studies conducted at both levels during the four-year period are as follows:

Community setting

1 Changing patterns of bilingualism in interpersonal and social domains (Canagarajah 1995b)
2 Code-switching strategies between buyers and sellers in market places (Canagarajah 1995a)
3 Ethnography of argumentative discourse strategies in a Saiva Tamil village (Canagarajah 1992)
4 Bilingual discourse strategies of the local academic community (Canagarajah 1996)
5 Modes of negotiating vernacular and English discourses by creative writers (Canagarajah 1994)

Classroom setting

6 A year-long ethnography of a tertiary-level ESL course on the attitudes, motivation, and learning strategies of students (Canagarajah 1993b)
7 Classroom observation of ESL teacher trainees in secondary schools for the manner in which they negotiate L1 and L2 with students (Canagarajah 1995c)
8 A year-long observation of tertiary-level ESL teachers adopting a task-based teaching method (Canagarajah 1995d)
9 The process of streaming students in tertiary-level ESL classes, and its connection to the socio-economic background of students (Canagarajah and Iyer 1993)
10 Case studies of research writing by postgraduate students (Canagarajah 1997a)

It is important to note that these studies cover a wide range of settings and discourses. The extra-classroom data represent the village and the city, the market and the university, fisherfolk and professionals. The classroom research covers teachers and students in tertiary and secondary contexts, negotiating different language skills.

Although the *approach* used to elicit, collect, record and interpret the data from the above studies was primarily ethnographic, a variety of *methods* were employed. While research approaches provide an overall orientation to the study in the light of a coherent set of philosophical assumptions, disciplinary tradition, and analytical focus, each approach could be realized by a variety of specific methods. I incorporated a range of methods to collect data with a clear focus on the community's point of view as it emerges through everyday language, behavior, and other cultural practices in the natural social contexts of occurrence:

1 Field notes (deriving from participant and non-participant observation)
2 Formal and informal interviews with teachers and/or students
3 Recording of linguistic interactions (audio-recorded, delayed-recalled, and/or spontaneously transcribed)
4 Textual analysis of written products (students' notes, essays, assignments; teachers' records, lesson plans)
5 Questionnaires

These methods were used as appropriate for the different research purposes and settings. The different sources of data would check any eccentricity in interpretation.

The focus of the data was primarily linguistic and discursive. That is, priority was given to observing the manner in which the words of the teachers and students embodied or generated changing attitudes, values, roles and relationships. Of course this is to be expected in a linguistically-motivated study, where the learning of language is the object of analysis. The interplay between the competing languages (English and Tamil) is central to this study. However, since the focus is on the lived culture, language is a complex medium that can reveal the stated and unstated attitudes quite insightfully. As we discussed in the previous chapter, language is also the most subtle and effective vehicle of ideologies and cultures. The linguistic interaction between the different subjects dramatizes the subtle negotiation of statuses, values, and identities that typically takes place in the community and classroom. However, language cannot be used as the sole means of interpretation in the fashion of much relativistic, acontextual readings in contemporary humanities. It is for this reason that social practice, institutional structures, and historical forces are actively employed in the contextualization of interpretation.

Some of the studies here were conducted while I was the teacher of the classes concerned. While the teacher/researcher role does create certain tensions, it is not always inimical to producing insightful findings. Much of this sort of work (Canagarajah 1993b, 1993c) follows in the tradition of *action research* (Nunan 1990). The dynamics behind action research are not unlike the challenges in ethnographic participant-observation, which I have used extensively in my research activities. While ethnographic/classroom observation keeps one detached from the study, participant observation enables closer involvement in the processes of schooling and community life, providing deeper insights into the participants' orientations. For example, my daily interaction with the students in negotiating meanings through English and participating in the students' successes and failures, with the attendant need to revise my own teaching strategy, provided a vantage point over their perspectives. Moreover, I enjoyed natural access to their daily work and activities, without having to flag my role as researcher.

Studying my own community makes my research status somewhat unique amongst studies on periphery ELT. My insider status in periphery communities has helped me to avoid some of the limitations foreign ethnographers would face in lacking sufficient background information, or in gaining access to socially intimate sites. It has also helped me to overcome the power differentials they would encounter in coming from colonial communities. However, there are other challenges periphery researchers have to face in such an ethnography. While defamiliarization comes easily to alien researchers, an insider has to struggle to adopt such a perspective. Being an insider does not guarantee an 'accurate' or 'correct' understanding of the cultural and attitudinal processes of the community in question. The culture that the local ethnographer presents is no less a 'construct' of the different contextual and discursive forces at play during the research process. Although ethnographic studies of one's own community are peculiar, they are not rare. In recent times many center ethnographers have realized the need for 'studying up'—observing their own urban institutional cultures—as a corrective for the earlier practice of 'studying down' remote, less developed, colonized villages (Marcus and Fischer 1986: 152–7).

It is important to realize, however, that since cultures and subjectivities are multiple and hybrid it is difficult for anyone to claim that he or she is fully native to a culture or community. We enjoy different levels of membership in the different discourse communities within a single geographical (or national) boundary. In my case, I am in many ways a relative 'outsider' in my Tamil community: while the dominant religious identity is Saivite, I am Christian. While the emergent linguistic nationalism favors the Tamil monolinguals, I am a bilingual. My profession as an English teacher holds low academic and social status in the community at a time of linguistic nationalism. My middle-class bilingual identity would enjoy a coveted status among educated circles, while being stigmatized by monolingual groups. On the other hand, my male gender and *vellalla* caste identity provide certain forms of power in the local social hierarchy (although this status is also being increasingly questioned). Yet, born and raised in this community, and having been schooled in the vernacular-based educational system here, in some senses I enjoy in-group solidarity. The different levels of insider/outsider, higher/lower statuses I enjoy according to the different caste, class, religious, gender, and linguistic parameters create quite complex tensions. I realize the need to negotiate my own subject positions during the research and writing, in terms of the different subjects and contexts I encounter. This realization is a powerful reminder of the theme articulated above—that research is itself a form of social practice, and enjoys no immunity from or transcendence of the contextual realities governing any activity.

Conclusion

The challenges to the Enlightenment paradigm of knowledge construction (which I articulated in the last chapter) have a bearing on the methodologies I employ in my research. It is futile attempting to suppress the mediations of the context, the researcher's subjectivity, and the discourses of the researchers and the participants in search of unconditional objectivity. We should actively engage with these contextual factors in order to develop reliable findings from our inquiry. In this vein, I describe in the next chapter the salient historical and political tendencies in periphery communities that should inform our consideration of micro-level classroom life.

Notes

1 Note, for example, that ethnographic research has a critical ethnography (Willis 1977, G. Anderson 1989), and text analysis has a critical discourse analytical school (Fowler 1985, Kress 1985, Fairclough 1989). Similarly, the other approaches can be given a critical orientation, although they do not boast of similarly well-known sub-schools: e.g. classroom interaction (Canagarajah 1995c) or learning strategies (Canagarajah 1993b).

2 The book has already been praised for its 'eloquent' and 'stimulating' discussion by center scholars (Holborow 1993, Ricento 1994). However, a periphery-based perspective on the book will be radically different; see Canagarajah 1995e for a more complete discussion.

3 In Chapter 8, 'English language teaching in action', we are made to expect a discussion of classroom practice. What is actually discussed here are directions in ELT research, and policies and practices of educational aid.

4 In the final chapters, Holliday introduces ethnography to expatriate teachers, drawing on illustrations from his own methodology, from which it is presumed that we will glean the approach he takes to gathering his data.

5 Sociolinguist Labov (1972) offers an interesting example of how power difference affects research findings. He has explained the notion of cognitive and linguistic deficiency 'discovered' by Bereiter and Engelmann (1966) in Black youth as being a direct result of the interview situation, in which aged Caucasian middle-class researchers intimidate urban underclass Black teenagers into silence, or 'grunts and moans'.

6 Anthropologists like Geertz (1983) and Marcus and Fischer (1986) are of the opinion that the relativistic tradition of ethnography is already well motivated to deal with the post-modernist realizations, enabling one to interpret cultural descriptions with an awareness of the conflicting discursive influences going into their construction.

3 Resistance to English in historical perspective

It's good that everything's gone, except their language,
which is everything.

Derek Walcott, *North and South*

The English language has had a history of imposition for political and
material reasons in most periphery communities, often in competition with
native languages. It is still deeply implicated in struggles for dominance
against other languages, with conflicting implications for the construction of
identity, community, and culture of the local people. In opting to learn and
use English, therefore, students are making complex ideological and social
choices. For users of English in these communities, the language embodies its
controversial history since colonial times. The fact that their perception of
English is colored by these conflicts of the past makes it important for English
teachers to develop a historical perspective on their profession and the
language.

Unfortunately for contemporary researchers, who need access to reliable
and balanced sources, the colonial history of English is often shrouded in
stereotypes, half-truths, and myths. On the one hand, there are the legislative
records and memoirs of colonial administrators, which largely considered
the teaching of English as one more 'white man's burden', undertaken for the
improvement of uncivilized communities. On the other hand, there is the
later revisionist historiography, which reflects the nationalistic political
temperament by projecting natives as holding a collective hatred towards the
language imposed on them for ulterior material and ideological purposes. It
is unfortunate that center scholars feel compelled to use whichever set of
histories happens to be readily accessible, since such sources can lead to
exaggerations of one form or another. Alternative sources of information
must be tapped: past and present records of oral history, and vernacular texts
of the local communities, in particular, can provide a window to the impact
of English on everyday life at the grassroots level. It is understandable that
many center scholars may not know the local languages or have ethnographic
field experience to gain access to such materials, but it is important to delve

deeper into periphery communities to recover their occluded narratives, and develop a more complex perspective on how they have negotiated the hegemony of English.

Ambivalences in the reception of colonial English

Pennycook's recent *Cultural Politics of English as an International Language* is exceptional in grappling with the paradoxes and ironies in the status and functions of English in the periphery. He goes beyond the usual dichotomies and stereotypes that characterize this historiography to acknowledge greater tension in the roles of English and the vernacular. He captures what he calls the 'critical ambivalences' in which English is caught up, embodying conflicting attitudes and values. Surveying the role of English in the colonial period under the dual discourses of Orientalism ('policies in favor of education in local languages for both the colonized and the colonizers') and Anglicism ('policies in favor of education in English'), Pennycook (1994a: 74–5) explores the complex ways in which both policies existed side-by-side to serve the interests of the colonial agenda in the periphery. He thereby corrects the stereotypical view that Anglicism brazenly triumphed over Orientalism (which other scholars, including Phillipson 1992, have adopted).

Pennycook (*ibid.*: 103) theorizes the complementary relation of Orientalism and Anglicism thus:

> First, both Anglicism and Orientalism operated alongside each other; second, Orientalism was as much a part of colonialism as was Anglicism; third, English was withheld as much as it was promoted; fourth, colonized people demanded access to English; and finally, the power of English was not so much in its widespread imposition but in its operating as the eye of the colonial panopticon.

Foucault's notion of the panopticon is employed to theorize how certain discourses serve to conduct subtle surveillance and control by providing constant knowledge for the powerful on the dominated groups. Pennycook also invokes Said's broader conception of Orientalism (Said 1979), theorizing the European scholarship on the Eastern languages and cultures as both enabling, and being enabled by, imperialist interests.

Although Pennycook presents both Orientalism and Anglicism as orchestrated to serve the reproductive agenda of the colonizers, we need to go further and see how the dialectic between these discourses also spawned native resistance against the colonial project. Although Pennycook generally acknowledges the sources of resistance in the post-colonial world, he documents little signs of resistance before decolonization. Paradoxically, within Anglicism itself there were the seeds for its destabilization—planted by English education, which created a breed of natives influenced by enlightened liberal democratic discourses, who demanded such values from colonial rulers. Opposition to colonialism and Anglicism was expressed by natives in subtle and sometimes partially expressed ways. Encouraged by local discourses, cultures, and philosophical traditions, this tradition of resistance later played an important function in the post-colonial context, engendering related forms of linguistic resistance and appropriation. Incorporating this strand into the colonial dialectic adds even more complexity to the historical background of English. This is not to deny that, despite these sources of resistance, colonialism and Anglicism had many ways of imposing their reproductive agenda.

Another more vibrant and ideologically sturdy resistance to Anglicism—also expressed in subtle forms of opposition in everyday life—needs to be taken into account if we are to do justice to periphery resistance to English. Following local English teacher Chelliah 1922 (who wrote his history of ELT in Jaffna while the British were still present), we might call this movement 'vernacularism'. Orientalists shared with Anglicists a belief in the superiority of Western to Eastern literature and learning; they also favored the study of Oriental languages as a means to exercise social control over the populace, and to inculcate Western ideas. Not surprisingly, the position of vernacularists was different, as I will illustrate later. Vernacularism promoted the superiority (or at least the equality) of indigenous languages and cultures; it also saw through the reproductive agenda of Orientalism, and generated ways of retaining indigenous discourses and cultural traditions with or without learning English.

Pennycook's treatment of the post-colonial status of English, especially in Singapore and Malaysia, also goes beyond stereotypes to show the manner in which Anglicism thrives in the local communities at a period of intense nationalism. He surveys discourses such as pragmatism, meritocratism, and internationalism, that make the local people still 'desire' English. Some features of this positive valuation of English jostle besides oppositional perspectives. Therefore

> it is both the language of modernity and the language of decadence, the 'first language' (the medium of education) but not the 'mother tongue' (the racially assigned language), a neutral medium of communication yet the bearer of Western values, the language of equality and yet the distributor of inequality, the language of Singaporean identity and yet the mother tongue of few (1994a: 255).

However, Pennycook sees such attitudes of natives as still favoring the hegemony of English. He does not explicate the complex sources of resistance in everyday life, though he does introduce a chapter in the end to discuss how resistance to English and appropriation of English by local languages and cultures is expressed through Third World literature. But a discussion of resistance in literature might give the wrong impression of there being no linguistic resistance and/or appropriation in everyday discourse. It might suggest that resistance is an élite activity, restricted to educated bilinguals alone.

Pennycook's discussion of the post-colonial status and functions of English in the periphery stops short of answering some of the crucial questions evoked by the narration. It is possible to extend his analysis closer to the linguistic domain to understand how the conflicting attitudes towards languages are expressed in everyday face-to-face interaction in the periphery communities. Such an approach would help develop a more micro-social perspective. Because Pennycook situates English in different domains in order to understand its status and functions—such as religion, education, and mass media, somewhat in the tradition of Fishman 1967—he overlooks such considerations. We can take some of Pennycook's insights to their logical conclusion and ask the following questions: If there are conflicting attitudes towards English, how are they sustained? How do such attitudes manifest themselves in the linguistic interaction among speakers? What implications do such attitudes have for the structure, values, and functions of English in the periphery? How do speakers in the periphery resolve these tensions linguistically?

Colonial period: white man's burden vs. brown person's tact

The processes by which the British spread English in the colonies and the motivations for this activity have been well described. As in other colonies, when the British brought the ethno-linguistically diverse island of what they called Ceylon under one political umbrella in 1796, they set up English as the language of official interaction above the indigenous languages of Tamil and Sinhala. It was therefore considered economical to employ local natives proficient in the language in lower-level administrative posts (as interpreters, court clerks, and regional headmen). These functionaries would also serve as linguistic and cultural mediators between the colonizers and the subjects. In order to develop the necessary local workforce, an 'English education' system was set up at secondary and tertiary levels.[1] In fact, it was mandated that all native teachers (even those in vernacular schools) had to display a knowledge of English to be employed. Although English was introduced primarily to boost the colony's financial turnover, the British were cognizant also of the ideological and cultural rewards.

English education meant not only teaching the English language, but adopting the modes of instruction, curriculum, and teaching materials used in British public schools.[2] It is clear from the records that a rigorous schedule was instituted to 'discipline' the students according to the Protestant work ethic and to wean them away from their relaxed, personalized, non-formal *guru-shisya* learning system (Tennant 1850: 101). Students were expected to be boarded for the duration of the course so that they would be protected from the cultural and linguistic influences of the home. Apart from thus regimenting students for the imperial bureaucracy, the 'foreign' curriculum and Enlightenment sensibility suppressed the tradition-based, scripture-bound learning styles, and philosophical traditions of the Saiva Tamils.

According to Lankan linguist Wickramasuriya (1976), English education quickly became a 'craze' in the island. In one sense, locals had little choice, since it was the key to status and affluence. The secret of the social reproduction carried out by English was that it did not radically change the intra-community status quo; it merely became one more criterion for maintaining the power of the dominant caste groups. Since fees were levied for this élite education, only those who already possessed the necessary economic capital could enjoy access to this linguistic capital. Because pedagogical resources and native English staff were limited, the few English schools were concentrated in the towns; this meant that only vernacular education was available in the villages, and that most rural folk remained monolingual in Tamil. Furthermore, since Tamil 'family ideology' stipulated that only male offspring should study and work hard in order to boost family status and prosperity (Perinbanayagam 1988), women did not compete for English education. It was also the case that Christians were given preferential admission to English schools, and that others who went through English education often ended up becoming Christians. Thus English reinforced the social stratification in place, providing status, wealth, and power to the largely Christian, rich, upper-caste, urban males. Despite their enlightened democratic sentiments, the British did not radically challenge the caste system, but used it to carry out their goals in the periphery.

It was also the case that certain internal social contradictions and cultural peculiarities of the Tamil community enabled English to take root in the local social formation. Although it was an imperialist language symbolizing alien culture and religion, English was associated by natives with power, learning, science, and civilization. For these reasons the local community devised ways of accommodating English into their life. At the time, for Jaffna Tamil society, religion served as the 'core value' (Smolicz 1980) of ethnolinguistic consciousness. That is to say, Tamils defined their identity primarily in terms of religion, and not language. This is why the Saivite revivalist movement of the 19th century, headed by Arumuga Navalar (1872), fashioned an ideology according to which Tamils could acquire English and Western scholarship, provided they continued to be Saivites. Moreover, the Saiva *siddhantha*—the Tamils' religious code of ethics—had leanings toward a puritanical work ethic. The fact that the mission schools of English education encouraged their own brand of Protestant work ethic struck a resonant chord among the natives. Influenced (ironically) by such Christian discourses, Saivism made a cult of excellence in education and employment, which helped to unleash the irrepressible drive for English education. The Annual Report of the American Mission in Ceylon stated in 1902: 'The mission no longer holds the monopoly of English education, the Saivites having nine English Schools besides 03 High Schools and 02 colleges' (quoted in Vignarajah 1994: 16).

The caste division also functioned to turn the natives towards English education. In the initial stages it was the lower castes, disgruntled with Hinduism for endorsing the caste system, who turned to Christianity and English education in order to escape their oppression. But when the upper-caste members saw that it was lower-caste groups who were prospering in the new order introduced by the British, they quickly abandoned their opposition and turned to English education with a vengeance. For Tamils, successful education in English schools assured them of socially-respected white collar employment in an arid terrain where agriculture and industry held no prospects for advancement. Thus the natives competed among themselves to acquire English and the privileges associated with it.

The fact that such native social and cultural characteristics were conducive to colonial rule did not escape the attention of the British. Missionary Strutt noted: 'The moral character of the Tamil naturally makes the strongest appeal to the heart of a missionary... Their enterprise has caused them to be called the Anglo-Saxons of the East ... untiring industry may be safely attributed to them as well as enterprise' (1913: 66). This work ethic was often translated into educational activities. Furthermore, the Tamil community gave priority to classical textual learning—as encouraged by the study of traditional Hindu texts. Perinbanayagam records that 'Jaffna's scholars were by and large classicists, content to learn and understand the treasures of the past and rarely venturing forth into uncharted territories—a philosophy well suited to the demands of an imperial bureaucracy' (1988: 97). What the above narrative illustrates is that English did not have to be brazenly 'imposed' on the Tamil community; to some extent, its social and cultural conditions influenced the community to participate in its domination.

Modes of opposition

While acknowledging the paradox that many factors in the local community aided the reproduction of Western cultural and ideological structures through the English language, we must not fail to note forms of local resistance against English colonialism. What partly enabled these movements of protest were the uncertainties and conflicts over educational policy among the British themselves, which served to demystify the colonialist ideology for the natives. From the beginning of British rule, there is evidence of a sincere and complex debate among colonial educators on the competing claims of Anglicism and Orientalism. The proposal for opening Batticotta Seminary in Jaffna showed them clearly favoring an English-medium education, with a secondary role for the vernacular. The chief reason motivating this decision was the value of English for introducing natives to what they perceived to be a 'superior' civilization and culture:

> A leading object will be to give native youth of good promise a thorough knowledge of the English language. The great reason for this is, that it will open to them the *treasures* of European science and literature, and bring fully before the mind the evidences of Christianity ... Their minds cannot be so thoroughly *enlightened* by any other means. (Emphasis added; quoted in Chelliah 1922: 6.)

At other times the British educators sounded more defensive. They rationalized their divergence from their fellow missionaries in Serampore, who provided a vernacular-dominant education, by arguing that India had a better developed print culture that had enabled it to translate English works into native languages, which was not the case in Sri Lanka. They assured everyone that the larger goal of English education was to eventually produce more translators who would turn English texts into the vernacular and thus usher in a period when English would not be necessary for schooling.

Articulating the place for the vernacular in their education, they acknowledged that 'Tamul (sic) language like the Sanskrit, Hebrew, Greek, etc. is an original and perfect language, and is itself highly worthy of cultivation' (*ibid*. 1922: 9). In this way they attempted to steer clear of prejudices, providing some excellent linguistic reasons why literacy in Tamil should be encouraged. They noted that diglossic High Tamil was difficult for the unschooled to read or write, and that a systematic 'cultivation of Tamul composition' was necessary to develop a more intelligible prose. It is worthy of note that before the advent of English, Tamils had no prose tradition; even their scholarly texts were written in verse. The development of prose, and the resulting changes in Tamil syntax, have since left an indelible mark on the vernacular (Sivatamby 1979). However, the educators of those earlier times went on to provide other reasons for teaching Tamil which smack of an imperialist agenda. They expected a knowledge of High Tamil to help their students to criticize classical religious texts: this 'would bring into their service those poetic productions which are written in opposition to the prevailing idolatry, and thus assist their attempts to destroy it' (quoted in Chelliah 1922: 9). The paradoxes of Anglicism and Orientalism were well exemplified through these very public debates surrounding the Batticotta seminary experience. In sum, the colonists encouraged the vernacular as well as English for a mixture of controversial reasons; while genuine development of the vernacular took place, it was achieved for certain ulterior ideological motives.

Despite the careful strategizing of their educational project, the missionaries felt defeated in the end. This was because they found that after gaining an English education, native students used their new-found skills to gain government jobs, defeating the expectation that many of them would become native preachers. The seminary was therefore pressured by the trustees to conduct vernacular education. They realized that English education was not only unhelpful to develop preachers who could proselytize effectively in the vernacular, but also provided new 'temptations' and ambitions to local students. The Jaffna educators, however, disagreed with the trustees on turning purely to vernacular education. They therefore chose to close down the seminary amidst much dismay, after 33 years of running English education. The moral behind this experience was that whatever policies the colonists adopted, the locals carried out their own personal agendas, and foiled the expectations of their masters.

We must also note that there was conflict between the church and the state on the place of English, much against the stereotypical view that they fully collaborated in the imperialist project. Both envisioned different benefits from language education. The colonial administration wanted education to develop a cadre of functionaries who could help economize their rule; the church wanted workers who could communicate the faith in the native language and convert locals. This meant that, while the government insisted on English education, missionaries preferred the vernacular. In fact, many of the missionaries in Jaffna were from churches in the United States who did not owe much allegiance to Britain. Similarly, the Catholic missionaries who arrived with the Portuguese regime before the British favored vernacular education. Those such as Rev. Christopher Bonjean, of the Roman Catholic Mission in Jaffna, identified the limitations of English education thus: 'I believe the system has failed in nearly all those things which would be aimed at in a good National Scheme of Education ... It constitutes a social evil, and perhaps, a political danger also' (Sessional Paper 1867: cccclxxiv). He saw that English was making natives faithful subjects of the imperial power, and disuniting them along linguistic lines. This led the British colonial administration to become suspicious of the missionaries' endeavors. The Colebrook–Cameron commission (sent in 1832 to make recommendations on the economic efficient administration of Sri Lanka) chided the church, pointing out that: 'The missionaries have not very generally appreciated the importance of diffusing a knowledge of the English language through the medium of their schools' (Mendis 1956: 73). Such friction between the agents of colonialism would have helped the natives to discern the competing interests behind English education.

The subtlest form of resistance was in the everyday behavior of the locals. Natives practiced many forms of dissembling to defeat the goals and expectations of the colonial educators. While the locals desired English education, there is ample evidence that they learned it in their own terms. Although many were compelled to become Christians in order to gain English education, they practiced Hinduism on the sly. While the colonists expected the locals to imbibe Western culture and Christianity through the learning of English, the locals developed strategies of maintaining strong roots in their native religion and cultural traditions, while pretending to have accepted Christianity. Many are the stories (in oral history) of locals being baptized and accepting biblical names to symbolize their new faith—and then returning home for Hindu rituals. Others enjoyed English education on the promise of becoming preachers, only to abandon the ministry for lucrative secular positions on completion of their education. Chelliah's chronicle of English education in Jaffna includes such revealing stories as the following:

> There was one great cause of discouragement in the moral tone of the school in 1843. A large number of students and several teachers were found guilty of having attended Hindu religious festivals where there was nautch dancing. Worse still, a large number were found to have been involved in grossly immoral practices. This resulted in the dismissal of many students from the various classes and all of a select class which was being trained for Christian work (1922: 37).

The 'grossly immoral practices' didn't amount to anything more than drinking the local brew of toddy or eating the food offered to the Hindu deities. But these were indicative of the other cultural practices and values influencing the students of these missionaries. In other words, locals were selectively appropriating the Western culture and values, while benefiting from the economic and social rewards from English education.

Although they might have desired the advantages promised by English, locals were not blind to the politics of this alien language. Even students could see through the reproductive function of English education. In 1853 a writer calling himself 'Henry Candidus' wrote in the student journal *Young Ceylon*:

> They give us a poor English education merely to suit their own selfish views, that is to say, they must have Natives to fill the minor offices and they train them up to do the drudgery; and those who have by dint of their own exertion exceeded the standard ... benevolently prescribed by the gentlemen of the School Commission, all that they get for their trouble is irritation at their present condition and ambition without the means of gratifying it.
> (Quoted in Wickramasuriya 1976: 20)

Note, however, that the writer is not rejecting English education, but requesting parity in content and rewards.

Apart from this spontaneous grass-roots level opposition (which is sometimes ambivalent and ideologically unclear, since the subjects still desire colonial institutions), other forms of resistance were more vocal and uncompromising. Paradoxically, English education itself might be considered to have worked against its interests by producing locals with liberal values who eventually questioned the status of English education. They carried out this critique from many sophisticated perspectives: its educational value; its impact on personality development; its influence on identity formation; its effect on native social and cultural systems; and its value for the development of local material and economic resources. Tamil scholars such as Sir Ponnambalam Ramanathan, Sir Arunachalam, and Ananda Coomarasamy were vocal on the limitations of an 'English only' education. The deracination which this education led to was well expressed by Ananda Coomarasamy, who called the English-educated natives 'a generation of spiritual bastards' (1946: 32), adding by way of explanation that 'A single generation of English education suffices to break the threads of tradition and to create a nondescript and superficial being deprived of all roots—a sort of intellectual pariah who does not belong to the East or the West, the past or the future' (1957: 156). Considering other evils for the intellectual and personality development of local children, Arunachalam said: 'The policy of ignoring the pupils' mother tongue is educationally vicious and impedes the due development of his mind ... The root of the evil in Ceylon is that the vernacular is neglected' (undated: 261–2).

While Orientalism was supportive of the colonial regime in many ways, vernacularism turned out to be a more vibrant tradition of resistance constituting primarily the response of local monolinguals. Although Wickramasuriya (1976) considers that this movement was sufficiently distinct and significant to constitute a 'tradition of radical protest' against English education in colonial Sri Lanka, we must acknowledge the complexity of the motives, modes, and agencies of resistance in this tradition. The protests should not be unduly glorified. As we have seen in the examples above, in most cases the natives were not calling for the total abandonment of English, merely criticizing the lopsided nature of exclusive English education. It would have been considered impractical and premature to totally reject English at that time. Many argued for parity for the vernacular and, in some cases, that it should be accorded greater importance. Others, however, were trying to get more rewards for themselves through English education. After the closing of the Batticotta seminary, for example, the local alumni met and collected funds to continue English education at the same site on their own initiative—probably in order to preserve their vested interests.

In some cases the oppositional stance of the natives was quite complex. While resisting the reproductive functions of English, they saw value in learning English along with the vernacular. This dual position is best summarized by the life and work of the Hindu reformist Arumuga Navalar (1872), who was himself an eminent product of English education. Although he played an important role in translating the Bible into Tamil, when he reconverted to Hinduism in later life, he effectively appropriated the discourse strategies of Christians to do missionary work among Hindus and to debate the aliens. This discourse strategy accounts for his very effective reform and apologetics. Navalar's tracts, books, pamphlets, and face-to-face debates with missionaries exemplify the indigenization of Western discourses to serve native cultural and religious needs. Quite proficient in English, Navalar also used the alien language for fighting the Hindu cause and communicating Saivite thinking. He provided the clearest example of a discursive practice that was to take a definitive shape in later times—the appropriation and indigenization of English for local purposes.

Decolonization: global village vs. separatist states

Although Sri Lanka was granted independence in 1948, it has not been easy to dislodge the power of English. While the English-educated élite who took over power were not interested in changing the lingua franca from which they themselves profited, a left-oriented populist government (still led by the Anglicized élite!) subsequently attempted to change the linguistic status quo in the name of the disgruntled Sinhala monolingual masses. The controversial Sinhala Only Act of 1956, introduced 'democratically' in the Sinhalese-dominated parliament, suppressed with increasing militancy the Gandhian-style *satyagraha* by Tamil politicians claiming parity for their language. Thus language became the 'core value' of Tamil ethnolinguistic consciousness. Although Sinhala became the official language of administration (with reasonable use of Tamil), and both vernaculars took over primary and secondary education (with English taught as a second language), it was difficult to root out English from many other important domains. In fact, the raised status of the vernaculars did not radically alter the local social stratification. Sinhala and Tamil monolinguals simply gained mobility into certain mid-level positions as teachers, clerks, and administrators. The professions and other élite vocations were still dominated by the English-educated. One effect was that since Tamils faced another colonial language in Sinhala, they now found English to be a relatively neutral language in which they could find escape or reparation from Sinhala dominance.[3]

After independence Tamil parliamentary politicians tried for about 30 years to negotiate parity for Tamil with Sinhala in the unitary Sri Lankan polity. Their failure to achieve gave rise to an armed struggle for a separate linguistic state for Tamils, provisionally named Eelam. Since establishing a *de facto* separate state in the considerable land 'liberated' from the Sri Lankan government in 1990, the Tamil military regime has also challenged the dominance of the English-educated bilinguals in the community, using its civil institutions and political infrastructure to promote Tamil as the dominant, if not the sole, language. What makes the language policy of the local regime effective is the partly state-imposed and partly self-imposed isolation of the Tamil region from the outside world. English newspapers and other literature published outside hardly enter the region. The economic and fuel blockade, and the denial of power supply to the 'liberated zone' by the

Sri Lankan government, reduce access to radio and television transmissions, and other forms of entertainment and information relayed trilingually (i.e. in Tamil, English, and Sinhala). Whatever is substituted by the local regime is broadcast solely in Tamil. The continuing hostilities have also led the Sinhalese and Muslim residents to vacate the Tamil 'homeland'. All this is gradually leading to the cultural and linguistic homogenization of this society. The *de facto* Tamil state may be considered an example of the many militant nationalistic communities in the periphery today which are defined strictly in ethnolinguistic terms.[4] As such, it is a test case for the scope and status of English in post-colonial communities. We must examine whether the 'new order' has greater success in resisting the hegemony of English.

At one level, English is opposed with a vengeance. Even in face-to-face interactions, local officials take care to enforce the use of unmixed Tamil. Interactions such as the following in a 'pass office', where permits are issued after inquiry for traveling outside the liberated zone, are quite typical:

1 Officer: *appa koLumpukku een pooriinkaL?* 'So why are you traveling to Colombo?'
2 Applicant: *makaLinTai* wedding-*ikku pooreen.* 'I am going to my daughter's WEDDING.'
3 Officer: *enna? unkaLukku tamiL teriyaataa?* England-*ilai iruntaa vantaniinkaL?*
   'What? Don't you know Tamil? Have you come from ENGLAND?'
4 Officer: *enkai pooriinkaL?* 'Where are you going?'
5 Applicant: *cari cari, kaliyaana viiTTukku pooren, makan.* 'OK, OK, I am going to a wedding, son.'

In a context of heightened linguistic consciousness, even a single borrowing from English gains saliency. The applicant (a woman from a middle-class bilingual background) is forced to drop the English loan 'wedding' and use the Tamil equivalent.

As in the above example, the military regime has publicly insisted on using 'Tamil only' in formal and informal interactions, and that the Tamil spoken should be purified of any foreign mixing. Their paradoxical objective is to develop Tamil to be fit for all modern purposes, while at the same time returning it to its classical purity. Local officials 'police' language use when they refuse to process petitions or applications tendered in other languages or in mixed Tamil to legal institutions, village councils, and other organizations. The alternate curriculum and teaching materials being developed by the regime use unmixed Tamil as the medium of instruction. Street names and billboards, which used to be bi- or trilingual, now have to be exclusively in Tamil. The public has been obliged to adapt its language use, although not without difficulty. In order to avoid English loans, new words are coined and periodically announced to civilians through local mass media by the military regime. Thus 'hotel' has become *uNavakam*, 'factory' *toLilakam*, and 'ice cream' *kuLirkaLi*.

Apart from such enforced linguistic changes, Tamil has been gaining ground in other domains as well, causing a leak in the diglossic situation. Formal meetings in educational and professional institutions are held mostly in Tamil. Ironically, even the speeches made by the chief guests in the traditional English Day celebrations in schools are now in Tamil. When I used English to address a school English Day celebration, the principal spoke wholly in the vernacular, translated my speech, and concluded by wishing that I had spoken in Tamil rather than English (field notes, 5 May 1992). The proceedings of the university statutory bodies, which were always held in English, are held increasingly in Tamil, and minutes are maintained in either language depending on what the speaker uses. There is also strong social pressure not to use extensive English for conversations in informal contexts. Even gate-keeping processes, such as interviews and selection tests for jobs in mainstream institutions, are increasingly held in the vernacular. As a result, an L1-monolingual stratum is beginning to emerge as a new élite group. It happens that most leaders of the military regime are monolingual, and come from the previously non-dominant caste/class groups.

There has been a noticeable decline in English proficiency in the community (Suseendirarajah 1992). Even the traditionally élite bilingual segments of the community, drawn from professional and intellectual circles, are either totally monolingual or L1-dominant. Faculty members from the local university do not have the proficiency to sustain a conversation or read an academic paper in English. Locally trained doctors, engineers, and lawyers are also monolingual, or display only passive bilingualism. A small percentage of senior members in the social groups mentioned above—especially those who have gone abroad for training, or studied in the older educational system—display more proficiency in English. In fact, it is only the relatively older generation that displays English proficiency, and even they find fewer opportunities for sustained use of the language. Most locals today are therefore L1-dominant, or passive bilinguals with a stronger rooting in their native culture, since English has passed out of use at home and in other informal social contexts, and social pressure encourages solidarity with Tamil culture and its values.

Granted this general weakening of the status and currency of English, it would be a mistake to consider that English has no future in Sri Lanka. At least in slightly altered forms, it still plays important communicative functions in this society (as I have displayed through extensive linguistic data in Canagarajah 1995b). Some groups still use English quite openly in certain situations: the more prestigious intellectual and professional groups feel compelled to use some English during in-group communication as a mark of their learning and status; teenagers exchange a few phrases loudly in public to display their participation in international pop culture and the world of fashion; drunks and street brawlers (with the advantage of loosened inhibitions) may switch from Tamil to show their familiarity with English expletives; manual laborers, farmers, and fishermen speak some English in order to present a macho image. Despite the censorship, English words are also essential when discussing military matters: *shelling, gunboat, supersonic jet, bomber, sentry, heli* (the local abbreviation for what might be called a 'copter' or 'chopper' elsewhere), *camp, base, army, navy, sniper, anti-aircraft guns* are in the daily lexicon of all age groups. Modern Tamil political poetry, too, cannot avoid English mixing, as displayed by the title of a recent poem 'Phoenix' (Pushparajan 1985). Ironically, the 'official' resistance songs published by the regime, which had been written and composed by senior cadre members, include English borrowings, as in the refrain of a popular lyric:

6 *tuppaakki cattankaL keeTkum* 'Gun shots will be heard.'
  sel vantu enkaLai taakkum... 'SHELL will blast us.'

The spread of English lexicon is so widespread that even traditionally monolingual speakers from rural backgrounds can code-mix for rhetorical effect. In some fish vendors' bargaining discourse, I found significant occurrences of English words related to marketing: number + rupees (e.g. twenty rupees); nouns relating to seafood items (e.g. *fish, crabs, prawns*); and adjectives like *fresh, good, tasty,* and *cheap* (Canagarajah 1995a). In a two-hour recorded interview with a traditional folk-dance artiste of a Saivite village, I found the following uses of English words: *show, select, make up, ticket, light, original, social, school, interview, entry, hire, camera, television, foreign, video* (Canagarajah 1995b). In the last two data sets, the speakers knew Tamil equivalents, and used them in other instances or with other interlocutors; they chose English purely for rhetorical effect. While some of the above may be linguistically simple borrowings, they are nevertheless motivated by complex rhetorical and pragmatic considerations.[5]

Such use of English is so pervasive, cutting across discursive boundaries, that English may be considered to have infiltrated all domains of 'pure' Tamil speech. Just as opportunities for using 'pure' English for social interactions are becoming infrequent in this society, the chances of using unmixed Tamil are now slim. When I spoke unmixed Tamil in formal gatherings (with much effort and self-consciousness after my return from postgraduate studies abroad), members of the audience remarked that it was stilted and unnatural. They considered a code-mixed Tamil as being common even in such formal contexts. What we find, then, is that English has infiltrated both forms of diglossic Tamil. It is such an 'Englishized' Tamil that is becoming the unmarked form (Scotton 1983) for many contexts, while unmixed English and Tamil are becoming marked (or rare). English forms, whether used as loan-words or as code-switches, perform dynamic social and rhetorical functions in a society that has a high linguistic consciousness and is subject to various forms of censorship. The very fact that people have to make an effort to use unmixed Tamil is an indication of the 'naturalness' of Englishized Tamil. At a time when even such simple mixing is officially frowned upon, the persistence of English in such contexts is quite significant; what is remarkable is not that Tamil is gaining power, but that English still has so much currency in Jaffna. There is an ironic reversal of roles here: amidst powerful forces of Anglicist reproduction during the colonial period, there was a vibrant tradition of vernacular resistance; in the post-colonial period, in subtle ways, English resists the militant vernacular nationalism.

Accounting for the persistence of English

By a strange paradox, at a period when Tamil separatism is most militant and politically successful the community is also very 'internationalist'. The community is aware of, linked with, and influenced by the West, possibly more than ever before in its history. This is partly because the political struggle itself had to be 'internationalized' for its success. There are Tamil lobbying groups in Western capitals, collecting funds and seeking recognition for Eelam. Tamil information centers operate hotlines, electronic mail, and news networks to keep the world informed about the struggle. The need for arms and specialized training requires liaison with Western military and diplomatic officials, with the result that, as shown above, the techno-jargon of modern warfare accounts for many of the English borrowings which have passed into common Tamil usage. Additionally, as a side effect of the fighting, thousands of Tamils have sought economic and political refuge in European and North American cities. The local community is very much in touch with the diaspora, and in most cases is only able to survive in war-torn Tamil regions through the cash and gifts sent by their acquaintances outside. To the extent that almost every other person is thinking of going abroad under some pretext, the need for an international language is very widely recognized.

The international hegemony of English still looms over the Colombo government's ministries of education, commerce, and communications. It serves as the link language between these institutions and the civilian population, so the Education Ministry, for instance, is forced to use English, rather than Sinhala, when it corresponds with Tamil parents, teachers, and education officers. The Tamil community also needs English as a bridge to the symbolic and material rewards that are tied to the international educational and professional centers: A mother sending a telegram to a son studying in Sweden will have to write it in English, for the benefit of the local postal department; someone wishing to obtain a professional certificate in accounting or architecture will have to study, and write the test, in English.

The post-colonial Tamil community has been characterized by an ideological tension that could affect attitudes towards English. On the one hand, there is the Saiva–Tamil strand, which as well as displaying a religio-linguistic chauvinism also endorses caste hierarchy; on the other hand, there exists a liberal-democratic tradition, inculcated by the missionary educational institutions and epitomized by the Youth Congress of the independence period, which militantly opposes casteism, and encourages interaction with other cultures and 'enlightened' contemporary philosophies (Sivatamby 1990). While the former strand can be expected to oppose English, the latter favors it. Such internal cultural contradictions explain the persistence of English.

The foregoing should make us expect the mode of social stratification to be quite complex. Although a new monolingual élite has certainly come into prominence, English still props up the status of the bilingual professional élite who have traditionally dominated this society. It is possible therefore to speak of two parallel élites in the Tamil community: the bilinguals dominating the professions enjoy social status and economic security, but hold no political clout; the monolinguals dominating the local administration and politico-military hierarchy enjoy significant power, but lack economic security. It is still important, however, for the bilinguals to display proficiency in Tamil in order to appeal to the local solidarity that will assure their status, and for monolinguals to at least code-switch in English to prove that they are not inferior to the professionals. Thus English is perceived in the local context as a class marker (i.e. as the language of the educated and rich), although it is not rigidly marked for caste, gender, region, or religion. English is therefore well embedded in the society, and still exercising its influence on socio-economic stratification.

The linguistic stratification of codes will enable us to appreciate the currency of English in the post-colonial Tamil community. Certain discourses require a heavily Englishized Tamil: politics, military activity, music, cinema, sex and romance, education, medicine, law, current affairs, fashion, Western cuisine, and travel. Certain other discourses demand relatively unmixed Tamil: folk religious rituals, folk arts, domestic relations, rural cultural practices, local cooking and dress. Unmixed Sanskrit is used for orthodox Hindu temple rituals, and a Sanskritized Tamil for religious discourses and the arts (such as Bharata Natyam) belonging to the Hindu classical culture. In terms of situations, the language of formal use could be Tamil (in rural, traditional or Hindu institutions) or English (in urban, administrative, educational, and professional institutions). Mixing is relatively less in formal communication. In semi-formal or semi-official contexts (in educational and vocational sites) and informal contexts (in family relationships, intimate interactions, or polite social intercourse) an Englishized Tamil is in use. All this should be qualified by a consideration of the addressee: those who appear educated, rich, urban, professional and of the older generation are expected to reciprocate in English; those with the reverse identities are expected to possess less competence in English. This pattern suggests, then, that notwithstanding the decrees of the nationalistic regime English is still employed by the people for some important discourses, to claim material and symbolic rewards in their daily social interaction.

Negotiating language choice: Jihad vs. McWorld

It is important at this point to explore the negotiation of codes in micro-social encounters, to see how resistance and accommodation to English are manifested in interpersonal communication. This level of analysis will also shed light on the ways in which people reconcile the demands of competing codes and ideologies in their everyday communication. By manipulating to their advantage the prevailing sociolinguistic stratification of codes, speakers can tap complex rhetorical resources and social meaning. Important in this process is the social dynamic of speakers attempting to alter or redefine the status quo. Speakers may attempt to use codes to renegotiate and perhaps resist the established identities, group loyalties, and power relations.

Even traditionally monolingual speakers from rural backgrounds can deploy certain English borrowings to claim dual ethos, or straddle group membership. In the example previously cited (data 1–5), note how the officer who chastises the petitioner for using an English loan uses one himself. Although the Tamilized form of 'England' is *inkilaantu*, he chooses the former. He is probably indicating to the petitioner that his insistence on the use of the vernacular should not mean that he is himself rustic, ignorant, or uneducated. By using English borrowings he is implying to the addressee that he is at home in her culture also. The strategy might be aimed for leveling the inequalities of status in the relationship (Heller 1992: 134). Although the monolingual official has more power in political terms, he may desire to level off the symbolic inequalities with those proficient in English.

Monolinguals can strategically employ the few English tokens at their disposal to considerable economic advantage. In my study on the use of English borrowings by fish vendors, I have explored the many functions performed in the bargaining process (Canagarajah 1995a). Consider the following interaction in a crowded fish market when a vendor notices a trouser-clad buyer turning away from another vendor after finding the latter's fish too expensive:

7 V: *ayyaa Raal irukku vaankoo. ancu ruupaa Raal.* 'Sir, come, I have prawns. Prawns for five rupees.'
(Buyer does not respond; goes toward other vendors.)
8 V: FAY RUPI. 'Five rupees.'
(Buyer, turns round, and comes toward V.)

The same message repeated in English dramatically elicits the attention of the buyer. In using English (the code being highly marked in the market place, where Tamil is conventional) this vendor has greater chances of attracting the middle-class buyer to himself. Often this also functions to specify the addressee, as English-competent bilingual buyers are alerted to the fact that the vendor is specifically addressing them. Few in the market can be presumed to be competent in English. Many buyers, when interviewed, admitted to being flattered when they are addressed in English, as the vendor was perceived to be 'accommodating' (Giles 1984) to the buyers' preferred code. By using such skillful strategies in the bargaining process, the vendors are often able to persuade the buyer to pay them a favorable price.

Bilingual élites, for their part, are forced to use some Tamil even in conventionally English-only contexts, in order to court vernacular solidarity. After an English drama competition in a school, when the judge began his prefatory comments before reading out the placing to an avid student audience, the formal silence of the auditorium was punctured by two sarcastic calls in English: 'Don't speak in English!' and 'We can't understand you!' The audacity of the demand (ironically, made in the language the speakers claim not to know) gained serious attention, and the judge was forced thereafter to self-translate his comments. There is a subtle power struggle here: if the speaker had persisted in speaking English, ignoring the veiled threat of the audience, the latter would have booed and jeered him off the stage (as monolinguals were clearly in the majority in the unlit auditorium). This would have seriously damaged the status and identity of the 'judge'. In effect, the monolingual audience enjoyed the threat of drawing an 'élite closure' (as defined by Myers-Scotton 1990), that would ostracize the English-speaking 'judge' from their circle. So even if English is the conventional code for this context, the judge had to give in to the use of Tamil.

The strategy of self-translation adopted by the judge—first uttering a unit of thought in English, and then paraphrasing it in Tamil—was an effective reconciliation of the conflict he had to face. While he was asserting his right to use the conventional code for the context (and thus saving face among the educated bilingual circles, who would consider his use of Tamil for the occasion a scandal), he was also making a concession to the immediate audience by using Tamil. This strategy enabled him to maintain solidarity with the educated bilingual community, while at the same time bonding with the vernacular community. He was thus able to hold dual identities at once—cosmopolitan and local. This strategy is increasingly adopted by bilinguals to accommodate to monolingual addressees in formal contexts.

The interactions discussed here complement the somewhat macro-social description of linguistic and social stratification in the previous section. Sometimes the code chosen can violate the conventionally expected code for that context. This serves to modify any rigid compartmentalization of languages we may posit. Through code alternation strategies, both L1-dominant and L2-dominant bilinguals can shift their identities, roles, and group solidarity, thus also qualifying any rigid (pre-linguistic) establishment of these features for the community. Since these unconventional code choices and negotiation of identities result in gain or loss of status, power, and material benefits, they prevent a rigid stratification of this society and constitute it in dynamic tension. The significance of such code alternation strategies for the status and currency of English should not be missed. The fact that English can be used creatively—even by monolinguals, in unconventional situations with complex socio-economic implications—suggests the continued life of English in this society. English is so much a part of this social formation that it functions dynamically to negotiate meanings, identities, and material rewards in day-to-day, face-to-face interaction, from the lowest social stratum upward. The activity is, furthermore, quite radical. Through code alternation, people are subtly resisting the prescriptions of the regime and the dominant social opinion proscribing English. Perhaps it is the mechanism of code-switching that enables them to do this. They are able to get away with using English since they are using it with Tamil. This activity enables them to pretend to others and themselves that they are only using the vernacular, when if circumstances necessitate it, they are quite ready to claim the benefits of English.

What, then, is the position of English in a militantly nationalistic post-colonial state? The micro-social description above suggests the vibrant afterlife of English. It is now well noted in sociolinguistic literature that mixing of codes can enable a speech community to reconcile the psychological and socio-cultural tensions it faces between two conflicting languages, and thus maintain both codes (Romaine 1989: 39). This serves to explain the persistence of English in many periphery communities. Blanc and Hamers (1982) have posited that Chiac (a hybrid of French and English) reconciles the conflict of New Brunswick youth in Moncton who cannot afford to be left out of the economically powerful urban North American English, nor lose their traditional rural Canadian-French identity. They satisfy both needs by mixing the codes in their conversation. Heller (1992) demonstrates how French–English switching similarly serves Quebecois, while Swigart (1992) accounts for French–Wolof mixing in Dakar the same way.

It is a measure of the pervasive influence of English in post-colonial communities that it has Englishized the vernacular itself in a subtle, unconscious, and deep-rooted fashion (through mixing), apart from itself getting vernacularized. Apart from Chiac (mentioned above), sociolinguists have begun to identify the development of hybrid languages in other periphery communities. Swigart (1992) has noted a Frenchified Wolof in Dakar, and Pandit (1986) has posited an Englishized Hindi in India as distinct codes, assuring the continuance of bilingualism in these politically-charged communities. A thorough grammatical and sociolinguistic description of these hybrid codes is currently being attempted.[6]

Our consideration of the language question has served to produce significant insights into the socio-political dynamics of a nationalistic periphery society.

English continues to subtly stratify and regulate such a society, despite the intensification of ethnolinguistic nationalism that has considerably checked its overt forms of dominance. Periphery communities, then, must still contend with the international hegemony of English. Blommaert (1992), to take one example, shows the irresistibility of English despite the nationalistic *ujamaa* experiment in Tanzania. However, if Tamil is becoming Englishized, it could be said that local communities are getting even with English by Tamilizing it. This process has oppositional implications in the context of the burgeoning 'English-only' and 'standard English' movements of the center. The subtle forms of vernacularizing English we have seen above show the extension of the tradition of linguistic appropriation established by local scholars such as Navalar during colonial times.

It is important to situate this micro-social perspective on Tamil society in the context of larger geopolitical tendencies. We must realize that globalization (spurred by technology and mass media) and nationalism are competing tendencies in the late 20th century. Ben Barber (1995) has recently explored this dialectic in his insightfully-titled book *Jihad vs. McWorld*. He is correct to say that these two trends—i.e. globalization (in the terms set by Western superpowers) and factionalism (in terms of ethnic, religious, or regional differences)—exacerbate each other. The more one becomes prominent, the claims of the other gain strength. (The growth of militant religious and ethnic groups in the United States and Europe proves that factionalism is not limited to periphery communities alone.) So the challenge for periphery communities is this: while the demands of globalization and internationalism would encourage the learning of English, the equally strong pull of nationalism would motivate resistance to English. How can these contradictory demands be reconciled? Rather than asking which tendency is going to win over the other, the more important questions to pose are: How do people learn to live with these tensions in their everyday life? How do they transform these constraints in their favor? How do they creatively manipulate these tensions to conduct their life with dignity and self-determination? The manner in which the Tamil community appropriates English to dynamically negotiate meaning, identity, and status in contextually suitable and socially strategic ways, and in the process modifies the communicative and linguistic rules of English according to local cultural and ideological imperatives, is very instructive. These are the strategies by which the powerless carve a niche for themselves in the face of historical forces.

Conclusion

To return to ELT, both Pennycook and Phillipson explore the colonial history of English to show how the discourses of 'English as an international language' and ELT derive from the colonial expansion of English and Anglo-American imperialism. They explain how the colonial experience helped to construct the functionalist, scientistic, and apolitical strands in these discourses that indirectly favor the linguistic imperialism of English over the vernaculars in periphery communities. While this is certainly true (and I have shown above how the natives themselves participated in the construction of these discourses to some extent), another important development should not be ignored. The same historical conditions generated a significant tradition towards the resistance and appropriation of English which is currently finding fresh impetus in post-colonial communities. The ways in which this periphery tradition of appropriating English may serve to redefine ELT are explored in the following pages.

Notes

1 For a historical account on the motivations accompanying these activities, see Mendis 1956.
2 The prospectus of the Batticotta seminary (which in 1823 was the second university-level institution to be founded in South Asia, after that in Serampore, India) records the educational objective as follows: '[T]hrough medium principally of the English Language it is designed to teach as far as the circumstances of the country require, the sciences usually studied in the colleges of Europe and America' (quoted in Chelliah 1922: 10). Chelliah 1922 provides useful insights into the syllabus, teaching material, and pedagogies adopted by the missionaries in Jaffna.
3 For a detailed account of the developments in the status of English *vis à vis* the vernaculars, see Kandiah 1984 and Canagarajah 1995b.
4 The 'liberated zone' is quite fluid in its boundaries, since the fighting between Sri Lankan and Tamil forces continues. Although much of the northern peninsula and considerable areas of the north and east of the mainland constituted the *de facto* Tamil state during the period of my study, the power of LTTE (Liberation Tigers of Tamil Eelam, the militant organization that is spearheading the fight for separation) has been restricted to the north-east of the island since 1996.
5 For a detailed argument on the ways in which borrowings can be rhetorically complex and constitute code-switching in post-colonial communities, see Gysels (1992) and Myers-Scotton (1992).
6 This project has been inspired by the recent calls of Y. Kachru (1994) and Sridhar (1994) for more research into how English co-exists with other languages in periphery communities, to redress a 'monolingual bias' in second language acquisition scholarship.

4 Conflicting curricula: interrogating student opposition

I'm just a red nigger who love the sea,
I had a sound colonial education,
I have Dutch, nigger, and English in me,
and either I'm nobody, or I'm a nation.

Derek Walcott, *The Schooner Flight*

Armed with the theoretical and methodological constructs outlined in the preceding chapters, we will now explore how periphery students and teachers negotiate curricular and pedagogical concerns in their everyday classroom life. An ethnographic orientation will enable us to penetrate beneath the surface activities to discern the hidden agendas, interests, and values that shape ELT in the periphery. The emphasis in the following chapters falls on the discourses students and teachers develop to variously accommodate, escape, oppose, and/or transform the forces of domination they confront in the classroom.

In this chapter we will consider the policy and practice pertaining to the ELT curriculum in periphery classrooms. I broadly define curriculum as the *what* of language teaching, and pedagogy as the *how* (which I will discuss in the next chapter). The following curricular issues are taken up for special consideration here: the linguistic skills, competence, and purposes targeted for the different levels of learning; the communicative situations and discourses presented; the textbooks and teaching material used; and the social content informing the lessons. Decisions about such curricular issues are ideally motivated by the sociolinguistic realities of the community in question, including the language needs and attitudes considered in the last chapter, and should in principle be systematically applied. But this rarely happens in practice. There are many institutions and agencies involved in the policy-making process. We have to keep in mind that curricular decisions in post-colonial communities are shaped considerably by various state, commercial, and educational agencies at both the center and periphery levels. This can lead to multiple curricula for ELT that are often at conflict within themselves. Not only are there divergent curricula defined at the level of policy (by the different policy-making institutions), there are also different curricula existing in practice in actual classrooms at the local level. In addition, there operates a less conscious but potent *hidden curriculum* deriving from the politico-economic agendas of different interest groups. Contesting these three dimensions of curricula (i.e. curricular policy, curricular practice, and hidden curricula) is a fourth type which is the focus of this chapter: the students' curriculum. By this I mean the educational expectations students bring to the classroom.

Orientating to the classroom

It is important for the purposes of this and the later chapters to understand the different domains and influences that constitute the typical ELT classroom in the periphery. The multiple influences on classroom life have important ideological implications. The fact that the classroom is shaped by multifaceted socio-cultural and institutional forces, with different levels of conflict between and within them, suggests the difficulties in predicting ideological domination unilaterally by any single force. Giroux has reminded us that social institutions such as the school 'are governed by complex ideological properties that generate contradictions both within and between them' (1983: 102). The classroom, therefore, is not inexorably *determined* by the interests of any specific macro-level institution, although it may be considerably *influenced* in its functions by such institutions. Bernstein points out that hiding these unpredictable multiple tensions might itself be an ideological ploy by dominant institutions to create the myth of efficient organization, monolithic structure, and uniform function:

> Power relations accomplish their reproduction by establishing a principle of classification that suppresses its own contradictions and dilemmas through the insulation it creates, maintains, and legitimates. (1981: 336)

By insulation (i.e. the suppression of gaps and dislocations evident in society and institutions) dominant agencies can reduce the complexity of social reality so that it appears more pliant and tractable. People may also fail to discern the potential for resistance underlying the inconsistencies and complications characterizing social reality. Perceiving the contradictory socio-cultural strands at work in the classroom will enable us to understand the scope for resistance against the dominant reproductive forces which are only partially effective in their control. On the other hand, we can appreciate the subtlety of these forces which have to work through multiple layers of influence to carry out their reproductive agenda.

I consider the classroom as a heterogeneous site whose cultural domains overlap.

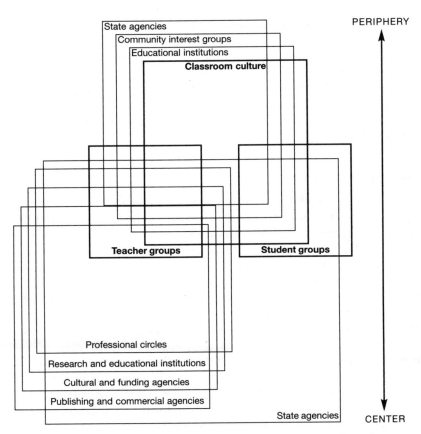

Figure 4.1: Periphery English classroom as a cultural site

Classroom culture is a site where the agendas of the different interest groups get played out, negotiated, and contested. However, it has a degree of autonomy to develop its own agenda. In fact, each of the spheres represented above enjoys a certain amount of autonomy while it is open to influences from other institutions. Thus each sphere displays diverse cultural tendencies within itself. Center ELT professional organizations, such as TESOL and IATEFL, for instance, are considerably influenced by the commercial interests of publishing and research institutions, and by the ideological interests of the state agencies, even though they are functionally independent to develop their own programs. Nor is it always possible for cultural agencies (such as the British Council and the Asia Foundation), educational and research institutions, and publishing organizations (involved in the production of textbooks, scholarly expositions, and journals) to separate their own interests from those of the state.[1] Note also that there is considerable interaction between the center and periphery institutions. Periphery ESL teacher groups, for instance, display the influence of center professional and/or educational organizations, as well as indigenous teaching traditions and local academic institutions. Similarly, student groups in the periphery show a plurality of influences—including contemporary Western popular culture, as well as local nationalist political ideologies.

To illustrate how the different agendas of the various interest groups are present in the classroom, I wish to focus on a tertiary-level ESL course, and to outline the discourses that shape the curriculum as a background to understanding student responses to this course.[2]

Incommensurate agendas

To begin at the most significant level of curricular influence at the periphery, we must consider the Sri Lankan government's attitudes towards ELT. English has been subject to different pressures at different times, according to shifting political priorities. Recently it has been promoted by the government as a link language between the warring ethnic groups—Sinhalese and Tamils. The liberalization of the economy in the 1980s has created a need for a language of wider communication with multinational commercial enterprises, and for those working in the burgeoning tourist and textile industries. For these reasons, the utilitarian purposes of English have been gaining importance in the curriculum.

However, the curricular influences of the local communities are at odds with the official agenda set by the ministry. The heightened linguistic nationalism of the Tamil community, for example, inspires a different orientation to ESL. Although English is not totally proscribed, for the local community its uses may appear to be strictly academic. Students may not appreciate the significance of the communicative functions emphasized in the official curriculum: being largely rural, with the meager technological resources in the community further depleted by civil strife, they have been cut off from the latest systems of transport, electronic communication, and mass media which are featured in the lesson situations. Furthermore, the use of English for intra-community purposes, even between teachers and students in the classroom, creates considerable strain for local students, who would prefer to acquire a narrowly functional literacy in English through a course conducted in the Tamil medium.

The curriculum in each university is established separately, since universities enjoy greater autonomy from the state than the elementary and secondary schools. Although all courses in the humanities, social sciences, and certain natural sciences are taught and tested in the vernacular, faculty members in these and other disciplines realize that is important for students to have at least the competence to read English reference material. At the tertiary level, therefore, English is considered to be essentially a 'library language', to be used for reference purposes. In the University of Jaffna (hereafter UJ) the courses take an ESP orientation in the second and third years, as students are taught the text structure of the different disciplines. Academic literacy features prominently in the curriculum, apart from formal and semi-formal uses in institutional contexts. In a largely skills-based program, the emphasis falls heavily on reading and writing, with a final written test. There is thus considerable difference between the policy of the state and that of the higher educational institutions. Where the state plans English for interpersonal communicative functions in the many non-traditional modes of employment (such as the tourist industry), the higher educational institutions develop literacy for academic purposes and professional contexts.

The inconsistency *within* the higher educational institution itself is that while English is valued in policy, in practice it has a restricted place on the campus and in classrooms. It has been often pointed out by students that hardly any lecturer specifies reference reading in English, or employs English during their teaching. For most purposes, and increasingly, the day-to-day functioning of the universities is in the vernacular. These tensions have recently started to affect the ESL policy itself, motivating changes in the university requirements. When a pass in first-year English was mandatory to earn the Bachelor of Arts degree, many students who could pass their other content-area courses effortlessly (especially since English was not crucial for following them) could still not earn their degree because of repeated failure in English. In 1993, after a lengthy debate, the faculty at UJ decided to drop the compulsory requirement of a pass in English. Strong nationalistic sentiments were expressed at the prospect of 'an alien language' hampering the employment prospects of local students. Such tensions in the policy and practice of the faculty and administration of higher educational institutions send local students confusing messages about the place of English, and affect their motivation.

To add further to the already complex tensions in the periphery ELT scene, we must understand the role played by center-based agencies in directly and/or indirectly defining the curriculum for the periphery university. The expertise, research findings, and curricular assumptions of center institutions usually percolate down to local classrooms through the activity of cultural agencies such as the British Council and the Asia Foundation. Few critical studies are available on the role of these cultural agencies in Sri Lanka. Such interrogation may be perceived by locals as harming the continued services of these agencies, which many teachers still consider to be necessary. A senior ELT professional, (Fernando 1994), in her comprehensive history of ELT in Lankan universities still manages to express through her guarded language the tensions between the practices of local educational institutions and center cultural agencies.

The involvement of the Asia Foundation in the ELT programs of the local universities has increased since 1980. Fernando (*ibid.*: 6) documents the multifarious ways in which it has shaped ELT: sponsoring the visit of short- and long-term ELT American consultants, establishing pre-sessional intensive courses for new entrants, holding annual teacher orientation seminars, and donating books and equipment. She also notes that 'ELT policy ... became much more the concern of the administrator and funding agency, emerging as a top-down model ... But the dominance of top-down and outside-the-system activity held potential dangers.' Fernando highlights one source of curricular tension when she says that the popularization of communicative activities was a result of the involvement of the Asia Foundation. Given that local professionals had previously introduced grammar-oriented, structural-linguistic syllabi, this suggests a significant change of orientation.

Through such activity, Western cultural agencies serve as a conduit for the influence of center institutions, in particular commercial organizations involved in textbook production, and educational institutions involved in teacher training. The special potency of the cultural agencies in influencing periphery ELT enterprise lies in their ability to side-step the other macro-level periphery organizations (such as the state agencies and educational bureaucracy) and reach directly into the language classrooms. For example, by supplying textbooks, the agencies can shape the curriculum and by conducting teacher training courses they can influence instructors' values and orientations. This means that whatever policy the periphery institutions and administrators may develop, classroom practice may be considerably shaped by a center agenda.[3]

The place of the textbook in periphery classrooms needs to be understood in order to appreciate what a powerful instrument it can be for center agencies wishing to influence the local curriculum. First of all, many of the center textbooks are increasingly produced and marketed in order to satisfy all the needs of the course. With their teacher's manuals, testing kits, and audio tapes for listening activities, these textbooks limit 'the traditional role of the teacher as an intellectual whose function is to conceptualize, design and implement learning experiences suited to the specificity and needs of a particular classroom experience' (Aronowitz and Giroux 1985: 149; see also Apple 1986). Added to this is the inability of periphery teachers to readily print or photocopy their own material for classes. Due to limitations in time, funds, stationery, and printing facilities, teachers find it difficult to produce teaching material for the very large classes they teach. These practical difficulties, which are common to many periphery communities (Holliday 1994: 56–61, Phillipson 1992: 223–39) drive teachers to an attitude of dependence on the prepackaged, ready-to-use material freely provided by Western cultural agencies. Although teachers are often aware of the cultural inappropriateness of these materials (Canagaratne 1982) practical reasons eventually overweigh other considerations, so they continue to use them. Even if some teachers use secondary texts for supplementary purposes, and devise additional tasks for classroom use, they have no alternatives for core texts. These textbooks therefore gain importance in the periphery classroom, providing a structure for the entire course—even though the official curricula (as defined by the local institution) may be different from that contained in the textbook. Such donations enable the center to penetrate into the heart of local classrooms, side-stepping the other institutions of curricular policy-making in the periphery.

Ideological tensions in the ESL classroom

How do the curricular tensions outlined above affect the classroom? What implications do they have for what gets done in ESL courses in the periphery? I wish to explore the ways in which periphery students in a tertiary-level ESL course cope with a textbook published in the center and recommended for use by a funding agency. Although teachers do mediate the way students use the textbook, I will focus on the attitudes and strategies of teachers in the next chapter. The purpose of this discussion is to develop a keener sensitivity to the cultural background of periphery students, the agendas they bring to the ESL course, and the strategies they employ to negotiate the ideological tensions in the classroom.

The textbook and its hidden curriculum

This discussion focuses on a course employing *American Kernel Lessons: Intermediate* (1978). These materials were donated to many Sri Lankan universities in 1980 by the Asia Foundation, and have been the core text for first-year ESL courses in UJ for over a decade. Teacher orientation on how to use this text was originally provided by center experts in a program which was also sponsored by the Asia Foundation. Some five universities have been using these books as a core text for several years. In Jaffna it is still the main textbook for first-year students, since subsequent donations of alternative textbooks have been on a smaller scale. These textbooks undoubtedly show their age, but, anyway, local teachers have no choice.

Before we explore the classroom culture of local students, it is important to describe the professed and hidden curricula of this textbook. *AKL* takes a situational language teaching approach (Richards and Rodgers 1986: 31–43). (See the response by the principal author, Robert O'Neill, at the end of this chapter.) Presenting grammatical and lexical input in meaningful situations, the course focuses on the acquisition of form. Although each lesson is organized around a chosen grammatical item, communicative functions are not ignored. Although intended for students at intermediate level, *AKL* begins with the simple present, and progresses in a spiral to more complex syntactic structures and verb forms in Unit 25. Each unit is uniformly structured in four parts: Part A introduces the grammatical item through a set of well-illustrated situations. The passages are first presented aurally, before students read them aloud for fluency. Later, cues are given for oral exchanges with the teacher or among students, to work out the meaning of the passages. Part B, labeled 'Formation and Manipulation', contains substitution tables, pattern practice, and other structured drills that provide more direct practice on grammar. Part C is a serialized 'detective story' that introduces carefully-graded new vocabulary, and provides practice in listening and reading comprehension. Part D presents a conversation for role-playing, with a concluding section on guided composition.

The assumptions about language and learning that inform the book's approach are expressed in the note 'To the Student and Teacher' at the beginning. What stands out is the concern with providing practice in 'the fundamentals of English' which intermediate-level students 'still cannot seem to use correctly, easily and as automatically as they would like' (*AKL* 1978: vi). The language echoes behaviorist thinking in assuming that given sufficient drilling or practice students can be made to display habit-oriented, 'automatic', 'correct' responses. In its concern with 'correctness' the book arrogates to itself the authority in the classroom to arbitrate, evaluate, and thus define knowledge. The 'fundamentals of English' are considered to be autonomous, value-free grammatical structures (much in the fashion of American structuralism) excluding the cultural and ideological values that inform the language. Little consideration is given to how the students' own linguistic and cultural backgrounds might affect or enhance their language acquisition. The fact that 'correct' English is taken to be Standard American English, rather than the 'Englishes' students bring with them, means that the students are further isolated from their social context.

In fairness to the situational approach, we have to note that the textbook is concerned about meaning and context, even though it is organized around grammar. *AKL* (1978: vi) does acknowledge the need to make learning an 'enjoyable experience', and presents exciting reading passages and opportunities for collaborative pair-work which enable students to discover or generate meaning within the curricular framework set by the textbook. It advises students that 'the situations themselves are more important than isolated words', and that they should try to 'understand the whole situation' (*ibid.*: vii). However, the situations represented—such as commuting by plane, cooking with a microwave, or shopping in department stores—assume an urbanized, Western culture that is still largely alien to rural students, and likely to clash with their traditional values.[4] It may be that such cultural content is motivated by a curriculum intent on giving students the fullest possible introduction to the Anglo-American speech community. Even the patterns of conversation and genres of talk represented in these situations are influenced by discourse conventions of the West. The dialogs presented in the book for role-playing confront students with certain cultural biases regarding appropriate language use. The conversation in Unit 2, 'A Talkative Lady', is a supposedly comical episode between an elderly woman and a sales agent at a railway station ticket office, in which the lady misses her train because she gets carried away by the conversation. The message indirectly and unintentionally conveyed to students by this passage is that they should value a strictly focused, goal-oriented, utilitarian conversational style, whereas Tamil discourse values the digression and indirection typical of predominantly oral, rural communities. Another example can be found in Unit 4d, where Joe and Susan are calculating their weekly expenses. Joe's casual remark that he will shortly have to hold a party for 35 colleagues, to celebrate his promotion, angers Susan because of the short notice, and the extra expenses involved when they have just purchased their house. Such 'budget talk', based on the middle-class values of consumerism, thrift, delayed gratification, and social mobility, are quite alien to rural students, whose circumstances are such that they can only spend as and when they earn.

The narratives in the textbook also embody certain partisan values. While the intention may not have been to propagate a particular set of values, the effect is to project ideologies taken for granted by center communities as natural and legitimate. One such narrative relates the experiences of a black woman, Jane, who is undisciplined, careless, and always late—to get up in the morning, to catch the bus, to get to work, to meet her date, and to go to the movies. She leaves her room untidy; she leaves her umbrella in the cinema. At the beginning of Unit 9a, when she and her boyfriend miss the bus, she begins to think that she should find a boyfriend with a car, and before the unit concludes, she gets a ride. In the next unit, we see her in the cinema with her new boyfriend, who is introduced as the person who gave her the ride. This episode suggests that her relationships are motivated by selfishness, expediency, and materialism. In portraying stereotypes of colored people through Jane, and using her as a foil for characters from the dominant community, the book assumes the values of the Anglo-American community.

The discourses that structure *AKL* represent a hidden curriculum of controversial values and ideologies. What we cannot tell is whether the authors and publishers of this and similar courses are aware of this fact, or understand how little relation their subliminal messages bear to the life of students and teachers in periphery communities. The dominant pedagogical discourse of structuralism—characterized by deterministic, positivistic, and technocratic values—displays what Giroux has termed instrumental ideology (1983: 209–16). The possible effects of such an ideology on the social and cultural life of the students are not difficult to discern. The book's guiding principle, that knowledge is value-free, pre-defined, and universal, encourages a deferential attitude that would discourage students from questioning the 'reality' or 'truth' presented by the textbook (and authority figures). The textbook thus illustrates the consequences of what Phillipson (1992) terms the 'narrowly technical' content of center expertise, which discourages an exploration of the social and political implications of learning. Moreover, the linguistic ideology of the textbook tends to reinforce the dominance of a 'standard English', by ignoring the existence of indigenous Englishes in the periphery. The assumption that L1 cannot mediate the learning of L2 is hardly calculated to foster a healthy attitude towards the vernacular among the students. The structuralist orientation fails to acknowledge the association of grammar with values, and to develop a critical language awareness among students. As a result, the situations and activities take the communicative norms and cultural values of Anglo-American communities for granted, and do little to encourage a critical exploration of such discourses. The pedagogical assumption that language learning is a value-free, instrumental activity communicates itself to students, which is why textbooks have a potential to influence them according to these center-based discourses. While some students may feel alienated by such a curriculum, on the grounds that it has little relevance to them, others may be strongly attracted by images depicting a lifestyle of comfort and affluence beyond their reach.[5]

Coping strategies of students

The effectiveness of the discourses of the curriculum and textbook in transforming the ideologies and cultural practices of the students is contingent upon how students respond to the textbook. Depending on their own cultural and discursive backgrounds, students can adopt various strategies to receive, resist, or reconstruct the messages of the text. Their values and practices will mediate their reception of the curriculum and textbook. It is therefore important to understand the discourses favored by the students. To begin with, I wish to use the glosses, comments, scribbles, or graffiti scrawled by the students in the margins of their textbooks to characterize their discursive background. These glosses will also provide insights into the attitudes of the students towards the textbook, and their strategies for dealing with the hidden curriculum of the course.

The writing of glosses in the margins of textbooks is a widespread student activity that usually passes unnoticed by teachers and researchers. But it is useful in many ways for understanding the motivations and learning strategies of students. This data source gets around the supposedly inevitable *observer's paradox* that hampers classroom research in particular (Nunan 1991: 48) and participant observation in general (Labov 1984: 30). As a result, the glosses are relatively free of researcher mediation, having been written secretively, on the assumption that they will not be read by the teacher. For this reason they can be considered to represent illuminating evidence of students' own attitudes to the textbook, the curriculum, and the course. The fact that they are usually scribbled spontaneously and almost unconsciously makes it likely that they represent impressions whose implications have not been analyzed by the students themselves—thus providing access to less conscious levels of their perspectives and strategies. I distributed the books to my students before each class and took them back at the end, since we had limited stocks and frequent losses. This meant that my students wrote their glosses during class sessions, which gave us access to a level of verbal and social interaction in the classroom that usually eludes the eyes of the teacher. Beneath the level of classroom activities usually observed by teachers or researchers, there is a second (necessarily hidden) plane of student interaction which these glosses enable us to decipher.

What do we find in the marginalia of UJ students? Many of the glosses consist of symbols and motifs inspired by the ongoing nationalist struggle. and characterize the political discourse of the students (Schalk 1990). Refrains from popular Tamil resistance songs are penned all over the textbooks. Songs such as the following display their nationalist sentiments:[6]

Our proud possession called Tamil Eelam
What will we do if misfortune overwhelms it?

Fletcher, seated in a prison cell in the first unit, has been given the traditional honorific mark of *tilakam* on his forehead, a mustache and spectacles, and is referred to as Thileepan (a popular Tamil resistance fighter who fasted to death in 1987 in protest against the Indian occupation army). When Fred joins the army in Unit 25a, the guns in the background of the visual are labeled AK47 and T57—the type of weapons typically used by Tamil militants.

The second set of glosses employ visual and verbal symbols from traditional Tamil-Saivite culture, which constitutes the dominant religio-linguistic discourse of the community (Sivatamby 1990). Laura and Susan frequently appear with *poTTu*, a painted mark on the forehead which is supposed to ward off evil, and indicate one's Tamil-Saivite identity. They are also given a *kondai*, the traditional way women wear their hair. Other characters are given traditional dresses, such as *sari* or *verti*, to Tamilize them. Tamil proverbs, aphorisms, and riddles also fill the margins of the books. As Bruce moves into a higher-paying job in his quick rise up the social ladder (in Unit 4a), and purchases a new car and house, a student writes the proverb 'New footwear hurts', implying that novelty is not always pleasant.

Glosses are also composed from titles of films and refrains taken from songs heard in films. Cinema occupies an important place in the popular culture of contemporary Tamils, and a recent ethnographer expressed the view that films function as a 'mythology of modern life' for the community (Lindholm 1980: 137). It is not surprising, therefore, that glosses are created relating to film titles and refrains from cinema songs. The students read the situations in the textbook in terms of films they have seen. Bruce's 'success story' (Unit 4a) has film captions added at each stage in his development, for instance, with apt comments on the message or moral to be drawn. The illustration of Fletcher escaping from prison in the moonlight is given the title *citrapavurNami* (April Full Moon) by some, and *muunRaampiRai* (Moon's

First Quarter) by others. These are names of popular films which have similar plots and situations to those in the textbook. The phases of the moon referred to are considered auspicious according to Hindu astrology. Students also voice their frustrations with the course through cinema songs:

The trial is still not over,
there's nobody to complain to;
being the eldest child I've never cried,
and there's nobody to turn to.

Romance and sex inform the fourth set of glosses. Such experiences are stereotypically associated with university life, as the liberal environment in the campuses is perceived to be tolerant of intimate relations between the sexes. Since such sexual relationships are often identified by Tamils with what they consider a permissive Western culture, different from the stereotypically conservative Asian ethos, most of these glosses were, interestingly, written in English. The picture of Fletcher driving alone at night with Marilyn (Unit 14c) appears romantic for most students, when both are in fact hotly pursuing a group of criminals. In one book Fletcher is presented as saying 'I love you darling', in another Marilyn says 'My dear lover'. Laura, leaning towards Bruce (Unit 1a), is made to say 'Kiss me', while Susan, whispering to Joe next to her (Unit 9a), says 'Love me'.

Students' attitude to physical sex is expressed through their erotic painting. The private parts of characters in the book are highlighted with ink. Such painting usually occurs when male and female partners are found in close proximity—as when Jane and her boyfriend are presented in the cinema. Visuals of this nature appear to titillate students, since such levels of intimacy are taboo in their own culture. There are also innuendoes that refer to the sex act. Naked women in different postures verbally invite readers for sex. Perhaps it is difficult to miss the impression, however, that some of these drawings are aimed at insulting the English instructors, or the publishers of the textbook, or the American characters presented.

The glosses characterize the discourses that interest the students. They show a mixture of cultural backgrounds: romance, sex, and cinema all show influences from international 'pop culture', and the lifestyle of Western entertainment media and youth groups; traditional cultural values and practices are based on Hindu religious roots; the modern Marxist-influenced political discourse is slanted towards nationalistic tendencies. The discourses described above straddle such familiar cultural dichotomies as traditional/ modern, East/West, and conservative/progressive. They remind us of the argument made by post-colonial thinkers that periphery subjects and communities are characterized by a hybridity of complex values (Bhabha 1991, Said 1993). There are, in fact, subtle tensions within the cultures students bring with them—consider the uneasy relationship between traditional Hindu values and Western sexual freedoms, or between the nationalistic political values and cosmopolitan pop culture. We will take up these cultural contradictions later as part of a critical interrogation of their ideological and pedagogical implications.

Of special importance for our present purposes is the way in which the glosses reveal the strategies students adopt to cope with the discourses represented by the text and curriculum. They symbolize the counter-discourses the students use to detach themselves from the ideologies of the textbook, forestall cultural reproduction, and construct for themselves more favorable subjectivities and identities. The textbook's discourses put students at a disadvantage, making them feel alien, incompetent, inferior, and powerless; their own discourses provide them with confidence, familiarity, respectability, and greater power in their own socio-cultural milieu. In other words, the students see the textbook as threatening to remove those desired discourses, and the rural, Tamil, Saivite, activist identities they value, in order to replace them with their own. Faced with this reality in the classroom, the glosses allow students to construct a universe of discourse in which they can feel comfortable, confident, and sheltered.

At times, the content of the textbook is reframed, reinterpreted, and 'rewritten' by students' counter-discourses. They go on to absorb the verbal and visual symbols in the text, and provide alternate meanings. Although we only have slight and occasional indications of how students' interpretations will proceed, those few instances speak loud. For instance, many symbols from Tamil nationalism occur in the serialized detective story in the book, revealing an attempt to understand the narrative in the students' own terms. The story of an innocent man fleeing from the agents of the law to prove himself would inspire students to remember Tamil resistance fighters who were (from the Tamil point of view) perceived as selfless and noble fighters for the rights of their community, unfairly incarcerated by the state. Even the Tamil clothing and appearance given to American characters might be seen as attempts to understand some center situations in terms of local life. It is through such interpretative strategies that students seek connections to their cultural and social context from visuals and narratives that lack local relevance.

The glosses also reveal an oppositional attitude towards the course. To some extent, students wrench the textual signs from their original context and make them objects of ridicule in an act of 'resistant reading' (Fetterley 1978). The glosses sometimes perform acts of violence on the images and symbols of the textbook. The fact that students spend time writing such graffiti in class time could also indicate a lack of interest in classroom activities and the curriculum. Some of the elaborate drawings suggest that students must have taken the whole hour of class time to do them. In many cases, students communicate their shared antagonism to the course more explicitly: one student, for example, wrote 'This is a job for the jobless' over a pair-practice exercise on grammar.

The ironic nature of the glosses could suggest that the students are demystifying or demythologizing the ideologies inscribed in the textbook. In fact, humor, sarcasm, and parody are well-known modes of resisting power in subtle and non-direct ways (Scott 1985). The film titles that caption the episodes in Bruce's path to success through sheer determination and effort (in Unit 4a) perform such a function. By further exaggerating the romantic nature of Bruce's progress, the captions ridicule middle-class values such as social mobility, the work ethic, and material advancement. The first episode, in which Bruce proudly stands in front of his huge factory, a lifetime achievement, is called *vasaNtamaaLikai* ('Palace of Summer')—a film about the wasted effort and unfulfilled expectations of a man who builds a large mansion for his intended wife. The final episode, where the newly successful Bruce marries for a second time, and is depicted together with his children, is ironically entitled *viiTu manaivi piLLai* (i.e. 'Home, Wife, Children')—borrowed from a film that romanticizes the ideal family life.

The glosses reveal how students resist the strait-jacketing and boredom of the alien curriculum and teaching materials, and try to retain an element of independence and creativity. Many glosses show the students distracting themselves by elaborately and laboriously painting the dresses of the characters in the narrative situations. Some show the students letting their imagination run riot, breaking the closed bounds of the exercises and instructions—as when they let insignificant visual details engross their attention, neglecting the grammatical input these visuals are supposed to illustrate. So when a bank hold-up is presented to teach the simple past and past continuous tenses (Unit 13a), students embellish the visuals by providing cigarettes for the gunmen, sparks for the guns, and wads of notes for the cashier.

In essence, the glosses provide evidence of a vibrant *underlife* in the classroom, where students collaborate in providing social, emotional, and psychological sustenance and solidarity against the perceived lifelessness and reproductive tendencies of the course. The student who wrote the refrain 'The trial is still not over . . .' (Unit 11f) was revealing his difficulties with this and other exercises in the textbook. Such comments suggest a caring community, and shared frustrations with the textbook and curriculum. There is gossip on various personal issues (such as exchanging news about the latest classroom romance) and messages such as 'Kumaran and Selvi from Changanai made love'; 'Ruthragantha and Nathiya are in love'. The latter confirm Widdowson's (1987) observation that students come to classrooms for *interactional* purposes (i.e. peer group agendas) as well as for *transactional* purposes (i.e. educational agendas).

This sense of quiet collaboration extends into pedagogical and transactional domains as well. Hoping to defy the inductive, process-oriented approach of the textbook, students often find correct answers and hints to solving grammar problems in the margins of their handed-down books, or written beside the exercises. There are also cases where the students have playfully peer-corrected each other's mistakes in glosses written in English. Other glosses provide Tamil synonyms for English words, or transcribe in Tamil the pronunciation of English words. Content words such as 'response' and 'informal' are translated; proper names and nouns such as 'Kansas' and 'Hooper' are transliterated. In general, students make considerable use of the vernacular in negotiating the lesson material. Classroom observation provides additional evidence for the preference of the vernacular in the learning process (Canagarajah 1993b): the students tend to put pressure on their teachers to use L1 for classroom communication by responding in Tamil, even when discussions have been introduced in English. The places where students spontaneously use English syntactic and lexical items show which discourses they prefer, as in 'I love all of the girls peautiful (sic) in the Jaffna University', and 'Reader: I love you. Bleave (sic) me', and the reply 'I do not love you because I do not believe you. You are terrible man.' Such lexical items, picked up by students outside the class, are being used creatively in quite complex syntactic constructions.

The underlife we discover through the glosses, together with the range of strategies displayed to mediate the alien ideologies and cultural values of the textbook, are of immense significance in understanding student opposition. There are many everyday manifestations of underlife and oppositional behavior in the classroom that teachers will have to note more carefully in order to understand the students' response to the curriculum. By communicating through secretive whispers, exchanging notes and messages among themselves, deviating from the classroom agenda, and cheating the teacher, students enjoy a secret community life and a dimension of curriculum and culture that means a lot to them. It is interesting to imagine the ever-expanding oppositional community that successive batches of such students may be forming through these essentially subversive glosses, in textbooks which are used for many years, and pass through many hands.

Contextualizing student opposition

Why do students resort to developing oppositional behavior in classroom underlife? What prospects are there of student opposition being expressed more constructively and openly? To answer these questions, the discursive data from the margins of the textbook have to be situated in the larger context of classroom behavior, and students' stated views. We will consider to what extent this additional layer of data reveals other dimensions of classroom behavior. While the marginalia provide significant insights into the *lived culture* of the students—the dimension of culture that is instinctively and unconsciously lived out in everyday life without rationalization or theorization—their stated opinions, conscious behavior, and considered attitudes could be different. Although lived culture is important for understanding the hidden attitudes and agendas of the students, to adopt a balanced perspective on resistance, we need to situate it in macro-level data.

Understanding student motivation is important for appreciating the agendas they bring to the course. In a questionnaire survey at the beginning of the course, the reasons for learning English emerged as predominantly intra-community functions. About 76.1% stated 'educational need' as their first preference (including 61.9% who considered this their sole choice). 'Job prospects' was cited by 19.2%, and 'social status' by 4.7%. Since 'To travel abroad' was cited by none, it can be inferred that none of the students was considering learning English for interacting with the Anglo-American community. However, the motivations students themselves proffered in more open-ended interviews suggest a range of motives that are narrowly pragmatic, on the one hand (a–c), and idealistic on the other (d–h). Students needed English (a) because ESOL is mandatory in the university, 5.8%, (b) because a pass is required in the first-year examination, 5.8%, (c) to pursue post-graduate studies, 5.8%, (d) to understand other cultures, 11.7%, (e) to interact with a wider group of people, 14.7%, (f) to gather more information, 20.8%, (g) to know an international language, 23.5%, and (h) 'to become a complete person', 11.7%. While some students would appreciate the cultures and information presented by *AKL*, such a curriculum cannot satisfy those whose motivations relate to intra-community functions.

Student groups from the most marginalized backgrounds were the most open in their opposition to the course curriculum. Supendran, who came from a remote rural community, and whose parents lacked any formal education whatsoever, wanted English in order to serve his own village: 'To enable me to help my village folk to draft official letters to institutions, to read documents we receive from the government, to understand foreign news broadcasts, to read labels on fertilizers and farm equipment.' He wanted a curriculum that was rooted in local community background and needs: 'Rather than talking about apples, talk about mangoes; rather than talking about apartment houses, talk about village huts. Are we all emigrating to America? No! Some of us will continue to live here.' Such students were not served by the curriculum provided by the periphery institutions (which focused on academic contexts) nor by that of the center agencies (which focused on Western and urban discourses)—both discourses are of limited significance for this largely rural group of students.

In order to understand the multiple tensions that can be produced against the classroom discourses, it is important to understand the range of motivations and expectations of the student community. It is clear, for example, that not all students want to follow the curriculum offered by the local universities, which tends to be heavily oriented to English for Academic Purposes, just as others do not share the state's vision of vocational English in terms of urban developmental needs. Nor are students motivated towards interacting with the local or foreign English-speaking communities (known to applied linguists as 'integrative motivation').[7] The functions they envision are different from those addressed by the periphery and center institutions. However, while their language needs are more pragmatically rooted in their immediate rural contexts, they acknowledge the value of English to empower them personally and socially, which is why they do not share the extreme forms of linguistic nationalism sometimes present in local community politics.

In general, the students showed evidence of a remarkably high motivation towards ESL throughout the course. The glosses show that the students were engaged with the course—albeit in a paradoxical way, and from a safe distance. The need they expressed in the initial questionnaires for ELT in university education, and for the language in their social life, were repeated in interviews with me at the end of the course (Canagarajah 1993b). This unwaning interest in learning English suggests that their opposition is not generated by the language *per se* but by the encounter with the curriculum, teaching materials, and the discourses embodied in them. The cultural conflict evident in the glosses is confirmed by some of the more overt classroom behavior and activities, which make it clear that the content of the material was interfering with the learning process. The textbook publishers had expected teachers to use the visual aids to help students formulate interpretative schemata for listening comprehension passages. In practice, the students were often frustrated by the presence of unbridgeable cultural differences in the visuals themselves.

The implications of English for their identity and group solidarity placed a large degree of strain on many students. Some felt that their use of English for classroom interactions would be interpreted by classmates as an attempt to discard their local rural identity and pass for a member of an anglicized élite, or even for a foreigner. It was probably for this reason that in the questionnaire, although 50% stated that they would use English 'with a foreigner who also knew Tamil', all except one rejected the possibility of using English 'with a Tamil who also knew English'. This goes some way towards explaining why students were reluctant to engage in the conversation pieces they had to role-play in each unit.

Other tensions in the course resulted from the learning styles encouraged by the textbook. The students seemed uncomfortable with the collaborative, task-oriented approach, for example. Most preferred to sit, pen in hand, and write down whatever was on the board, or simply listen to the mini-lectures given by the teacher between tasks. They also expected to be provided with the abstract forms and rules of the language quite deductively, to store in their memory, rather than be asked to formulate the rules inductively for themselves through active use of the language in communicative interactions. Recommendations the students made in the final set of interviews with me, for a more effective course, confirmed this product-oriented and examination-focused learning strategy. In fact the attendance rate picked up in the final weeks before the examination to notch a high 90%.

What the lived culture of the students suggests is a dual oppositional trend. On the one hand, they oppose the alien discourses behind the curriculum and textbook. On the other hand, they object to a process-oriented curriculum, and would prefer a product-oriented one. Both trends show a connection: seeing few possibilities of relating what they learn to their socio-cultural background or linguistic needs, students see little meaning for the course beyond the formal, academic ritual of passing the examination and satisfying the English requirements of the institution.

At a more general level, we need to account for the somewhat conflicting attitudes and behavior displayed by the students in this course. I consider that their continuing protestations regarding the high motivation to study English, and the hidden levels of opposition displayed through the glosses dramatize a complex response to the course. The dual attitudes (i.e. motivation and opposition) display the conflicts students face between the threats of cultural alienation experienced subconsciously, and the promises of a socio-economic necessity acknowledged at a more conscious level. The students experience discomfort in the face of the alien discourses confronted in the course (although they did not extensively theorize or analyze this in their interviews with me). However, this alienating experience has to be juxtaposed with their awareness of the powerful discourses which glorify the functions of English, the pressure from the educational system to display proficiency in the language, and the promises of social and economic advancement English holds. Their conflict, then, is this: how to learn English, or earn a certificate of proficiency in English, *without* being inducted into the values embodied by the language and curriculum?

The grammar-based, product-oriented learning which students ask for is part of a strategy they adopt to reconcile this conflict. In their view, grammar learning enables them to be detached from the language and the curriculum, to avoid active use of the language which could involve internalization of its discourses, and thereby continue their opposition to the reproductive effects of the course. At the same time, this strategy enables them to maintain the least contact with the language necessary to acquire the rules of grammar—which they consider to be the most efficient preparation for getting through the examination. This strategy, while enabling students (however tenuously) to preserve their cultural integrity, also enables them to accommodate the institutional requirement of having to pass English and thus bid for the socio-economic advantages associated with it.[8] In a study that comes close to my explanation for student opposition, Resnik (1993) has made a similar observation regarding the attitude of Puerto Ricans to ESL. Opposing the hegemonic thrusts of English against their dominant Spanish culture, yet realizing the economic necessity of being able to speak English in the North American market context, Puerto Ricans adopt a formalistic approach to the acquisition of the language. They acquire a rudimentary grammatical competence sufficient for institutional purposes, while forestalling the spread of English into other intimate areas of social life, which they associate with Spanish. Others such as Delpit (1995) and Muchiri *et al.* (1995) have argued that minority students desire the immediate satisfaction of the codes of dominant social groups in a product-oriented manner, considering process-oriented approaches as misdirected, irrelevant, or hegemonical. Along these lines, Pennycook (1996) shows how memorization-based product-oriented learning strategies of Chinese students can have oppositional possibilities.

We must not fail to reconstruct from the glosses the curriculum students themselves bring to the class.[9] Students seem to want a course that would help them use English with consideration for their own socio-cultural milieu, characterized by an intense nationalistic consciousness and rural living conditions. They want a course that employs discourses, narratives, and situations related to their political aspirations, traditional Saivite religious culture, and contemporary popular culture (chiefly cinema). Only formal English is required for strictly institutional and educational purposes, so their needs are grammar or code-focused. They are looking for a form of functional curriculum which would use L1 as a significant medium of classroom interaction, since in their social milieu English and the vernacular function in a mixed and integrated manner, as a multi-vocal or hybrid medium of communication. We will wrestle with these conflicting agendas in the final chapter, when we develop alternate curricula.

Although it is important to become sensitive to the students' curriculum, we must not fail to interrogate it critically for its hidden ideologies. We must resist the somewhat misleading tendency in critical pedagogical circles to romanticize student opposition and minority discourses as being always liberatory and progressive.[10] We must also note that the students here are adopting an examination-oriented motivation and an outwardly accommodative learning strategy that fails to engage with the course reflectively for critical learning. Their curricular preferences expose an attitude that turns learning into a convenient route for correct and easy answers, rather than a process of self-discovery and exploration. Their discursive background also shows a range of values which includes questionable assumptions and beliefs about social life. While the nationalistic discourses and the Saivite religious sentiments may have radical potential, students' discourses on romance, sex, and popular cinema are controversial. Tamil cinema is largely melodramatic and sentimental, usually avoiding confrontation with the harsher socio-political realities. Similarly, the discourse on romance as private and emotional, may encourage an escape from the social world. The presentation of women as sex objects (obviously glossed by male students) dehumanizes women, and suggests their gender-based biases.

It becomes important, therefore, to unravel the ambiguous strands of students' behavior with the help of Giroux (1983: 109), who warns that the concept of resistance must not be allowed to become a category indiscriminately attached to every expression of 'oppositional behavior'. Giroux distinguishes between *resistance*—which he sees as displaying ideological clarity and commitment to collective action for social transformation—from mere *opposition*, which is unclear, ambivalent, and largely passive. Having analyzed the classroom behavior in the larger discursive and social contexts, we can say that the responses and attitudes of the students do not fall under Giroux's definition of radical resistance. In most respects, theirs is a vague, instinctive, oppositional form of behavior that lacks ideological clarity. It fails to sustain consciousness-raising or collective action for change. Students' behavior in the class is ambivalent, containing elements of accommodation as well as opposition in response to the conflicting pulls of socio-economic mobility, on the one hand, and those of cultural integrity on the other. Although at one level the grammatical approach enables students to resist the ideological thrusts of the curriculum and textbook, it is doubtful whether we can interpret the students' behavior as a form of radical resistance.

It is important not to take students' opposition at face value, therefore, but to interrogate such behavior in the light of the larger social and historical background. We need to explore how student cultures could display conflicting impulses and influences. The attitudes and responses students display contain a range of mixed values which hold ambivalent possibilities for resistance or accommodation to dominant ideologies. Teachers have a responsibility to unravel the conflicting strands of student behavior in order that the more productive insights and strategies can be tapped for a critical pedagogy. Of course, they must not look on this as an opportunity to impose their own ideologies unilaterally; this task has to be negotiated by teaching staff who are sensitive to the aspirations of their students. In Chapter 8 we will consider how teachers can help students to interrogate these conflicting impulses in their classroom culture, and to develop a potential for resistance that will result in them fashioning a curriculum that is ideologically liberating, as well as educationally meaningful.

Conclusion

Despite their possible limitations, the discourses that students use to engage the classroom curriculum are significant. It is important, therefore, to be sensitive to the multiplicity of cultures students bring from outside the classroom, and the ways in which these mediate the lesson. The behavioral strategies of the students show that they are not passive in the face of ideological domination by center curriculum and teaching materials. Their cultural background mediates center ideologies and generates various subtle ways of opposing and/or appropriating them. Such behavior of the students shows the limitations of adopting deterministic models of center domination in ELT.

Notes

1 It is for this reason that I include the state agencies as active spheres of influence in the classroom, deviating from Holliday's similar—but less complex—model (1994: 29). His model is of course consistent with his view that any cultural domination from the center results solely from the interests of the professional circles in ELT.

2 The ethnography reported here is of a first-year ESL course on English for General Purposes at the University of Jaffna. The observation—complemented by surveys and interviews—took place during the 1991 academic year.

3 In recent years some attempts have been made to break away from the unilateral influence of the center agencies. ELT units in Sri Lanka's universities have been forming a national decision-making body, and organizing annual conferences. They have also published two collections of studies representing the local scholarship of the past ten years (Raheem *et al.* 1987, Gunesekera *et al.* 1994). However, periphery professionals have limited financial and technological resources with which to organize themselves, and to conduct and/or publish research on their pedagogical challenges. The Asia Foundation has had to partly fund the publications and conferences organized by local professionals.

4 My interpretation of the cultural content of the book here assumes the perspective of a general rural student community. I will, however, provide data from my students' responses later in this chapter to discuss the extent to which they find the cultural content alien and intrusive.

5 Phillipson documents cases of textbook donation by center agencies without adequate consideration for the needs and background of classrooms in India, Kenya, Nigeria, and Zambia (1992: 253). That center curricular models and teaching materials violate local cultural norms is demonstrated by other studies in periphery contexts (Maley 1986, Osterloh 1986, and Miller and Emel 1988. Swales (1980: 64) talks aptly of an 'educational shock'—analogous to culture shock—for periphery students confronted with alien material in Khartoum University.

6 The glosses that follow were originally written in Tamil, except in the few cases specified which were written in English.

7 I find the terms integration/instrumental (popularized by Gardner and Lambert 1972) as well as the recent alternative of extrinsic/intrinsic (championed by Brown 1991) too limited to talk about the range of unique motivations displayed by periphery students.

8 The paradox of periphery students being highly motivated for English education (often despite teachers' limitations and institutional failures) while also showing opposition to curriculum and pedagogy has been noted by other researchers. But the 'apparent contradictions' which Holliday observes (1994: 153), remain a passing mention. Chick (1996) brings out how, in South Africa, Kwazulu students adopt taciturnity and rote learning as a 'deference strategy'. Holliday (1994: 154) also finds that Egyptian and Iranian students adopt 'coping strategies' to deal non-confrontationally with classroom problems.

9 Holliday (1994) refers to this as 'students' lesson'. Widdowson (1984: 189–200) has called this 'the curse of Caliban', to capture the idea that whatever the teachers might teach, students still take from the course only what they wish.

10 On the limitations of idealizing student culture, see Giroux 1983. The care with which teachers should undertake to critique student behavior is discussed by Ellsworth (1989) and Giroux (1992: 34–5).

A reply by Robert O'Neill

My full reply cannot be included here for reasons of space. I argue that there are many different ways of reading the texts and narratives in *American Kernel Lessons*, and that the interpretation Mr Canagarajah places upon them tells us more about his own ideological preoccupations than it does about the effect those texts are likely to have upon language learners. In addition, I argue that although foreign language textbooks may have many faults, they should not be criticized because the characters and texts in them are 'foreign'. *American Kernel Lessons* is an EFL (English as a *foreign* language) textbook. Yet Mr Canagarajah criticizes it because the characters in the book seem 'foreign' and use English for purposes in ways which are foreign–or different from the ways and purposes for which Tamil speakers use Tamil with other Tamil speakers. People do not learn a 'foreign' language in order to communicate with speakers of their own language. They learn a foreign language especially an international language like English–to communicate with people who do not speak the same language–and this inevitably involves using that language in ways and in styles that may seem 'foreign'–and sometimes even 'alien'.

I am particularly sensitive to the charge of racism, and do not accept that the charge is justified simply because a character in it who is not stereotypically 'white, Anglo' sometimes comes to work late or misses a bus. All the other characters have far worse faults, ranging from gross incompetence, dishonesty, and cowardice to blackmail and betrayal.

Most of all, my disagreement with Mr Canagarajah focuses on the proposal that Tamil students need a programme of 'ideological liberation' and protection from the alleged 'hidden agenda' in *American Kernel Lessons*, or any other textbook that is likely to be an adequate vehicle for the learning of English as a foreign or even a second language. I believe that Mr Canagarajah's program for 'ideological liberation' is really 'ideological insistence on ignorance' and that the results of it are unlikely to be even what Mr Canagarajah appears to desire, especially at the end of this century, in which more people than ever before have been murdered in the name of various kinds of ideology.

Author's note: Robert O'Neill's response is important because it shows the wide gap between the intentions of textbook writers and the reception of their material by periphery students and teachers. The ideological stance, attitudes, and educational goals articulated in his response should be taken into consideration as we grapple with the many conflicts in the ELT enterprise. Our exchange on these issues can be read in full from the Oxford University Press ELT website at:

http://www.oup.co.uk/elt

Follow the link to the ELT catalogue and Applied Linguistics, and then select the book title:
Resisting Linguistic Imperialism in English Teaching.

5 Competing pedagogies: understanding teacher opposition

We repeated the meaningless phrases
Like the yellow birds
In the *lajanamara* grass

The teacher was an Acoli
But he spoke the same language
As the white priests [. . .]

And he tried
To force his words
Through his blocked nose.

He sounded like
A loosely strung drum.

p'Bitek, *Song of Lawino*

Hitherto, ELT pedagogical thinking has been obsessed with instructional methods. Methods are believed to offer practitioners an integrated conception of theoretical approaches and classroom techniques for teaching purposes. They provide teachers with ready-made ways of dealing with the complexities of strange student populations, alien socio-cultural contexts, and peculiar learning styles. In the positivistic tradition, methods are considered value-free instruments that avoid the clumsy mediation of human subjects and, thus, accomplish one's objectives efficiently. Especially if these methods are formulated through systematic research, they are believed to offer final solutions to the complicated pedagogical problems in language acquisition. It is understandable therefore that teachers and researchers have been searching for the 'best method' that would set language teaching on a surer footing. This search has spawned periodic fashion shifts, as methods rise and fall, with superlative claims made on behalf of each succeeding approach in tune with the prevailing pedagogical orthodoxy.

However, the idea of method has recently come into criticism. Many scholars realize that, purely from a pedagogical point of view, what teachers practice in language classrooms rarely resembles any specific method as it is prescribed in manuals. What is supposed to be the same method can differ from teacher to teacher, and class to class, depending on the many logistical, cultural and institutional forces at play. It has been pointed out that classroom realities rarely correspond to any recognizable method. Even when teachers start with a specific method in mind, they are influenced by classroom contingencies to make changes as they teach. Therefore, scholars doubt whether there is anything called a 'method.' Furthermore, applied linguists now recognize that we can never discover the 'best method' (Prabhu 1990, Kumaravadivelu 1994). Sheen (1994) analyzes the area of Methods Comparison Research and highlights the different levels of effectiveness of specific approaches in diverse learning contexts. Scholars in ELT have therefore started speaking of the emergent *postmethod condition*, in which teachers are compelled to give up thinking in terms of predefined methods, and begin to creatively devise pedagogical strategies to suit their specific classroom conditions (Kumaravadivelu 1994).

Apart from this strictly pedagogical critique, there also exists an ideological questioning of the methods concept. Following the thinking of philosophers such as Feyarabend (1975), ELT scholars realize that methods are 'constructs' put together by specific social groups for particular ends on the basis of their social practice and interests (Pennycook 1989, Phillipson 1992). Methods are not value-free instruments of solely pragmatic import. They are ideological in embodying partisan assumptions about social relations and cultural values. Methods can reproduce these values and practices wherever they are being used. The empirical claims and efficiency criteria serve only to blind teachers to the hegemonic implications of methods.

Consider how the methods industry parallels commerce in the international market place. The center's unfair monopoly over trade in industrial products with periphery nations is extended through the trade in language-teaching methods. The dominance of center applied linguistic circles stems from their ability to conduct sophisticated research using hi-tech facilities and then popularize the knowledge globally through their publishing networks and academic institutions (Canagarajah 1996). As in other areas of commerce, new methods (and sometimes old methods in new packaging) are marketed under different brand labels, first of all to create and then to maximize demand. It is not surprising that many teachers in periphery communities succumb to center claims that the methods propagated through their glossy textbooks, research journals, teacher training programs, and professional organizations are the most efficient. This dependency on imported products has tended to undermine the alternative styles of thinking, learning, and interacting preferred by local communities. Beyond this, of course, every new method sold to periphery institutions is a drain on limited educational budgets, which may be further depleted by the cost of paying center experts to retrain the teaching cadre. In these ways, the intensive promotion of center methods helps to draw periphery communities ever deeper into a vortex of cultural, financial, and professional dependency.

Few can dismiss the ideological and economic implications of methods for the periphery, as raised by critical ELT scholars, and when we come to observe what actually takes place in classrooms we will find that there are further complications. For instance, the methods and materials of the center may not be implemented as originally intended. As we saw in the previous chapter, periphery teachers and students may have different ways of translating or applying the resources they take from outside. The specific uses to which they put such resources may feature subtle forms of resisting and modifying pedagogical prescriptions. Apart from cultural processes of appropriation, there are other local material and institutional influences that mediate the use of center methods. Therefore an important research perspective is to closely observe classrooms, and describe how competing pedagogical traditions are negotiated in them. After discussing the ways in which center and periphery pedagogical traditions relate to each other, I will describe the introduction of the recently popularized task-based method in a periphery institution.

Conflicting pedagogical styles?

Many ELT experts and professionals see center and periphery communities as having different pedagogical traditions. Thinking in this field is often informed by such stereotypes, so I shall start with a critique of some of the typologies that have been constructed to capture the center/periphery difference.

Although Holliday acknowledges variations within BANA (i.e. center) institutions, he characterizes their contemporary pedagogy as primarily based on a learning group ideal which functions as the basis for the development of their teaching methods. He says, 'This learning group ideal sets the conditions for a process-oriented, task-based, inductive, collaborative, communicative English language teaching methodology' (1994: 54). He refers to this as what is established in center ELT circles as 'the optimum interactional parameters within which classroom language learning can take place' (1994: 54). Research both in general educational psychology and second language acquisition are claimed to support this orientation as universally valid features of successful learning. This learning group ideal therefore becomes the criterion by which methods, teaching materials, and professional training are constructed and evaluated by center professionals.

Holliday (1994) goes on to describe the periphery pedagogical tradition as based on the contrasting principles of didactic, teacher-fronted, product-oriented approaches. Using the labels coined by Basil Bernstein 1977 (i.e. collectionist and integrationist), he employs the product and process paradigms as his framework for discussing center and periphery pedagogies, respectively. He presents examples such as the following: while periphery teachers provide English through explicitly grammar-oriented approaches (resembling courses in descriptive linguistics), center communities focus on the skill of using language in actual communication; while periphery teachers give formal lectures, center practitioners orchestrate the learning experience with collaborative participation from students; while learning necessarily involves the presence and help of a teacher in the periphery, center communities encourage the autonomy of students (Holliday 1994: 80-5).

Needless to say, periphery pedagogical styles acquire a pejorative cast. In the light of the popular notion that center has actually 'progressed' from product-oriented to process-oriented pedagogies (Tuman 1988), periphery practices will look anachronistic if not ineffective and irrational. Add to this the association of process-oriented, learner-centered approaches with democratic values originating from egalitarian social systems (Tuman 1988). Product-oriented, teacher-fronted pedagogies end up being associated with totalitarian values stemming from the traditionalistic and non-egalitarian social systems of the past. From this point of view, then, periphery classrooms are considered to be reproducing undemocratic and conservative tendencies in their students, while center methods are considered progressive. Furthermore, many teachers are influenced by Bernstein's (1977) argument that those who prefer integrationist (process-oriented) pedagogies come from middle-class families which have democratic family relationships and develop expansive thinking and communicative skills, while working-class subjects who are socialized into somewhat rigid/authoritarian family relationships and linguistic practices prefer collectionist (product-oriented) approaches. Thus, even critical pedagogues sometimes readily assume that process-oriented methods are more radical and empowering.[1]

As we deconstruct the above assumptions, we must first examine the association of process-oriented, student-centered, task-based pedagogies with the most efficient means of language acquisition. Sheen (1994) argues that there is not enough research in SLA to make such conclusive statements about any method. We have simply scratched the surface of language acquisition. There are in fact studies that show that deductive pedagogies serve useful functions—at times enabling a more successful acquisition of language in certain grammar structures (Doughty 1991, Gass 1982). Others point out that some variants of product-oriented methods produce better results than process-oriented methods either overall or in particular skills such as reading and writing (Casey 1968, Levin 1972, Smith 1970, and von Elek and Oscasson 1973). Therefore the wholesale denigration of product-oriented pedagogies has to be questioned.

Turning to the ideological issues at stake, it cannot be assumed that process-oriented methods are inherently empowering. Tuman (1988), considering the American pedagogical context, argues that process methods may in fact serve purposes of domination. Process pedagogy can give the illusion of freedom and equality in the classroom which may not be available in the larger society.[2] Students are thus fed on false optimism through a classroom empowerment that does not help them interrogate oppressive tendencies outside. In other words, process methods may constitute newer and subtler forms of domination. Tuman is influenced by the later writing of Bernstein (1981) which theorizes why not all change is progress and not all existing methods are reactionary. Bernstein points out that pedagogical change must be motivated by a realistic assessment of the social world whose dominant institutions may continue their reproductive function in subtle ways, whatever the pedagogical agenda or practice.

Moreover, there are testimonies from researchers that challenge the relevance and effectiveness of the process approach in periphery classrooms. It is important to consider this growing body of scholarship in order to understand how empowerment is contingent upon contextual factors and does not inhere in a method. Lisa Delpit (1995), an African-American teacher ethnographer, points to the limitations of process methods from the point of view of Alaskan and African-American student communities. She points out that when these minority student groups lack a knowledge of the very grammar and/or rules required to enter the mainstream, to postpone these in the name of discovery-processes is to perpetuate their disadvantage. A group of African scholars have recently supplied evidence from universities in their continent to show that process methods are ineffective in their context of limited pedagogical facilities (Muchiri *et al.* 1995). Such scholars point out that process methods are based on the interests of student groups from the dominant community who already possess the required codes and skills to develop higher level communicative skills through interaction. It is not surprising therefore that periphery students oppose process approaches. We must also remember here the discussion in the last chapter that students adopt product-oriented learning processes as a strategy of resistance.[3]

The purpose of critiquing the assumptions of center ELT professional circles is not to generate a backlash against process methods or to bring product-oriented methods into fashion. Similarly, it is not necessary to dispute teachers who have reported success in using process approaches in periphery contexts (Pennington 1995, Holliday 1994). The purpose here is to highlight the role of determinants such as contexts, students, and purposes in developing relevant pedagogies. Process and product take different values in different social, cultural, and historical contexts depending on the needs and interests of the student groups.

Periphery pedagogies in perspective

With the above qualifications in mind, we can delineate the dominant pedagogical tendencies in periphery communities. The preference for didactic instruction in many periphery ELT programs has been attributed to ancient ethno-religious practices. It is said to be based on a Koranic culture in Egypt (Holliday 1994), Buddhist culture in India (Bowers 1980), and Islamic culture in the Middle East (Dudley-Evans and Swales 1980, Osterloh 1986, and Parker *et al.* 1986). We need to understand, however, the pedagogical variety that exists and the complex determinants of the pedagogies practiced there.

Taking the Tamil community in Sri Lanka, for example, from pre-colonial times there have been wide variations in teaching approaches (Jayasuriya no date, Sirisena 1969, Somasegaram 1969). In the traditional learning system, one can distinguish at least three methods of learning. These were conditioned by the different purposes and contexts of instruction. The dominant system was, of course, the deductive, teacher-fronted method in the *guru-shisya* (i.e. teacher-disciple) tradition. Typically the teacher (always male) passed on his stock of received knowledge orally to the disciple at his feet. The disciples had to cultivate the art of listening meditatively and memorizing accurately the huge stock of information to be preserved without corruption. The reverence paid to the guru, as to the knowledge he transmitted, was almost religious in character. This pedagogy was partly a consequence of the dominant oral culture in this community. In oral forms of communication and knowledge transmission it is necessary to pass down information across generations—from one source who authoritatively preserves that knowledge to students who would memorize it accurately to pass it down to the next generation.

Traditional descriptions of language and pedagogies of language teaching have also displayed a penchant for prescriptive and formalistic methods. The well-known Dravidian scholar Emeneau notes (1955: 145-6): 'Intellectual thoroughness and an urge toward ratiocination, intellection, and learned classification for their own sakes should surely be recognized as characteristic of the Hindu higher culture ... They become grammarians, it would seem, for grammar's sake.' As evident from Emeneau's statement, this formalistic approach was more than a linguistic orientation; it was the dominant intellectual orientation of Hindu higher culture. Similarly, as late as the colonial period, the teaching of local languages to European administrators was primarily based on studying and memorizing learned grammatical treatises (Wickramasuriya 1981).

But there was also a second pedagogical tradition, different from the above monological one. This was a dialogical learning method, based on exploratory exchanges between the *guru* and the *shisya* (somewhat in the sense of Platonic dialogs). Discourses on religion, logic and philosophy were held in this manner. Although it cannot be said that this was an exchange where teacher and student enjoyed an equal relationship, at least the approach held the possibility of being more inductive and collaborative, since students could at least initiate topics and questions. Their attitude to the subject matter could also be more discovery-oriented.

The third pedagogical tradition was an informal learning approach, where the learner lived with the family of the teacher and 'picked up' knowledge and skills as he or she worked in the teacher's house. The learner accompanied the teacher on his various practical rounds related to his work—in the farm, dairy, fields, and workshop—to be apprenticed into the 'trade' through personal interactions. This learning system was considerably more non-formal with the blurring of distinctions between philosophical and technical knowledge, facts and skills, and knowledge and life. This was more process-oriented and inductive. There was greater scope for the student to gather knowledge non-didactically—by observing, inferring, performing, and practicing. This learning style was mostly reserved for practical skills in the training of artisans, whereas the other two were usually for formal knowledge in areas of literature, religion, philosophy, and philology. Thus the tradition of ancient learning systems displayed much diversity, straddling the process/product divide. The pedagogy differed according to the learning context, purpose, and (to some extent) subject matter.

It is possible to argue that a rigidly systematized and uniform product-oriented pedagogic tradition was in fact introduced by the Western colonial regimes when they began administering periphery communities. In most periphery regions, such as that of the Tamil community, the indigenous educational tradition was suppressed by the education imposed by colonial European powers. Schooling was institutionalized: learning was separated from everyday life and the non-formal learning contexts; the subjects, syllabi, materials, and schedules were centrally defined and controlled; and the professionalism of the teacher replaced the religious authority and accumulated experience of the *guru*. Descriptions of missionary schools in colonial Jaffna show teacher-centered classes where students focus on uniform texts produced in Britain to extricate or retain information for competitive examinations oriented towards the individual display of knowledge (Chelliah 1922, Vignarajah 1994). It is well known that the center communities themselves practiced product-oriented pedagogies in those days. Therefore, if the periphery communities are predominantly product-oriented today (losing their pre-colonial pedagogical diversity), the responsibility lies with center hegemony to some extent.

There are some other reasons for the dominance of product-oriented pedagogies in contemporary periphery communities. They are not solely cultural or religious (as emerging from the scholarship of center scholars cited above), but also economic and material. Because periphery communities are impoverished, their funds for education are limited. Therefore classrooms often have few facilities—there is no blackboard, no chalk, and limited textbooks for students. Furthermore, class size is large because there are few classrooms and/or teachers available. In many classes students stand up for the whole lecture, or squeeze themselves uncomfortably in the few available seats. It is difficult in these classes to rearrange the furniture for collaborative work or initiate conveniently the small-group negotiation that can be monitored by a single teacher. Since only the instructor has the teaching material, he or she has to impart this 'secret' knowledge to passive students. Obviously these conditions do not encourage pleasant student interactions or a relaxed engagement with knowledge. Students would rather get the 'facts' from the teacher, write it down in their notebooks, and rush to the next class. Termed a 'large-class culture' (Murphy 1986), such conditions can pressurize teachers to adopt a teacher-centered, oral, didactic, deductive pedagogy.

Despite these pressures in some periphery classrooms for product-oriented instruction, there are reasons for diversity at different levels. This is partly because ELT instructors themselves come under competing pedagogical influences. As depicted in the diagram in the last chapter, they are members of periphery academic institutions and disciplinary communities in one sense; but in another sense they are members of the international professional circles. These influences pose conflicting implications for their philosophy and practice. First of all, there are often inconsistencies in the policies and practices of periphery teachers. Teachers may profess center pedagogical fashions, but practice traditional approaches in the classroom. They may show inconsistent preferences on pedagogical styles, approaches, and philosophies, torn between the center and periphery educational cultures. It is not unusual to find inconsistencies such as the following: though teachers believe that the sole medium of ESL courses should be English-only, they use considerable code-switching with the vernacular in the classroom; though textbooks are task-based, they use it in a product-oriented fashion; though they reward 'standard British/American English' in examinations, they themselves use Sri Lankan English for active classroom communication. However, these tensions also contribute to the dynamism and diversity in the periphery professional group which can inspire creative pedagogical thinking and practice.

Negotiating pedagogies

In the light of the conflicting pedagogical influences in the periphery and the divergent contextual factors which shape such influences, we have to find out how classroom life is negotiated. I will explore the strategies teachers adopt to accommodate or resist the methods popularized by center professional circles. To exemplify the processes underlying the negotiation of pedagogies in periphery classrooms I narrate an attempt to employ task-based methodology in UJ.[4] Teachers of first-year courses on English for General Purposes had been meeting voluntarily once a week to discuss their teaching practice. They were troubled by the lack of student involvement and the limited improvement in communicative competence in these courses. They hypothesized that these problems could be probably caused by the largely grammar-oriented, teacher-fronted instructional strategy we were using.[5] They decided to adopt a task-based method, which was already gaining a foothold in local secondary schools through the textbooks and tests produced with the help of foreign experts. Some were impressed with proclamations on the superiority of the task-based methods they were encountering in the professional literature.[6] They were also attracted by the new textbooks popularizing this approach that were gifted by the Asia Foundation to the department library.

Teachers initially educated themselves on task-based approaches (through the available professional literature) and prepared some model tasks which they distributed amongst themselves. They recognized that this pedagogy came into conflict with the grammar-based approaches they had been practicing hitherto. Whereas in the new approach the task is the unit of lesson activity, traditional methods focus on grammar. If linguistic structures are taught at all in task-based approaches, they are introduced only implicitly and inductively. Furthermore, traditional approaches focus on *what* is to be learned, while task-based approaches attend to *how* it is to be learned. The task-based approach also calls for changes in the roles of teachers and students, as a teacher-fronted pedagogy gives way to a collaborative approach. In order to realize these features, teachers prepared tasks that involved calculating distances, planning itineraries, using maps and charts, ordering or organizing details in a logical format, and predicting events based on schedules and timetables. These tasks contained opinion gaps, information gaps, and reasoning gaps which call for student participation and collaboration.

Classroom observation suggested, however, different realizations of the method. Some teachers persisted in using the approach, while others gave up after a cursory attempt. Teachers adopted various coping strategies that constituted a range of direct and indirect forms of appropriating the method. Consider, for example, the experience of one of the teachers:[7]

- *Malathy appeared to be rather too confident about the assumptions and procedures of the task-based method during the staff meetings. As a junior staff member with a locally-earned Masters in Linguistics, she did not want to give the impression that the new method was difficult or strange to her. She always claimed that her use of the new method was successful in her classes. As we walked to her class in a building slightly damaged by aerial bombardment, Malathy shared with me that she was bringing a list of bibliographical entries for an activity. The 18 entries were each organized according to a consistent bibliographical convention but without alphabetical arrangement. This presented the information and logical gap that constituted the task for the students. Apart from developing the academic skill of comprehending, identifying, and using bibliographical information, she expected students to engage in verbal interactions during the task to develop their communicative competence.*

As Malathy entered the class of 60 students, she had to find a way of getting through the chairs which barricaded her from the teacher's platform and lectern. As for me, a student was prepared to offer his chair and stand against the wall for the rest of the class with some of his friends. When Malathy finally managed to reach the platform, she greeted her students and marked attendance. She proceeded to write the bibliographical entries on the board to prepare for the activity. She asked students to note the conventions followed in the entries. Since the blackboard in that room was small (it had in fact broken into two), Malathy could write only four entries at a time. This meant that she had to let the students write the entries after her, as she erased one set and wrote another. It finally took about half her class time to get the entries written down. Meanwhile the students were getting restless, whispering among themselves, confused by the novelty of the activity.

Although according to her lesson plan, Malathy intended to conduct a pre-task activity (i.e. a warm up exercise to orientate the students to the task), she appeared to have changed her mind during the lesson. Instead, she took about ten minutes to explain the nature of the activity. This occurred as a mini-lecture. Students complained that some of the words in the entries were difficult and asked her to explain them: 'empirical', 'syllogistic', 'prolegomena', 'molecular', etc. They then glossed the meanings and pronunciation in Tamil in their notebooks. After asking students to arrange the entries alphabetically, Malathy asked a few questions to check their ability to identify the information fast: On what subject did Toulmin write his books? How many books on economics are in the list? If you are asked to write an essay on business to which of these books will you refer? In which year was the book on Biology published? How many books of David Smith do you find in this list? When was his first book published? How many of the books were published outside America?

Students mumbled their replies hesitantly as they tried to reply in complete sentences. Malathy corrected the syntax for them, helped them form complete sentences, and reminded them of the rules. She always translated her questions into Tamil. Much of this interaction resembled the typical IRF routine of classroom discourse (i.e. Initiation, Response, Feedback—see Mehan 1985, Stubbs 1976). When she found that many students faced problems in forming the simple present tense, she proceeded to take some time off from the immediate task to explain subject-verb agreement and verb-formation rules. Students were asked to turn to their notebooks and refer to a chart that Malathy had introduced in the previous class. This explanation was a mini-lecture that took about ten minutes. Students took notes on what the teacher said. Another cycle of IRF interaction occurred for about ten minutes after the mini-lecture. Malathy couldn't finish all the tasks she had planned before the end of the class.

When we discussed her class after the lesson, Malathy said she had skipped the pre-task activity and given a mini-lecture because she felt that students were getting restless while the entries were being written on the board. The arrangement of the class had dissuaded her from giving the small group activity she had planned: 'I couldn't shift the chairs to form smaller circles,' she said. Although both of us considered how xeroxing the entries would have saved her the time taken to write them on the board, we realized that this was impractical in Jaffna where stationery and xerox machines are not freely available. Malathy summed up her overall impression thus: 'I managed to do only some of the activities I had planned. If the classroom facilities had permitted, I would have done a few other activities... I must plan the sequence of activities more carefully, taking into account the available facilities in each room.' It appeared that a successful class for Malathy meant conducting the tasks in an orderly and effective way. Malathy's record book confirmed this impression. She was preoccupied with issues of timing, sequence, room organization, and task preparation. Perhaps since these practical problems demanded much attention, she didn't appear to give adequate consideration to the aims and processes of language acquisition. Although Malathy was enthusiastic about her pedagogy, she may have been giving too much attention to what Pennington (1995) calls the *procedural aspects* of teaching (i.e. a focus on the logistics, tasks, materials, and classroom management).

Turning to some of her pedagogical choices, I asked her whether it was not sufficient for the students to give the information required in short answers rather than in sentences. Malathy said that her intention was to use the task to reinforce grammar. Asked whether immediate grammar correction was important, she said, 'I agree that this is not the point of the tasks. But I feel that students expect error correction from me. If I failed to correct them, the students could be misled into thinking that their answers are correct.' Confronted with the possibility that the point of the activity may have been to identify information, rather than to teach the tense, Malathy felt that without a linguistic component the students would consider that the lesson was a waste of time. She justified her intermittent mini-lectures in the same way.

It appeared that the students also considered that the point of the activities was syntactical correctness. The fact that they spent most of their time writing down notes suggests that they were more interested in developing an abstract competence in form than in improving their communicative fluency through oral practice. The mixed reasons given by the students I spoke to suggested that they considered grammar-based pedagogy to be rigorous and useful, whereas the task-based approach was too relaxed and enjoyable. Kumanan said, 'Of course, they [i.e. task-based activities] are quite interesting and enjoyable. They are OK for adding variation to the teaching. Perhaps, these activities also provide relaxation for the teacher—relieving them of the painful task of preparing and explaining grammar points.'

In terms of participant structure, we can note some general patterns from this class. There were few student–student interactions, apart from gossip and whispers on topics not related to the lesson, and the students initiated very little interaction with the teacher. There were only four moves out of a total of 15 where students asked the teacher questions, and these were mostly to clarify difficult words. Most of the interactions were initiated by the teacher, who also regulated turn-taking and topic initiation, and gave her periodic mini-lectures. The teacher's tendency to monopolize classroom talk and control the flow of instructional activities meant that the students' opportunities to talk in English were very limited.

Although the class had been organized around tasks, its format was clearly teacher-fronted, and somewhat product-oriented. Even when the teacher employed certain exercises and material suitable for a task-oriented approach, her values and practices showed the considerable influence of the traditional approaches (the grammar-translation method, in particular) that she had used before. Although tasks were provided, the 'deep structure' of the lesson showed a form-oriented, teacher-fronted style of instruction. What we eventually found, therefore, was a method that was neither task-based nor grammar-translation. The instruction was not grammar-translation because the unit of analysis around which the lesson was organized was a task. Furthermore, although grammar was explicitly taught, it was not deductively taught. At the same time, this was too product-oriented and teacher-fronted to be described as task-based. Grammar is explicitly taught and linguistic correctness emerges as equally or more important than task completion. It is significant, however, that the teacher maintained she was using a task-based pedagogy.

It is possible to consider this teaching experience as a largely intuitive (untheorized) reconciliation of the contextual problems raised by the new pedagogy. Teacher and students are negotiating an alternate pedagogy—a third approach that is neither traditional nor novel, neither grammar-translation nor task-based—that suits their learning context. It is clear how the cultural, institutional, and material conditions of the local context (outlined in the earlier section) mediate the classroom practice. Similarly, the teacher's own grounding in the local pedagogical cultures give rise to tensions in her practice, despite her expressed desire to implement a center-based novel method. The pedagogy thus becomes a complex hybrid of the conflicting contextual forces impinging on periphery classrooms.

Coping with novel methods

Malathy's failure to acknowledge that she had selectively interpreted and implemented the new method was largely an unconscious outcome. Certain other teachers chose to adopt this approach as a conscious defensive strategy; they claimed that they had adopted the task-based method, but in practice they continued to use the familiar pedagogical approaches. After making minor adjustments in their pedagogy under the influence of the task-based method, they continued to use the approach they were most comfortable with. So the trappings of the novel pedagogy were present (i.e. use of tasks, group activity, etc.), but the basic structure of the course was traditional (i.e. focus on grammar with mini-lectures, teacher-authority, and deductive learning processes). This practice was especially true of younger staff members with recent degrees and an awareness of international developments in the field. It is a measure of center influence on the thinking of local teachers that they should feel themselves under pressure to prove their professionalism by using new-fangled methods.

Some teachers used the pedagogy with other forms of subtle modification to suit their values and styles of teaching. A typical strategy was to 'cherry-pick' the assumptions and techniques of the new method. For instance, Karuna interpreted the task-based method as being similar to the one he was already using: 'Well, I have always been giving tasks and activities to my students after I introduce certain grammar items. The task-based approach involves simply giving more weight to activities in the classroom.' Such teachers do not want to abandon the pedagogies they are already using, so they use tasks selectively, incorporating elements of the new method into their original repertoire of classroom techniques. They consider this cut-and-paste arrangement to be a happy marriage between the new and old methods in a manner that was convenient to them.

Others adopted subtler strategies to resist the method. If they were poorly motivated, or were instinctively opposed to alien methods, they employed the new method halfheartedly. They would go through the steps of the pedagogy, without showing any signs of personal involvement. Morris (1991) calls this process the 'busy work' syndrome—i.e. routinized or uninvolved activity carried out in order to be seen as implementing a plan. This approach usually functioned as a self-fulfilling prophecy. Since the teachers did not feel committed to the new pedagogy the students soon picked up their lack of enthusiasm, and began to share the same resentment. At which point the teacher could assert that the method was not proving to be effective, and stop using it.

Many of the senior teachers (who had settled into a comfortable teaching routine) gave rationalizations for why the pedagogy wouldn't work in their class. Some blamed the students. Moorthy said that the students in his particular class had such low proficiency that they would not be able to follow the instructions for the task. He therefore wanted to stick to the 'basics'—i.e. the mastery of grammar. He shifted the responsibility for trying out the new method to the teachers with more proficient students. A few others said that their students were confused or put off by the non-linguistic material (diagrams, graphs, and charts) in typical task-based material. Ratnam asserted more than once that 'My students want only grammar. They find the tasks a waste of time.' This he felt excused him from trying out the new method. Such coping strategies also served to project teachers' own prejudices onto students: since teachers *thought* that students *thought* that grammar was important, that is what they gave them. All of which meant that there were few opportunities for the new pedagogy to be tried out fairly in the classroom.

The more interesting group was made up by theoretically-sophisticated veteran teachers, who would employ sociological and anthropological arguments (the alien values of the center pedagogical tradition, the hegemonic influence of center ELT constructs, etc.) to reject the new method. Raj said that 'These new methods are constructed with Western students in mind. Because our culture is different, they are irrelevant to our concerns.' Some teachers seemed to have a stock reaction against anything that was claimed to be new. Ganesh, for example, said, 'The approach we are presently using is a time-tested one that we have found through long experience to be just the type that is appropriate for our students—the alien methods are risky. They will unnecessarily jeopardize the whole teaching program we have painstakingly developed.' Even though most of these views were relevant, they were adopted stereotypically. Many of the teachers didn't appear to be interested in actively negotiating with the new pedagogies for their appropriate use in local classrooms, so their responses stopped short of constructive or sustained pedagogical resistance.

All this should not suggest that all the teachers took an oppositional stance. Some of them were sincerely excited by the pedagogy, and reported that it was working in their classes. Ranji claimed that her students were quite enthusiastic and involved, which I was able to confirm for myself when I visited the class. However, a number of other factors helped to account for this success. In particular, the excitement surrounding the new pedagogy tended to cause a short-term success sparked off by the teacher's unusual state of preparedness, the periodic observations carried out by supervisors, and the break from the tedium of the traditional approach, could all have had a salutary effect on the learners (a case of 'observer's paradox'). Hawkey and Nakornchai (1980) warn us to allow for short-term effectiveness due to reasons of novelty, which they find usually dies off some time into the course.

It is important to examine the range of coping strategies and oppositional behavior displayed by teachers.[8] While a critical attitude to fashionable new methods is to be welcomed, there are teachers who will always object to any form of change. Their opposition is largely passive and unconscious; their response is insufficiently reflective, conceptual, or analytical; their opposition is at time too stereotypical; they don't consciously work out pedagogical alternatives according to their own traditions or needs; there is little collective intellectual mobilization for suitable pedagogical alternatives. In cases where pedagogical appropriation does take place, it emerges as a default or unconscious option. The question we have to ask, therefore, is: How can pedagogies be appropriated with greater theoretical clarity, reflective practice, and critical agency?

Appropriating methods

I want to contrast Malathy's classroom (presented earlier) with Rani's, below, to exemplify more promising strategies of pedagogical appropriation. Rani was older and more experienced than Malathy, but she had fewer academic qualifications. She was less cynical towards the new task-based methodology than some other teachers, but was interested in applying it in a very flexible manner rather than adopting it in full. Her main focus had always been on her students, their needs, and typical learning strategies. She also had a clearer sense of the physical constraints of the local classroom. Compared to the other teachers above, Rani adopts a more creative process of pedagogical negotiation.

- *While we walked up to her class, which was made up of mostly low-proficiency students, Rani talked excitedly about the activity she brought with her. This was the daily schedule of two families—the Browns and the Blues—each consisting of three members. Students would be asked to study a chart depicting a day in the life of each member of the family, and then perform a series of activities involving comparison, contrast, inference, and calculating. The chart juxtaposes verb phrases with different times of the day to describe the different member' activities, e.g. 7.00 am: 'have shower'; 8.00 am: 'eat breakfast'; 8.30 am: 'walk to school', etc.*

  The class consisted of about 40 students in a half-constructed building that let in the pleasant breeze from the fields outside. A blackboard without a stand was leaning against the wall. After greeting the students, Rani introduced the task. Eliciting some comments from them on how their daily routine was organized, she gave a mini-lecture on the differences of family lifestyle in the East and West. Since most of the students were from rural backgrounds, she pointed out how much their relaxed and spontaneous daily life differed from the routinized, strictly planned, busy schedules of the Blues and Browns in the chart. Rani asked students to look for other cultural differences while she wrote the schedule on the board in preparation for the activity. (It appeared that she had shortened the schedule to just a few typical hours—morning, noon, night, etc.—so that the text would fit onto the broken board.) Rani began by telling the students that they didn't have to write anything down for the moment because she would be giving them grammar exercises and notes at the end of the activity. Her thoughtful announcement left the students keen to participate in the oral activity, while her pre-task activities got them interested in the cultural issues raised by the information on the board.

Referring to the chart, Rani asked students to say what differences in lifestyle they could see between people living in the East and the West. A few students challenged the teacher's interpretation of contrasting lifestyles, and pointed to features that appeared to be common to both categories (family togetherness, goal-oriented attitudes, etc.). This gave students opportunities to initiate exchanges and to question the teacher, rather than continuing with the usual IRF routine. There was also a brief discussion on the causes of the different lifestyles. Some students who were following a sociology course offered examples from their textbook on the difference between rural and urban cultures. Such discussions provided opportunities for developing a critical cultural awareness towards their own and the alien culture. The fact that Rani let students use any language they wanted (while she mainly spoke in English) enabled students to participate fully in the discussion. When it was becoming clear that the students were getting carried away with the pre-task activity of cultural analysis (the class becoming a bit disorganized, with loud small-group discussions in different parts of the room), the teacher announced the linguistic task she wanted them to perform.

Rani conducted the activity in two large groups, divided into males and females. Since the students were already seated separately (conforming to the gender-based segregation in local classrooms), they didn't have to move their chairs. A leader from each group would answer the teacher's questions after consulting with the group. The leader had to answer in English only, although the group could discuss in either language. Then Rani asked the questions: What is Mrs Blue doing now? What does Mr Blue do at 8.00 in the morning? What does Mrs Blue do after the music class? What activities do the Blues do together? How long is Mr Blue working today? (She limited her questions to the simple present and present progressive.) Since Rani was awarding points, the competition gathered momentum, with students keen to participate actively. There was discussion in smaller groups and a debate before the correct answer was passed on to the leaders. Although these sorts of discussion can be rather disorganized, this one was more structured because students had to provide the answer through the group leader.

At the end of the competition, Rani told the students that they had been mainly using sentences in the simple present and present progressive. She pointed to sentences they had produced to show the differences between both tenses. She also gave them a chart showing the subject–verb agreement rule, then gave them a cloze exercise to practice the use of tenses in context. Rani spent the last 15 minutes walking around the room, correcting the exercise individually.

Chatting with Rani at the end of the class, as I informally interviewed her, she expressed satisfaction with the class: 'Did you see how competitive they were? Nothing gets them as excited as group competition.' In her class record book, the entry for the day read: 'Another activity that worked well! Kumaran protests that I am partial towards the girls. He says that I give them easy questions so that they always win. I must see that there is no bias… Can provide more difficult tasks in order to maintain the spirit of competition and interest in the activities.' It appeared that Rani was focusing on the interest of the students and the collective rapport. These are the *interpersonal concerns* (defined by Pennington 1995 as the implementation of the method based on student involvement and empathy), as distinct from the *procedural concerns* of the lesson displayed in Malathy's approach. It was clear, however, that Rani was intuitively drawing on her long teaching experience, and her awareness of student culture and classroom conditions, to make appropriate procedural decisions.

Rani manages to negotiate the cultural differences between the old and new pedagogies quite effectively. Note that she is just as much in control of her class as her colleagues; at the same time, she manages to encourage individual student participation, and some group work. Although she has to work within the constraints of a large class with very limited facilities, she manages to use the space well to suit her purposes. By dividing the groups into males and females, she is also recognizing some of the local norms of interpersonal interaction, and thus succeeds in increasing participation and collaboration among students. By promising to deal with grammar at the end of the lesson, she wins their trust, and ensures involvement in the activity. They have an enjoyable time with the task, but she still provides them with grammar notes in order to satisfy the form-focused motivation of the university-level students. She is also able to encourage critical thinking by inspiring students to challenge easy cultural stereotypes during the pre-task discussion and negotiate classroom authority with the teacher. So in various ways she manages to reconcile the process/product dichotomy in her practice quite well.

Malathy and Rani are both appropriating the new method according to their local conditions, but there are some interesting differences. Rani's interest in interpersonal aspects—in contrast to Malathy's procedural concerns—contributes to a better integration of the pedagogical conflicts. Moreover, Rani's approach moves from the ground upwards, since she is more focused on the classroom situation than on the features and activities prescribed by the method. It might even be said that their approaches show different levels of appropriation. Rani attempts a more creative and formidable integration of the new method in the local context in a manner that satisfies acquisition goals, student expectations, and critical thinking, whereas Malathy is only being faithful to the procedures of the method. However, even Rani's appropriation reflects a less planned and conscious pedagogical practice, with limited ideological awareness of the choices involved. In both cases, the pedagogical negotiation could go one step nearer to what Pennington considers the higher level of *conceptual concerns* (i.e. a meta-cognitive awareness for integrating theory and practice, deriving from the teacher's more reflective, personalized, and critical adoption of the method). It is at this level that both can move to a more conscious and theorized strategy of integrating the competing pedagogies, with a clearer notion of the larger goals of teaching, taking into account the needs of student empowerment and social relevance.

Empowering periphery teachers

The three terms we have employed above to evaluate the modes of pedagogical negotiation displayed by the teachers (i.e. procedural, interpersonal, and conceptual concerns) are part of what Pennington (1995) offers as 'the teacher change cycle' in an ambitious attempt to develop empirically a model that explains how teachers orientate to new pedagogies. As we consider ways of empowering periphery teachers to move to more satisfactory forms of appropriating methods for instructional purposes, we must consider her correctives.

Pennington's model assumes a universal progression from more concrete and intuitive levels of competence to more abstract and reflective levels, where teachers mature into using the new method effectively. Pennington incorporates sufficient loops in her model to allow teachers to work through the resistances they face at each level, as they progress towards deeper awareness. If teachers get stuck at any of the 'immature' levels of procedural or interpersonal concerns, Pennington advises that with sufficient encouragement and feedback, they can be inspired to move towards an accommodation of the new method. She is prepared to admit that, as instructors go through the teaching process, the pedagogy itself will change slightly in accordance with the contextual constraints, and the cultural biases of the teachers.

However, the model fails to accommodate more disturbing outcomes.[9] There is no awareness that behind the facade of development, teachers could be nursing hidden levels of suspicion, opposition, and disinterest—as we find in the case of the UJ teachers reported above. The model also assumes that while the method may undergo changes, teachers will still work within the same pedagogical paradigm, tailoring it to suit their values by incorporating the necessary features from their context. There is no possibility of teachers getting stuck on one level, or adopting a totally different method due to oppositional perspectives. Furthermore, if an appropriate pedagogy is to be developed, the reasons for resistance need to be taken seriously—not overcome by simply providing more positive feedback. It is also important to consider those teachers who would give up this paradigm altogether to take on a totally new one. In her wish to see the process-oriented pedagogy universally implemented, Pennington does not consider such outcomes.

Finally, there are questions regarding the precise nature of pedagogical appropriation. Pennington implies that the negotiation stops when teachers reach a psychological comfort level: 'They achieve a higher level of expertise, psychological comfort, and understanding of the innovation, thereby personalizing it to bring it into their own practice' (1995: 705). But to make this assertion is to wholly psychologize the achievement of pedagogical appropriation. In this sense, her ideal is similar to Holliday's 'appropriate methodology'. While Holliday sometimes implies that the process of adaptation will go on endlessly, at other times he recommends whatever approach is comfortable for teachers and students. But these are inadequate reasons for concluding that the method is sufficiently culturally adapted to become an effective pedagogical tool. To take this line of argument to its *reductio ad absurdum*, a method that accomplishes no pedagogical goals whatsoever could still be judged as successful purely on the basis of being psychologically comfortable to teachers and students. What is lacking in the models of Pennington and Holliday, therefore, is a clear set of pedagogical principles to motivate and arbitrate this process of cultural adaptation. The balance reached has to fulfill certain important pedagogical functions while finding cultural and contextual relevance. Pedagogical appropriation has to be achieved in terms of ideological and material empowerment, in addition to the goals of critical language development. Such features have to inform the 'higher' stage of conceptual concerns.

Conclusion

What we find exemplified through the experience of the teachers described here is that pedagogies are not received in their own terms, but *appropriated* to different degrees in terms of the needs and values of the local communities. Multifarious contextual factors—institutional, material, cultural—play a part in shaping the realization of the imported methods. The 'indigenous' pedagogies are themselves so heterogenous—straddling the process/product dichotomy—that local teachers have to negotiate the influences they would permit into their classrooms in a highly reflective and informed manner. As we unravel the many different attitudes and responses periphery teachers display towards center pedagogies, to appreciate the oppositional insights they embody, we must also acknowledge that they do not always display a principled sense of pedagogical appropriation or ideologically-informed sense of agency. In the midst of the conflicting influences from the center and the periphery, local teachers have to adopt creative and critical instructional practices in order to develop pedagogies suitable for their communities.

Notes

1 Myron Tuman (1988) describes how the change towards process-oriented approaches of writing in the American academy is automatically treated as a more progressive pedagogical development. Schenke and Pennycook (1995) also point out how student-centered approaches are considered sufficient to make a pedagogy progressive for many critical pedagogues whose instructional material they analyze.

2 Giroux (1983) shows how variants of the process methods which are focused on the development of self-discovery and self-esteem including the cultivation of spontaneity, sincerity, and originality of expression (which Faigley (1986) labels 'expressive process') simply provide a way for the students to feel good about themselves. This notion of psychological or personal empowerment does little to engage with the structures of inequality. Similarly, he critiques methods which encourage a rational engagement with language and texts (which Faigley calls 'cognitive process') which simply encourage a mentalistic approach to problems.

3 The oppositional potential of product-oriented learning strategies is supported by scholarship from a wide variety of settings—Resnick (1993) for Puerto Rico, Canagarajah (1993a) in relation to Sri Lanka, Muchiri *et al.* (1995) for Africa, and Pennycook (1996) for China.

4 The study involved a year of observation of first-year English for General Purposes (EGP) classes, in the academic year September 1991 to July 1992. Observations were complemented by formal and informal interviews with the teachers. The invitation to observe emerged from the teachers' discussion forum. It was decided that a member should visit each of the 13 classes being conducted to observe the classroom dynamics in order to generate issues for reflection and evaluation. As the co-ordinator of the ESL program, I served as the observer.

5 Note that I have provided a different explanation for these problems in the previous chapter—pointing to the attitudinal tensions for students between the promises of socio-economic mobility, and the threats of cultural reproduction.

6 Note claims such as the following by Long and Crookes (1992: 45–6) in the *TESOL Quarterly*: 'TBLT [task-based language teaching] is distinguished by its compatibility with research findings on language learning, a principled approach to content selection, and an attempt to incorporate findings from classroom-centered research when making decisions concerning the design of materials and methodology.'

7 This description of classroom life, and another that follows later in the chapter, are reconstructions from observation, notes, and interviews. They adopt the features of 'educational criticism' promoted by Flinders and Eisner (1994) as a form of research that can provide richly-textured perspectives on pedagogical issues.

8 There was an interesting demographic pattern behind the coping strategies of teachers. In general, female teachers were more receptive to new methods, while the men were more typically conservative in their pedagogical preferences. Younger teachers proved to be better acquainted with emerging pedagogical developments, and readier to experiment with new approaches. Teaching experience was mediated by the other social parameters. In the case of female teachers with longer service, their experience had a salutary effect. Their keenness for novelty was tempered by the ability their experience gave them to work out creative alternatives. Men with longer teaching experience tended to be more settled in their teaching practice, although in terms of education the few teachers with a postgraduate degree were favorable to experimenting with new methods; however, this mostly turned out to be a defensive strategy to validate their qualification. Naturally, such conflicting preferences often gave way to group rivalries between the young and the old, the scholars and the practitioners, the men and the women.

9 Some of the peculiarities in Pennington's research methodology weaken her model. The teachers in her study are implementing this pedagogy as a requirement for their Masters degree in a Hong Kong university. Their diaries are a primary source of data. The marginalized subject position of the teachers-as-students compromises their ability to articulate oppositional perspectives. They appear to be excessively enthusiastic about the new methods. We do not see the complex range of teacher responses discernible in the UJ example. Also, the researcher fails to use culture-sensitive ethnographic methods for classroom observation. She overlooks the cultural manifestations of ideology and power. Pennington's failure to adopt an insider perspective with sufficient sensitivity to issues of cultural politics limits her contribution.

6 Clashing codes: negotiating classroom interaction

Why not let me speak in
Any language I like? The language I speak
Becomes mine, its distortions, its queerness
All mine, mine alone. It is half English, half
Indian, funny perhaps, but it is honest,
It is human as I am human, don't
You see? It voices my joys, my longings, my
Hopes, and it is useful to me as cawing
Is to crows or roaring is to lions ...

Kamala Das, *An Introduction*

- *Ways of dealing with students' use of L1 in the class seem to be as varied as the teacher and his or her teaching philosophy and personality. My philosophy has been that, for students to learn [to] think in English, they should speak only English—in class, that is. However, I never could bring myself to fine them. Instead, I've used a plastic hammer (the kind you buy in toy shops) which makes a noise when you hammer it—to lightly 'hit' students who lapse into speaking L1. None of my students seem to have been particularly offended by this 'punishment ...'*

- *A friend of mine—Susan—told me about something she used to do. Students (young ones) would be issued with an egg cup and a set number of Smarties (M&Ms) to put on their desk. Every time they used L1 an M&M was taken away from the pot on the front of their desk. Susan said this worked.*[1]

These are two of the many messages in an electronic discussion forum where center-based teachers shared their experiences of dealing with the use of first language (L1) by students in their classes. These messages provide insights into popular pedagogical practices pertaining to the place of L1 in ELT. However well-intentioned and genial the tone of these comments, they shouldn't blind us to the damaging and oppressive effects of these practices. Indeed, as his protestations reveal, the first commentator is aware of the linguistic implications of his pedagogy. Although students might not take his 'punishment' too seriously at first, it could mean that they associate English with indelible feelings of exclusion and penalization. After all, in contemporary societies, being deprived of sweets for using L1 could be seen as reflecting the denial of material and symbolic rewards for not knowing English. Such practices recall the behavior of those terrifying expatriate teachers in colonial schools who also imposed heavy punishments on students who 'lapsed' into L1.

It is claimed that an impressive tradition of empirical research confirms the assumption that English should be the sole medium for instruction for non-native students, and that use of their first languages should be eschewed at all costs. The belief that use of the learner's native language interferes with the learning of English, and hampers the process of second language development, has now passed into the realms of pedagogical common sense and professional orthodoxy. Phillipson (1992) has called such notions and practices the *monolingual fallacy*. As in many of the other applied linguistic constructs discussed in the preceding chapters, this notion, too, is to a large extent motivated by economic and ideological interests.

Insistence on the classroom use of English (by which is usually meant the 'standard' dialects of center communities) strengthens the dominance of center professional circles of ELT, and ensures that classrooms all over the world will be predictable and uniform in their instructional practices. As a result, textbook publishers in the center can conveniently produce books for periphery classrooms, confident in the assumption that English will be the principal medium of instruction. It would obviously be uneconomical to employ speakers of a wide range of other languages to construct ELT textbooks that adopted the different vernaculars. The monolingual fallacy ensures that speakers of center-based Englishes can market themselves as teachers in periphery communities without having acquired any proficiency in the local languages. The monolingual fallacy is thus complemented by another fallacy that is dominant in ELT circles—the *native speaker fallacy* (Phillipson 1992), according to which native speakers of English are automatically the best teachers of the language. By implication, it follows that periphery teachers are second-best, if not expendable for teaching English. As a result, even periphery educational institutions still stubbornly insist that the English instructors must be 'native speakers', thus perpetuating the fallacy that the best way to ensure that only English is spoken in the classroom is to employ teachers who are monolingual in that language.

Apart from boosting the professional hegemony of center-based ELT institutions, the monolingual fallacy has other ideological implications at a geopolitical level. By strengthening the dominance of the 'standard' dialects of English, putting in question the validity of newer periphery English dialects, and keeping English 'pure' from contact with the vernaculars, this fallacy helps English to impose itself over other languages. By increasing the possibility that second language learners will develop competence in English while neglecting their vernaculars, such a pedagogy may also serve to reproduce center-based institutions, discourses, and ideologies in periphery communities. We have to situate this classroom practice of monolingualism in the feverish moves to impose English-only in the center communities, including the reduction of state funding for bilingual educational programs.[2] This means that we have to see the English-only pedagogies in terms of larger ideological and social consequences. Auerbach perceives this practice as 'serv[ing] to reinforce inequities in the broader social order' (1993: 9). Skutnabb-Kangas terms this imposition of English in the classroom as a form of 'linguistic genocide', leading to the suppression of other languages and communities (1994: 626). Such interests should be kept in mind as we examine the dominant constructs of *second language acquisition* (SLA) and seek meaningful alternatives for periphery communities.

Contesting SLA theory

Divergent streams of SLA research have colluded to endorse the English-only policy for second language classrooms. For example, the *contrastive linguistics* hypothesis that dominated language teaching during the 1970s considered that L1 interfered with the acquisition of L2. In the heyday of structuralist linguistics and behaviorist psychology, when it was assumed that second language acquisition was a matter of habit formation through repeated practice and exposure to relevant stimuli, old language habits were considered to mediate the formation of new ones. When divergent languages were involved, therefore, it was feared that the previously internalized grammar would hinder the acquisition of the new system. Understandably, from this point of view, large doses of 'good English' were considered necessary to stamp out errors, and produce native fluency.

Chomsky's transformational generative paradigm opened up the possibility that language learning might be a more creative cognitive enterprise, in which the learner makes dynamic and independent generalizations about the new language, though not necessarily by moving in a linear fashion from L1 to L2. In other ways, however, Chomskyan linguistics denigrated the influence of L1 in SLA. By upholding native-speaker competence as the norm for linguistic communication, it failed to consider the ways in which the learner's first language can contribute to the uniqueness of his or her second language, or co-exist with the L2. Considering native competence as the target to be achieved is meaningless, since the needs and contexts of L2 speakers differ in many ways from center-based speakers. These learners represent periphery speech communities with their own communicative conventions, norms, dialects, and language attitudes. The mentalism of Chomskyan linguistics thus ignores far-reaching social and cultural constraints on the learning and use of L2. Sridhar is correct to point out that 'the Chomskyan notion, because it idealizes away variation, performance, and especially bilingualism, is even less suitable to SLA than it is to linguistics' (1994: 801).

Selinker's (1972) interlanguage model holds considerable influence among ELT experts and teachers as an integrated model of SLA theory. Selinker assumes that what second language learners display through their errors is a series of approximative systems (or interlanguages) which evolve to resemble the system used by the 'native speaker'. This theory provides remarkable agency and autonomy to the learner in the acquisition process. However, since native-speaker competence is held to be the norm for judging the achievement of acquisition, the bilingual competence which includes other languages and dialects is considered to be an imperfect system. This bias is revealed, for example, by the notion of *fossilized* items in the interlanguage, which hinders progression towards native norms. Often the speaker's L1 is considered to be the culprit in creating fossilized items. Furthermore, code-mixed versions of bilingual communication can be stigmatized as fossilized forms that prevent progression towards native-speaker competence. This means that the unilateral movement towards native norms, and the uniform criteria adopted to judge the success of acquisition, ignore the positive contributions of L1 in the construction of unique communicative modes and English grammars for periphery speakers. Yamuna Kachru (1994) is correct to argue therefore that there is a 'monolingual bias' in the dominant models of SLA.

Alternative perspectives and research on the role of L1 are now emerging. From being considered an obstacle to mastering a second language, it is now argued that L1 can actively promote the more effective acquisition of L2. Ways are being explored in which L1 can enrich and complement the processing of another language. The acceptance and valuing of students' native language increases their openness to learning English by reducing the degree of language stress and culture shock (Auerbach 1993). At a time when periphery communities still associate English with colonialism and oppression, it is important to show local students that their vernacular is valued by actively using it in the ESL classroom. In addition to these social considerations, there are cognitive justifications for the accommodation of L1 in SLA. Cummins's (1991) *linguistic interdependence principle* explains that proficiency in L1 can enhance competence in L2 by activating a common underlying proficiency that enables cognitive/academic and literacy-related skills to transfer across languages. In fact, research findings suggest that 'one of the best predictors of second language proficiency is proficiency in the mother tongue' (Stanford Working Group 1993: 9). Not only do speakers become fully bi- or multilingual without suffering interference or confusion from other languages, they also develop complex meta-linguistic and meta-cognitive skills (Beardsmore 1993). Scholars in the field of bilingual education and literacy programs have also produced additional reasons to explain why L1 is imperative for the education of minority-language students. Since it is beneficial to the individual to be bilingual, since learners may be assisted in their learning of content if they make use of the native language as well as the L2, and since the schools can play a powerful role in revitalizing and retaining minority languages, it is being argued that L1 should be accommodated in the schooling of language-minority students (Faltis and Hudelson 1994). Insisting that the provision of the mother tongue in the educational process is a fundamental 'linguistic human right', Skutnabb-Kangas (1994) invokes UNESCO's call for all linguistic minorities to be guaranteed the right to the active use of L1 in early schooling in all classrooms.

The above considerations demand a fundamentally different model of second language acquisition. In order to conceive such a model, we need to understand that for many periphery communities English is one more code in a rich repertoire of multiple languages. Countless millions of people who live in a linguistically-rich environment acquire more than one language simultaneously from childhood. Furthermore, the codes are often mixed in usage—as in code-switching, code-mixing, style shifting, or borrowing. In such a community, SLA (and usage) necessarily involves the active, integrated role of the local languages. We must also remember that for many speakers in the periphery, English is 'native', since as we saw in Chapter 3, some of its dialects are acquired from childhood and actively used for intra-community functions, according to the local norms and conventions. Such learners are not trying to be English monolinguals, but good polylinguals. They are not attempting to mimic center-based English speakers, but to be functional in the communicative norms and purposes of their own communities.

A model that takes account of such processes cannot be a substitutionary model (that assumes L2 taking over the place of L1) or a parallelistic model (that considers L2 to be a second separate code). It will be an additive or integrationist model that considers English as embedded in the rich repertoire of codes of the periphery speaker. The new model of SLA would be one that is more polyvalent in accommodating different systems of English. Y. Kachru (1994) and Sridhar (1994) are correct to argue that there is very little research on the process of everyday language acquisition in periphery communities to take into account their integrated processes of language use. Much of the existing research is based on socially-isolated immigrants and minorities in center communities whom Sridhar (1994: 801) appropriately calls 'transplanted learners', extricated from their typical speech communities in the periphery. The research is usually conducted in clinical settings, influenced by psycholinguistic orientations and structuralist–linguistic analytical traditions. The development of alternative models of SLA calls for an awareness of language socialization through everyday communication in periphery classrooms and communities. I turn now to such a research undertaking.

Juggling with languages in the classroom

In an effort to rectify the imbalances in SLA theory as it is currently conceived, I wish to consider in this chapter how English co-exists with the vernacular in ESL classrooms in periphery communities. We have considered in the last two chapters how students use the vernacular as a pedagogical resource for negotiating their textbooks and materials. Here we will orientate more directly to the use of L1 in teacher–student interaction. By analyzing how English and the vernacular are negotiated in secondary-school ESL classrooms, I wish to first bring out the complex functions such code-switching performs for classroom management and knowledge transmission. In addition to explicating the pedagogical functions of code-switching, I consider this classroom discourse as serving to socialize students into particular communicative practices, cultural values, and social relations for life outside the school. The use of L1 in the ESL classroom can be shown to play positive functions not only at the micro-linguistic level of acquiring grammatical competence in English, but also at the sociolinguistic level of developing bilingual communicative practices (i.e. negotiating values, roles, and attitudes through code choice). Similarly, while my primary mode of analysis is micro-social (i.e. the sequential analysis of talk in interpersonal relations), I also wish to demonstrate how classroom talk legitimizes or contests larger power relations in society.

Before considering the classroom interactions below, we must note that the teachers of most of these classes believe in 'English-only' as the desired norm for their classes.[3] They assert that their professional training and common sense predispose them to favor English as the sole medium of instruction. Those who eventually concede that Tamil *is* being used in their classrooms are usually apologetic, putting the blame on the low proficiency of their students, or the linguistic demands of a particular lesson. It is interesting to note that many of them only acknowledge the use of L1 when they are pointed to such instances from recorded data. We must realize, therefore, that in considering L1 to be detrimental to the process of acquiring English, local teachers have fallen under the influence of center pedagogical thinking. This is not surprising. As I have demonstrated in the last chapter, since teachers are influenced both by local communicative norms and the orthodoxies of the center ELT establishment, we must expect to find tensions in their policy and practice.

The instances reported below show that even when teachers do not actively encourage the use of L1, the vernaculars find a place in second language learning in quite spontaneous and unconscious ways.[4] As I will argue later, this is simply a measure of the 'naturalness' of the ways L1 is integrated in the use of L2 in such communities. As I described in Chapter 3, even when they wish to keep out English, the participants in linguistic interactions cannot do so. The ways in which classroom discourse is influenced by community linguistic norms again remind us that we cannot isolate the classroom from the society in which it is situated.

Classroom management

We will begin sampling some of the ways in which L1 helps manage the instructional process. It has been observed even in first language instruction that teachers develop a *modality splitting* to more efficiently manage the classroom (Merritt *et al.* 1992). Modality splitting is the reservation of specific codes or channels of communication for distinct functions. The students gradually become sensitive to this splitting and thereafter read the appropriate cues of the teacher to orientate their classroom behavior. For example, some teachers reserve the verbal mode for instruction and the non-verbal mode (gestures, silence, physical movements) for evaluation. So a teacher can walk round the classroom correcting students' written work individually, while simultaneously lecturing to the whole class. Code-switching can function analogously. While English is reserved for a specific set of functions (i.e. lecturing), the vernacular can be reserved for alternate functions (i.e. affective expressions and asides). Thus different pedagogical functions, genres of talk, and classroom activities can be distinguished by code-switching. When students become familiar with the linguistic cues, the different functions can be performed efficiently. Following are examples of such modality splitting to help classroom management.

In most classes, Tamil was used to prepare the students for the lesson (by giving them necessary directions regarding the arrangement of the chairs/room, for example) and English for instruction. Students learn to recognize that the opening remarks are not part of the lesson, and 'tune in' actively only when the language changes to English. For the teacher, the opening in Tamil helps to effect a smooth transition from the other classes in the school which are in Tamil medium. Furthermore, the utterance in Tamil functions to break the ice and establish rapport with the students for the instruction to follow. The following is an instance of this function:[5]

> 1 T: *piLLayaL, katirakaLai vaTTamaai pooTunkoo. cattam pooTaamal. ketiyaa pooTunkoo.//* Turn to page 40 for today's lesson. 'Children, arrange your chairs into a circle. Without making a noise. Do it quickly.'

Apart from indicating that the lesson has begun, the switch to English plays the function of attracting the students' attention.

A variation of the above function is for all task directions to be conveyed in Tamil, and for the activity proper to be conducted in English. In the following example, in order to set up a role-playing task the teacher has to get the class to assume that the student standing in front represents the person depicted in the card she is holding:

2 T: We will practice question forms next. (to S1) *niinkaL vaankoo.* 'You come.'
(S1 comes forward and T gives her a picture to hold.)
(to class) *cari, iva inta paTattu aaL enTu yosiyunkoo.* 'OK, imagine that she is the person depicted in the picture'.
(to S2) *ini niir ummuTaya keeLvikaLay vaasiyum.* 'Now you read your questions.'

S2: Who are you?
S1: I am a policeman.

Utilization of the distinct codes serves to separate the activity proper from the directions. The values associated with each language also serve to define the former as formal discourse and the latter as informal.

Similarly, any help students need is uttered in Tamil, while the tasks themselves are performed in English. In the following example, while two students role-play a dialog in front of the class, one student pauses to seek help from the teacher to pronounce a word:

3 S1: (reading) Who owns the red car?

S2: (reads) The red car belongs to// (to T) *itenna,* Miss, *eppiTi colluratu,* (spells) e-n-o-s-h-a? 'What is this, MISS, how do I say this?'

T: Enosha.

S2: (reads) The red car belongs to Enosha.

The switch to Tamil frames the utterance for help as being different from the utterances scripted in the role-play. So the class is able to keep track of the role-play, undisturbed by periodic appeals for teacher help. The coding of requests in the vernacular additionally has affective value—it conveys sincerity and an appeal for sympathy.

In situations where teachers needed to encourage hesitant, frightened, or nervous students for an answer, they switched to the less formal and more personal Tamil. This had the effect of putting students at ease, conveying teacher's empathy and, in general, creating a less threatening atmosphere.

4 T: What is the past tense form of 'swim'?// Come on.// *enna piLLayaL, itu teriyaataa? poona vakuppilai connaniinkaL.* 'What, children, you don't know this? You told me in the last class.'

S1: swimed=

S2: =swam

Although the words the teacher uses are not particularly endearing, it is the switch that performs much of the affective functions. Note also that the 'Come on' in English which precedes the switch is not as successful in eliciting a response as the encouragement coded in the vernacular. Teachers thus use either code to control or expand the access for student contributions in the classroom.

Whenever teachers found that the students were hesitant to follow their directives or commands, they repeated them in Tamil, with telling results. In the following example, many students don't obey the teacher's directive when she gives it in English; when she repeats it in the vernacular, they respond immediately:

5 T: Now close your books and listen to what I am going to read.//
Everybody must=
=*ellaarum puttakankaLai mooTa veeNum.* 'Everybody must close their books.'

The fact that the teacher begins to repeat the command in English but stops halfway to reformulate it in Tamil shows that she probably prefers Tamil as being more suitable for the purpose. While the command in English can be overlooked as being routine or formal, the one in Tamil (which nobody can pretend not to understand) conveys that the teacher 'means it'. The repetition in the vernacular also gains rhetorical force. The switch would indicate to students that the teacher is stepping out of the routine to make a special appeal. In fact, the switch in itself is dramatic enough (regardless of which codes are involved) to demand attention from inattentive students.

Back-channeling cues, particles, discourse markers, and tags were used in both codes quite fluidly. However, there was a subtle difference. Those in the vernacular had a warm, encouraging or mitigating effect. When teachers used Tamil, they were going out of their way to mitigate or modify their statements. It might be said that teachers were attempting to reduce the distance and power associated with their institutional role in order to establish rapport with the students. Code-switching can thus help teachers and students to change footing in their interactions:

6 T: What kind of letters do you write?//

There are different types of letters, no? What? Mention some types of letters.//

There are many kinds, *enna?* 'Isn't that so?'

appa, tell me a few? '*so*'

S1: letter of application?=

T: =*cari, veerai?* 'Right, what else?'

S2: letter to the [editor]?

T: [*oom*] 'OK.'

Note that the students do not respond to the teacher at first, and that her subsequent remarks in English do not help much. Her next statements are modified by the Tamil discourse markers for 'isn't that so' and 'so'. These convey a softer tone, and have the effect of reducing the students' inhibition. As the students begin responding, the teacher encourages them with more Tamil back-channeling cues.

The conduct of gossip between teachers and students in the classroom can provide a dramatic example of the linguistic process of symbolizing role relationships and genres of talk. Whenever teachers and students deviated from the lesson to discuss news about fighting in the region or any special happenings in the town, they always switched to Tamil. In doing this, both were stepping out of their institutional roles and assuming alternate roles as members of the local community. The switch also indicates the performance of a different genre of talk, namely gossip, as distinct from instructional discourse. When teachers wanted to refer to community happenings in brief 'asides' (of less extensive length than gossip) while teaching, they also switched to the vernacular.

At critical moments, such as when they had failed to carry out assignments or activities, the students were sometimes able to negotiate their roles and relationships with teachers in quite complex ways. Consider the following example:

7 T: What did I give for homework yesterday?

S1: Page forty.

T: OK, take them out, I want to correct your work first. (goes toward S2)

S2: *naan ceiya maRantuTTan*, Miss. 'I forgot to do it.'

Tamil is a more personal code, and signifies solidarity, so the student uses it when making excuses to the teacher, or asking for special favors. She is strategically switching to Tamil from the 'official' language of the context in order to request an altered relationship. Through this marked code, she is indicating to the teacher that she wants a different set of values to operate for the subsequent exchange, in contrast to the interaction defined as 'official' by the use of the English language. This signals that she wants the interaction to be considered as between two familiar members of the community, rather than between impersonal members of the institution who have an unequal power relationship. The dialog can therefore be construed as a request from the student for the teacher to temporarily lay aside her power and role in order to excuse her. The student taps the symbolic values behind the code to win the teacher's sympathy, and so avoid punishment.

Lesson content

We will consider next how the use of L1 is motivated by cognitive consider-ations to help in the transmission of the lesson's academic content. The conventional or established code for explicit instruction in the classroom was understood by teachers and students to be English, as I indicated above, but they frequently switched to Tamil—often unconsciously—with quite valuable pedagogical results. Many teachers resorted to L1 in order to explain points to students. Providing single-word definitions in the vernacular for concepts which would be difficult for learners to grasp in English is one of the universally performed functions in English classes (Merritt *et al.* 1992: 116). There were other, more elaborate, switches, as well. Code-switching provided many different strategies for explaining and/or reinforcing the matters taught: the strategies included repetition, reformulation, clarification (or qualification), and exemplification. Consider the following switch:

> 8 T: When you are forming yes or no questions, you start with the helping verb. *appa vinai collukku mun vaara vinayay munnukku koNTu pooviinkaL.* 'So you will take to the front (of the sentence) the helping verb that appears in front of the verb.'

The utterance in Tamil reformulates the previous statement in English. It provides additional information about where the helping verb usually appears in the sentence. However, the code switch assumes that the students have understood the previous statement in English, since it fails to specify crucial contextualizing details, such as the kind of constructions to which this rule applies. The teacher then assumes that the Tamil reformulation will build on the information already provided in English. Note that the discourse marker, *appa*, which means 'so' or 'therefore', also provides a different orientation to the same utterance. Students are given an opportunity to check their understanding of the English statement through the reformulation, and can thus confirm their comprehension.

The qualifications of certain information can have a similar effect:

> 9 T: You must shift to the front the helping verb which appears with the verb. *aanaal ellaa vinai coTkaLooTayum tuNai vinay varaatu.* 'But the helping verb does not occcur in all verb constructions.'

The teacher is probably switching to Tamil because he feels that this is a crucial piece of information that the students have to notice. The switch distinguishes the latter statement from the first (providing a neat contrast), and gives additional force to the statement in Tamil (which is the unconventional code for the ESL classroom). The teacher is thus able to highlight new information, as well as to convey the logical relationship between ideas. But, here again, the discourse marker *aanaal*, or 'but', indicates that he is banking on the students' understanding of the previous statement in English in order to communicate the new information. The code-switched Tamil utterance therefore 'piggy-backs' on the English statement, suggesting how both codes can complement each other (as in example 8 above). For this rhetorical strategy to work, therefore, the teacher has to assume that students have competence in both languages.

Teachers also code-switch when they want to provide examples, anecdotes, or illustrations in the class. Like their students, they also switch to Tamil when they want to delve into local knowledge in order to clarify the lesson content. Through this process, they relate the lesson to knowledge gained outside the classroom, and so bridge the gap between the school and home.

10 T: Today we are going to study about fruits. What fruits do you usually eat?//

inRaikku niinkaL viiTTilai enna paLankaL caappiTTa niinkaL? cila peer kaalamai caappaaTTikku paLankaL caappiTiravai ello? 'What fruits did you eat this morning at home? Don't some people eat fruits for breakfast?'

S1: *naan maampaLam caappiTTanaan*, Miss. 'I ate mangoes.'

T: Good, mangoes, eh? *Maampalam enRaal* mangoes. 'Maampalam means MANGOES.'

S2: *vaaLappaLam caappitta naan* Miss. 'I ate bananas.'

T: OK, bananas.

Note that while students do not respond to the general question posed in English, there is a torrent of response when the teacher reframes the question more specifically in Tamil, and relates it to their home background. The teacher proceeds thereafter to subtly introduce the English vocabulary items related to the lesson by translating the fruits mentioned by students in Tamil. The switch also serves rhetorical functions: it makes the illustration more personal, as distinct from the text-based information; it distinguishes abstract information (in English) from specific information (in the vernacular); it taps the everyday knowledge of the students encoded in the vernacular. Teachers would also switch to Tamil to initiate extended discourse, such as narratives, to exemplify lesson content.

On certain other occasions the items mentioned by students were so indigenous that the teacher could not translate them into English. In these occasions, Tamil is compulsory, and not motivated by rhetorical choice. On a lesson on the functions of trees, the teacher discusses their medicinal value:

11 T: Trees and vegetation are also used as medicine. Can you mention some trees which are used like that?// Quinine is produced from citronella. What else?

S1: *tulasi?*

T: Yes.

S2: *tuutuvalai?*

S3: *canTi.*

The items mentioned by students are mostly home-grown plants used in indigenous medicine. Students use the Tamil names for these. Merritt *et al.*

(1992) acknowledge the importance of this function in their research in Kenyan classrooms, and assert that it might be confusing and misleading to translate indigenous items into the closest English equivalent. By encouraging such answers in the vernacular the teacher is able to ensure that the lesson relates well to the cultural background of the students. Whereas the textbook limits itself to mentioning the abstract functions (furniture, food, transport, etc.) or mentioning stereotypical examples (e.g. quinine), by permitting the vernacular the teacher is able to proceed into greater detail and depth. The above examples are not suggesting laziness or incompetence on the part of teachers or students, since neither group is avoiding the challenge to grapple with the content in English. The last example actually shows a situation where they *cannot* discuss matters in English. Even in the other examples, the switch adds a qualitatively different dimension to the understanding (and experience) of the concepts, by tapping other forms of knowledge possessed by the students.[6]

Note that in the interactions cited above (examples 10 and 11) teachers use L2 for their turns of initiation and feedback, even though the students choose to respond in L1. In a sense, this is a strategy for having it both ways. While teachers permit the use of L1 by students, they enforce the use of English through their own turns, and thus re-establish the official code. Heller, in her research on French-language minority schools in Ontario, Canada, shows how the Initiation–Response–Feedback structure of teacher-centered classroom talk provides avenues for the legitimization of standard French as the official language of the classroom (Heller 1995; see also Arthur 1995). Micro-linguistic studies of this nature help us to understand how the structure of classroom discourse may serve to enforce official language policy, even though teachers and students collude in other ways to find interactional niches where they can use L1.

Underlife language

While the above uses of L1 were interactively achieved by the teachers and students, cases of 'unofficial' student collaboration unknown to the teacher were also evident. This is reminiscent of the student *underlife* we discovered in the classrooms in Chapter 4. These private exchanges, which were not initiated or recommended by the teacher, helped to explore the content in greater depth. Students prompted correct answers, translated sentences or phrases, repeated teacher's directives, and clarified the content amongst themselves in Tamil. Such acts had quite useful pedagogical consequences. Consider the following interaction:

12 T: (reads) . . . it is our duty to look after trees and replace them through reforestation. (To class) Reforestation means replanting trees and vegetation. (continues reading)

S1: (whispering) Reforestation *enRaal ennappaa*? 'What does REFORESTATION mean?'

S2: *umakku teriyaataa? kaaTaakkam.* Social science-*ilai paTiccam.* 'Don't you know? Reforestation. We studied about that in SOCIAL SCIENCE.'

S1: *enna? kaTukaLai aLikkiratoo?* 'What? Destroying forests?'

S2: *illai appaa. marankaLai tirumpa naTukiRatu.* 'No, man, replanting trees.'

The explanation of S2 serves to amplify the definition of the teacher by relating it to that knowledge students have gained from other subjects. Although S2 provides a one-word translation at first, she realizes that an expanded definition is required. This shows the occurrence of sensitive and intelligent peer help in the underlife of the classroom. Moreover, the students' discussion serves to reinforce not only the English lesson but also social science (much in the spirit of content-based ESP courses). In using the vernacular for peer interactions such as the above, the students define these informal learning situations as different from the official proceedings of the class.

Sometimes the students used Tamil as the medium for accomplishing the prescribed pedagogical activity. In one of the activities I observed, students had been divided into small groups and asked to arrange strips of utterances into a coherent dialog. The students conversed among themselves in Tamil as they correctly arranged the dialog and read it out in English to the teacher. Their conversation in Tamil included the following: translating the dialog strips into Tamil; judgments on the appropriateness of their attempted sequences; guesses at the probable purpose and direction of the dialog; and peer help on difficult words in the strips. Whenever such communicative activities or tasks were given, students used Tamil for interacting among themselves in order to produce the correct answer. Such collaborative interactions in the vernacular displayed more depth and involvement than the collaborative tasks teachers gave students to be conducted in English. The latter seemed to be performed perfunctorily as part of classroom routine.

When they conduct such interactions in the vernacular secretively (so that teachers who insist on English-only won't know) the students recognize that they are acting in what might be termed an anti-institutional way. They realize that if the vernacular is to be used freely, it has to be used in particular areas of the school. Despite their spontaneous use of L1 with teachers in the public forum of the classroom, students still have to find 'safe houses' to use their vernacular more consciously and uninhibitedly. Other researchers have found similar 'underlife' uses of L1. Pease-Alvarez and Winsler (1994) show how sites outside the classroom can house the insurgent discourses of the students. Locations such as the cafeteria and playgrounds are defined by students as safe houses where L1 can be used. Students (and sometimes teachers) identify sites and contexts which are removed from the official domains of the institution to use L1. Martin-Jones and Heller (1996) theorize that the existence of sites where students and teachers practice suppressed languages show how even totalitarian institutions may have gaps in their makeup. Such usage takes oppositional significance. These *interstices* of institutional power are exploited by the marginalized groups to resist and eventually transform oppressive policies.

Implications for language socialization

We have seen above how code-switching in the ESL classroom serves some positive functions in instructional processes. The code alternation helps teachers and students to manage their classroom interactions efficiently, and to negotiate the pedagogical content meaningfully. We must now consider how the use of L1 performs positive functions in the larger process of language acquisition and socialization.

Note that switching languages involves complex grammatical competence. To varying degrees, the students and teachers above employ competence in both codes in order to perform these switches. Since intra-sentential switches are categorized as more difficult (Poplack *et al.* 1987) compared to other types of switches, we will analyze them first for the grammatical competence they display:

— *inraikku naankaL* parts of the bicycle-*ai paappam*. 'Today, we will discuss PARTS OF THE BICYCLE.'

— Miss, *ivava paarunkoo, enrai* ballpoint pen-*ai eTukkiraa*. 'MISS, look at her, she is lifting my BALLPOINT PEN.'

In the examples above the students are integrating the English noun phrases into the typical SOV syntax of Tamil. In other words, the objects 'parts of the bicycle' and 'ballpoint pen' occur before the verb, unlike the typical position in English (indicated in the English gloss above). In addition, students are also adding an object marker—the Tamil morph (*ai*)—to the English items. Thus they are embedding the English borrowing into the Tamil syntax. In the example below, they are using the locative adverbial phrase sentence-initially, again adding a Tamil locative morph (-*ilai*) to the borrowing 'board':

— Miss, board-*ilai irukkiratayum eLutiRataa?* 'MISS, should we also write what's on the BOARD?'

In the following example, the students use the borrowing sentence-initially in a question where a question-forming *wh*-morpheme appears typically in English. In Tamil, the question-indicating morph (*enna*) in this type of sentence appears at the end of the sentence:

— Reforestation *enRaal ennappaa?* 'What does REFORESTATION mean?'

The morphemes and syntax show that Tamil is the base (or matrix) into which English is appropriated.

Even in the case of inter-sentential switches (where each code is used to form consecutive sentences) and extra-sentential switches (where the independent clause is in one language, while a tag or particle is in another) students require the ability to identify clause boundaries in both languages, for example:

> Inter-sentential switch: What fruits did you eat for breakfast? *kaalamai enna paLankaL caappiTTa niinkaL?* 'This morning, what fruits did you eat?'

> Extra-sentential switch: *appa*, we'll go to the next section. '"So", we'll go to the next section.'

Most of the examples above display the students' production skills, but it can be expected that they would be employing similar grammatical competence to decode their teachers' more complicated switches as well. Apart from developing students' competence in either language, these switches also display the development of meta-linguistic and meta-cognitive competence. Students need to know how to keep grammatically-distinct codes separate, but also how to bring them together in other places for rhetorical purposes. Juggling with two different grammatical systems is no mean cognitive feat. In addition to tapping the linguistic competence they already have, students are further developing their competence *and* performance in both codes through practice in the classroom. New syntactic constructions they confront will provide them with opportunities to make higher-order hypotheses about the languages, while also enabling creative experimentation with more complex switches.

There is the question of whether some of the above are 'incompetence switches' (i.e. motivated by lack of proficiency in English). But I want to argue that even if some switches are motivated by incompetence, they are loaded with social meaning and rhetorical implications. Note that to a large extent students can complete classroom routines solely in English if they want to. Teachers introduce certain stock expressions that can help the students participate. There is also the widespread use of 'broken English'—characterized by pidginized forms of simplified English—to participate in classroom interactions. So if students are opting to use Tamil in certain cases, giving up these other variants of English, this is motivated by rhetorical considerations. It is for this reason that I am also avoiding the traditional distinction between borrowing and mixing (which don't require much proficiency) and code-switching (which is considered to require a balanced bilingual proficiency). Sociolinguists now argue that even borrowings can have rhetorical significance in a context where speakers have the possibility of using synonymous words from different languages (Eastman 1992). They show that all kinds of code alternation can have social significance, and can be discussed under the umbrella term of code-switching. Finally, Merritt and her associates warn that 'mislabeling of content or conceptual problems as language competency problems' can lead to 'linguistic insecurity' for the teachers (Merritt *et al.* 1992: 103). *Unconventional* patterns of code usage, motivated by pressure from institutional policies, can also confuse the students. It is important therefore to realize that the inability to discuss the content of local cultural and geographical significance (as in examples 10 and 11 above) is not due to the subjects being incompetent in English.

Since we shall be considering communicative competence next, we must note that classroom code-switching enables students to be socialized into the value system associated with either code. A summary of the different functions performed by code-switching will enable us to categorize the competing values attached to the codes by teachers and students. While English is used for interactions strictly demanded by the textbook and lessons, for all other interactions Tamil is used; that is, Tamil is used for interactions that are considered personal or unofficial. The vernacular is also used to personalize or culturalize routine pedagogical transactions. This regularity confirms that English is the established or conventional code for the ESL classroom, while Tamil is the marked code. An indication of this is the fact that English was always written on the board, and never Tamil. Thus, English emerges as a code that symbolizes impersonality, formality, detachment, and alienation; Tamil emerges as personal, informal, spontaneous, involved, and homely.[7] Through classroom interactions students learn the values attached to the competing languages, and the ways to use the codes in recognition of the appropriate context, interlocutors, and topics. Therefore, in using Tamil to gossip about local news with fellow students between pedagogical activities, students show that the vernacular is appropriate for such communicative situations. On the other hand, students also learn how to manipulate these values for their purposes. So in example 7, the student who forgot to do the homework switches to Tamil (from the required code of English) to tap feelings of solidarity and to be excused by the teacher. Similarly, teachers use the vernacular in examples 1 and 6 to personalize routine interactions in order to establish rapport with students.

An additional feature is the implication of the codes for the identity and group membership of teachers and students. In the English class, teachers belong to a bilingual cosmopolitan discourse community, but they are also members of the Tamil vernacular community; in the same way, students are learners of English who want to become members of the cosmopolitan community as well as continuing to be members of the Tamil vernacular community. The code-switching indicates how they 'manage' both these identities. Whereas they can (and must) play the role of English teachers and English students in situations clearly framed as pedagogical, in other contexts they are ill at ease in these roles. In such contexts, they shift to Tamil to symbolize their vernacular (in-group) solidarity. Furthermore, through code-switching teachers and students manage the power difference in their institutional roles. Teachers reduce or heighten their power by moving in or out of Tamil. Similarly, students behave more or less like students (emphasizing through the latter their mutual Tamil community membership with teachers) by moving in or out of English. So when the student switches to Tamil in example 7 above, she is attempting to level-off the power of the teacher by offering to redefine the situation as one between in-group members. She is indirectly requesting the teacher to respond in the same way by using Tamil to express community solidarity. If the teacher responds in English, this will be interpreted by the student as a blunt message that he or she wants to maintain a detached role and authority (and possibly punish the student for failing to do the homework). These sorts of examples show that students not only learn to use the codes in contextually-appropriate ways, but also to linguistically modify the context to suit them. Students thus learn how to *redefine* roles and relationships in rhetorically-significant and socially-advantageous ways.

Through such examples we find that the ESL class becomes a site for the skillful negotiation of identities, roles, values, and group membership—which (as we saw in Chapter 3) is a complex discursive strategy used in everyday life by competent bilingual speakers. Thus the classroom prepares students for the patterns of bilingual communication practiced in multilingual periphery communities. Such practices include speech accommodation, code alternation, style shifting, and mixing, which function as discursive resources in everyday communication. The spontaneous practice students get in the classroom also helps them to build fluency and communicative competence in these everyday discursive strategies. Through such processes, the classroom prepares students for the specific types of communicative behavior they will encounter in the larger society and, thus, contributes to the continuance of multilingualism in the local speech community.

We need to adopt a more macro-social perspective in order to consider how such classroom language helps processes of language maintenance, language spread, and linguistic change. The use of L1 helps students to maintain positive attitudes towards their vernacular, and to develop competence in local languages and communicative practices even as they acquire English. Furthermore, while the use of English-only contradicts the well-substantiated development of periphery English varieties, the accommodation of the vernacular contributes to the development and legitimization of new Englishes. The negotiation of codes in periphery classrooms thus helps in the appropriation of alien languages by local communities. These are healthy developments that counteract the colonial and alien associations English holds in many periphery communities. Accommodation of L1 in acquiring English also helps in cognitive processes such as bridging the structural distance between disparate systems, reducing cognitive dissonance, and enriching the expressive and referential resources of the L2 in terms of local contextual conditions (Sridhar 1994: 802–3).

Since language participates in the reproduction of social and ideological values, we must finally consider the implications of such linguistic practices for political processes. The classroom interactions and discourse conventions are influenced by the communicative imperatives existing in periphery communities, contradicting the English-only policy imposed by the center-based ELT establishment. It is ironical, therefore, that the ground realities of multilingual periphery communities militate against the policies and scholarly constructs fashioned by the ELT establishment for teaching English globally. The fact that many of the rules and functions of bilingual communication between teachers and students are accomplished at a largely unconscious level is a testimony to the strength of the socio-cultural forces dominant in the community. This is further support to the argument that concerns of language acquisition, language teaching, and schooling should not be separated from the social context.

What we find in a growing body of research is that the vernacularization of ELT classrooms in periphery communities is a sociolinguistic reality. This is not a new phenomenon. We have simply started discovering what has always been true of language learning situations. Martin-Jones and Heller (1996), editing a set of papers for *Linguistics in Education*, gather studies from Botswana, Burundi, Hong Kong, Malta and Brazil (apart from classes of minority students in Canada, Britain, and Australia) to explore how such code negotiation may contest dominant social and educational policies on language. With muted irony, they point out that a key theme emerging from the studies is that students are taught which languages and discourses should be *hidden* from authorities! They say, 'The code-switching or code-choice practices of the classroom in the studies included here serve to send a strong message to students about what must be kept 'off-stage' and what can be publicly displayed' (1996: 10). More fascinatingly, even studies from center-based schools show ways in which the vernacular is actively employed in classes where the teachers from dominant communities are not proficient in it (Lucas and Katz 1994). Similar studies have been conducted by Pease-Alvarez and Winsler (1994), who are also troubled to find from a longitudinal perspective that students display more use of English and less of Spanish despite classroom code-switching. But their observation can also be interpreted to mean that the increased use of the vernacular in the classroom does not limit the acquisition and use of English. This strengthens the paradoxical thesis of this chapter: accommodation of L1 in English classrooms does not hamper the acquisition of L2, but enhances it.

Conclusion

The examples above suggest how teachers and students display agency in opposing the English-only policy of the ELT establishment. They creatively seek out opportunities for the use of L1, and practice code-switching. They work out coping strategies, such as the formation of safe houses, to practice their linguistic competence and ideologies under the very nose of the institution that attempts to suppress the vernacular. They maintain the illusion (through the ambivalence of code-switching) that they are adopting the English medium for classroom interactions, when they are in fact sneaking in the vernacular. These acts suggest their imaginative and resourceful oppositional strategies. In order to appreciate the significance of their critical stance, we need to understand that the teachers and students confront two forms of hegemony. While they face the Anglo-centric domination of the center through its monolingual fallacy, they also confront the vernacular-only policy of the local nationalist regime. Code-switching in the classroom helps students to subtly oppose both forms of domination. Teachers and students opt for a hybrid subjectivity and pluralistic ideology that resists both forms of monolingualist policies—i.e. from the periphery as well as the center. The limitation of these processes is that the modes of code-switching are still largely unreflective, unacknowledged, and surreptitious. We have also discussed above how the deep structure of classroom discourse still establishes the power of English (as in the ways the IRF structure sandwiches vernacular use). In Chapter 8 we will consider how L1 can be pedagogically sustained to enhance critical language awareness and cultural enrichment.

But the research significance of the above discussion is clear. This focus on classroom code-switching is a response to calls from periphery sociolinguists such as Sridhar (1994: 803) on 'the need to rebuild SLA theory from the ground up' towards 'a more functionally oriented and culturally authentic theory, one that is true to the ecology of multilingualism and views the multilingual's linguistic repertoire as a unified, complex, coherent, inter-connected, interdependent, organic ecosystem'. We certainly need more studies of everyday language acquisition in periphery settings to develop models of SLA that do justice to the complexities of English language acquisition in multilingual societies. Turning a blind eye to these linguistically hybrid interactions in order to be faithful to the English-only orthodoxies of the center will lead to grossly distorting SLA processes.

Notes

1 These comments appeared in the extended discussion entitled 'L1 in the classroom' in the TESL-L forum (*TESL-L Digest*. 1995a and 1995b).
2 After a brief period in the 1970s when bilingual education and vernacular literacy programs for immigrant and minority groups were encouraged,

North American and European states are currently reducing their financial and institutional support for these educational programs (Skutnabb-Kangas 1994). Schools are encouraged to 'mainstream' their students quickly into the English-only classes of students from dominant communities. The imposition of new funding categories, such as the Special Alternative Instructional Programs, allow districts to de-emphasize bilingual instruction in favor of instruction solely in English (Lucas and Katz 1994). Understand-ably, these policy changes are motivated by fears that the 'aliens' are taking over the center—imposing their languages, cultures, and values, while 'polluting' or delegitimizing those of the dominant communities. Groups such as 'U.S. English' are presently lobbying for a constitutional amendment that would establish English as the official language of the United States (Schmitt 1996). Opposition to accommodating L1 in ELT should be perceived in this context.

3 The data considered in this study derive from observation of classroom teaching by 24 teachers who represent a balanced selection of secondary schools in rural and urban areas in the Jaffna peninsula. The observation of each class was followed by extensive discussions with the teachers on their performance. I took extensive ethnographic notes on the context of each teaching situation and recorded the statements of teachers.

4 Employing a large sample of schools (i.e. nine exemplary K-12 programs for language-minority students nationwide in the United States) and broad range of languages, Lucas and Katz find that 'the use of native language appears so compelling that it emerges even when policies and assumptions mitigate against it' (Lucas and Katz, 1994: 537). In the majority of these classes, again, most teachers were monolingual in the dominant language and/or not fluent in one or more of the languages spoken by the students. This is confirmed by Pease-Alvarez and Winsler (1994) in their study of the classroom language of Spanish-speaking students.

5 The following conventions are used in the transcriptions:
   //   pause of 0.5 seconds or more
   =   latched utterances
   [ ] overlapping utterances
   ,   sustained intonation
   ?   rising intonation
   .   falling intonation
   italics for Tamil utterances
   '...' for translations of Tamil utterances in English
   SMALL CAPS borrowed lexical items

6 Antoinette Camilleri (1996) discusses a similar distinction between English-only teaching materials and oral interactions in the vernacular to negotiate the content in Malta. This is considered by local officials as a way of redressing the lack of teaching materials in Maltese.

7 Tamil should not be over-romanticized as a code of solidarity, empathy, etc. Although in a context where English is the official code of the classroom Tamil has such oppositional values, there are other contexts in which the use of Tamil establishes control, hierarchy, and power (see examples in Chapter 3 for such instances in the larger community).

7 Contrasting literacies: appropriating academic texts

So I am left to fend for myself
Walking in two different worlds
Trying my best to make sense
Of two opposing cultures
Which are unable to integrate
Lest they swallow one another whole

Ipellie, *Walking Both Sides of an Invisible Border*

To be academically literate in English, second language students have to acquire not only certain linguistic skills, but also the preferred values, discourse conventions, and knowledge content of the academy. To some extent, the academic discourses (especially of the 'Enlightenment' tradition) are historically associated with the values and interests of center-based English-speaking communities.[1] In writing in English to the academy, periphery scholars face the need to take on an identity and subjectivity constituted by these discourses. The conflict facing students from non-English backgrounds, then, is that they often face the pressure and/or temptation to give up their community-based indigenous discourses and adopt the academic discourses which enjoy power and prestige. This pressure is especially heightened when center-based teachers and scholars often expect a close conformity to the dominant textual conventions and consider any influences from the indigenous discourses of the students as an 'interference'. The psychological, social, and ideological costs of conforming one-sidedly to academic discourses in literate activity are all too evident to the students themselves. Periphery writers experience conflicts in having to indulge in a communicative activity from which they have to keep out their preferred values, identities, conventions, and knowledge content. The dire implications of such conflicts have not been explored adequately in ESL literacy research or scholarship, although they find powerful expression in the biographical and creative writing of veteran periphery writers in English.[2]

It is for the above reasons that we should stop conceiving second language literacy as an acquisition of decontextualized grammatical structures, rhetorical skills, thought patterns, or discourse conventions. We should develop a perspective that is grounded in the broadest possible social context. Our pedagogical approaches and rhetorical options should be sensitive to the ideological conflicts facing students. In order to venture into this challenging enterprise, I will first analyze the philosophical foundations of the existing pedagogical approaches. I will thereafter observe closely the writing strategies of three periphery students in order to understand the ways in which they cope with their discursive challenges. While reconceptualizing literacy instruction, this perspective will help identify ways of expanding academic rhetorical conventions in order to accommodate the multiple discourses of periphery students.

Revisiting ESL writing pedagogy

It is convenient to use for our purposes the classification of composition teaching offered by Raimes (1991) in her state-of-the-art paper on ESL writing. She divides the schools into four: those that focus on form, on the writer, on content, and on the reader. Although Raimes presents these approaches as constituting an ESL 'tradition', I will show how in fact they are borrowed from literacy instruction in English as a first language (hereafter FL) and that they are undergirded by philosophical movements of the center.

The form-focused approach (also known as product oriented) conceives of writing as the mastery of correct grammatical and rhetorical structures for text construction. Typically, sentence-combining exercises and imitation of model essays are prescribed in the classroom. This approach derives its roots from the 'current-traditional paradigm' (Hairston 1982) that was dominant in the mid-1960s in FL pedagogy and attended to the textual structures in the finished product of writing. The paradigm is so named because it is a revitalization of the classifications of rhetoric offered by classical Greco-Roman rhetoricians. It is undergirded by American linguistic structuralism and behaviorist psychology in its assumption that abstract textual structures can be drilled into students through controlled exercises in order to cultivate habitualized writing skills. The writer-focused approach attends to the mental skills that go into generating the finished text. Exercises for idea generation, organization, revision, and audience orientation are typical classroom practices to develop the required cognitive skills. This approach stems from cognitive process theory in FL which attended to the thought processes and cognitive strategies employed by writers, shifting attention from the written product. Perceiving composing as a dynamic cognitive activity that is recursive, generative, exploratory, and goal-oriented, the approach finds conducive soil in the Chomskyan revolution of transformational generative grammar and the related rise of humanistic psychology (Hairston 1982). Hence the trappings of scientism and empiricism that accompanied this paradigm, distinguishing it from the prescriptive tendencies and impressionistic scholarship of traditional rhetoric. The content-focused approach ties academic writing to the knowledge base which informs the texts of the respective disciplines.[3] Teaching is linked to the specific courses followed by the students, providing access to the related cognitive skills, linguistic structures, and information content characterizing each discipline. The reader-focused approach, according to Raimes, is a process of introducing students to the values, expectations, and conventions of the disciplinary communities addressed by the students, following pedagogical practices similar to the content-focused approach. McCrimmon's (1984) 'writing as a way of knowing' had already developed an emphasis on content within the FL process paradigm in the early 1970s. The reader-focused approach too had been anticipated by the Writing Across the Curriculum (WAC) school in FL context (Emig 1977, Fulwiler 1982, Beach and Bridwell 1984). However, not much purpose is served by considering the content-focused and reader-focused as separate approaches as Raimes does, since they have common influences from ESP, EAP, and WAC, and are usually treated as related movements (Shih 1986: 635–40, Spack 1988: 34–6). Both approaches are, furthermore, influenced by sociolinguistic and ethnography-oriented communicative approaches, and naturalistic or situational research methods. Hence the conception of writing as meaning-focused, communicative, and situated in the knowledge claims and discourse conventions of specific academic disciplines.

The moorings of ESL writing approaches in FL scholarship and Western intellectual traditions should be emphasized for many significant reasons. First, these approaches do not constitute the local knowledge (i.e. day-to-day classroom insights and first-hand observations) on writing of teachers and students in the ESL context. Hence these pedagogies do not grapple with the complexities of writing specifically for second language students, and cannot be expected to do so. Perhaps the underlying assumption here is that acquisition of second language writing follows the same processes involved in first language writing. This was in fact the dominant assumption (popularly known as the L1=L2 hypothesis) in language acquisition in the past. However, this has been challenged by the realization that there are many social, cultural, cognitive, and affective variables that mediate SLA (Y. Kachru 1994, Sridhar 1994). Nor are these writing approaches informed by the knowledge traditions of other minority communities from which periphery students come. They also fail to take into account the literacy conventions, hermeneutic models, and communicative modes traditionally practiced by periphery communities. All of which means that these pedagogies theorize challenges for periphery students from constructs developed in the center, especially in the FL context. It is therefore important, if we are to construct an effective pedagogy for such students, to focus on second language writing acquisition in its own right, and develop approaches unique or 'indigenous' to ESL.

With the above background in mind, we can now explore in some depth how these writing approaches orientate to issues of power and difference. To consider the form-focused school first, it is normative in considering a specific discourse and rhetorical structure as the correct form of academic writing. As such, it is quite prescriptive, so that teachers of this school look down on the rhetorical differences displayed by non-English students, sometimes considering that they indicate illogical, undisciplined, sloppy ways of thinking and communicating (as observed by Kaplan 1966). Teachers who begin by aiming to stamp out errors may actually stifle their students' different rhetorical traditions; they may also conceive of writing as being no more than the acquisition of form—a set of correct grammatical and rhetorical structures. Since these are defined in abstract terms, aspects such as content, discourse, and tone are considered to fall outside the province of writing pedagogy. Defining form as value-free (analogous to how grammatical items are treated in American structuralist linguistics), this school considers socio-cultural and political concerns as lying outside the domain of writing. Moreover, the acquisition of these structures is considered a matter of habit-oriented automatic skills. In line with behaviorist pedagogy, students are expected to master these textual structures through constant practice and imitation. However, by excluding 'thinking' from writing the school treats writers as lacking agency, subjectivity, or individuality. The students are prepared for formulaic writing, bordering on mechanical, thoughtless modes of text construction, similar to those demanded by bureaucratic institutions in a technological society. By refusing to problematize writing skills and textual structures, the approach not only ignores issues of inequality and cultural difference—by default, it makes normative the usual textual structures and rhetoric of the dominant social groups. This approach is therefore informed by what Giroux (1983: 205–31) calls *instrumental* ideology, and associates with the 'culture of positivism', technocratic social orientation, and behaviorist pedagogical practices.

Turning next to the writer-focused approach, its descriptive and empirical orientation provide it with much potential to understand the unique challenges confronting minority students in ESL writing. However, its over-riding mentalist tendency limits its inquiry, preventing it from addressing the socio-cultural, affective, and situational pressures that impinge on writing. This tendency has influenced proponents of this approach to insist that there is a set of universal cognitive strategies that generate effective writing; those who display such strategies are considered 'skilled' writers, and those who don't 'unskilled'. In considering the cognitive strategies as unmediated by situational and socio-cultural factors, this school ignores the type of differences that can characterize the production of texts. Furthermore, in considering those whose strategies are different as unskilled or 'ego-centric' (a term borrowed from Piagetian developmental psychology), this approach labels such students as infantile or cognitively deficient. Thus, cultural differences can be diagnosed as a type of deficiency.[4] The fact that this approach acknowledges the agency of the writer in producing the text is another corrective to the form-focused approach, which treats writers as passive. But in perceiving writing as simply an interaction between the mind and the text, or the mind and language, the approach reduces the complexity of the writer. Therefore, in some versions of this approach, 'writing with power' means negotiating the mind–text interaction and, in fact, ignoring the audience and the context (Elbow 1986). This school's perspective on power is further limited by its focus on the *how* at the cost of the *what* of writing. That is, mental strategies are considered in isolation from the rhetorical structures, discourse conventions, and knowledge content which characterize the product. Thus students are persuaded to accept the discourse conventions and rhetorical features of the dominant groups as the universal skilled means of communication. The writer-focused approach displays Giroux's *interaction* ideology, which conceives meaning as produced out of an interaction of the subject with the structures around him or her. Explaining rhetorical differences according to each individual's personality development and cognitive maturity, it simplifies (by personalizing) issues of inequality and difference in writing.

When considered together, it is clear that the reader-focused and the content-focused approaches avoid some of the limitations of the other approaches, and come close to addressing the unique cultural challenges facing second language writers. They avoid the prescriptivism and normative tendency of the form-focused approach, and acknowledge the different shapes texts take according to the diverse contexts and purposes of writing. They go beyond the finished product to consider the cognitive processes, knowledge content, and audience expectations that shape the text. So by contrast to the writer-focused approach, which reduces the writing process to individualistic and universal terms, these approaches accommodate greater pluralism. However, they stop short of addressing some of the more complicated ideological issues in writing. The notion of writing to different discourse communities means more than orientating the text to different audience expectations: it requires sharing the values, interests, and knowledge of the community more intimately. One must become an insider to the discourse community in order to write effectively to that circle. For this purpose, one must associate with the community extensively and intimately. A source of tension here is that the second language writer belongs to other discourse communities as well (i.e. to one's 'native' social group, as well as to other secondary groups of socialization) with different values and interests. Also, a disciplinary community might not accept each new entrant willingly, since it prefers to remain closed, and to preserve its vested interests. Communities have hierarchies, and relegate some members to the lower rungs so that a few can monopolize power. So there is conflict both within and between discourse communities (Harris 1989). The limitation of the content- and reader-focused approaches is that they impute egalitarian and democratic attitudes to discourse communities. Although they accept that the discourse conventions are different in different communities, they consider that they are all equally accessible to all writers, and hold equal value. Although they acknowledge difference, they do not relate it to power. As a result, they ignore the threat faced by minority students, in being dominated, alienated, or ostracized by the academic community. On the motive of inculcating communicative competence to talk to the chosen academic community, these approaches can indoctrinate second language students with the values behind these communities. They thus display an *assimilationist* ideology.

We can summarize the influences and assumptions of ESL writing approaches in the following manner:[5]

	Form-focused	Writer-focused	Content-/reader-focused
FL connection	current traditional paradigm	cognitive process theory	discourse analyses
pedagogical strategies	sentence combining, cloze writing, modeling	brainstorming, planning, revising	linked/sheltered teaching, rhetorical analysis
linguistic basis	structuralist	transformational generative	communicative competence
intellectual base	behaviorist, structuralist	rationalist	social cognitivist
	Skinnerian normative deductive	Cartesian empirical inductive	Vygotskyan relativistic situational/naturalistic
ideology	instrumental	interactional	assimilationist

Table 7.1: Approaches to ESL literacy

The purpose of this critique is not to reject the useful insights generated by these schools into the four obvious components of literate activity, but to situate form, content, reader, and writer more firmly in the social context. A suitable pedagogy must also go beyond certain stereotypical ways of perceiving the discursive challenges of periphery students into dichotomies such as L1 vs. L2, native discourse vs. Anglo-American discourse, vernacular community vs. academic community, or native culture vs. Western culture. As in SLA, the target of writing is conceived as pushing students from one end of the continuum to the other. We have to remember that the discourses of post-colonial subjects are multiple, hybrid, and overlapping. This means that second language students have to work with a range of competing discourses as they find ways of gaining voice and agency in academic literacy.

If we are to develop pedagogies that address their concerns, therefore, it is important to study the strategies second language writers employ to negotiate their ideological challenges. I wish to narrate the strategies displayed by three graduate students as they wrote a research report for a professional degree in ELT (M.A. in TESOL).[6] In the tradition of ethnographic-thick description, I fully ground the writing activity in the backgrounds and motivations of the students.

Contexts and texts in student writing

The three student-writers, who we will call Sri, Kumar, and Viji, are between 35 and 45 years of age, and each boasts of having considerable teaching experience. Sri held a B.Sc. in biological sciences, but after working initially as a science teacher turned to English language teaching in an urban secondary school. Like the other two students, he was from the urban, educated, professional, middle class. Like Kumar, too, he was from the Saivite persuasion, whereas Viji was a Christian. Sri was sufficiently hard working to do his reading and assignments consistently, but his attitude to the course was rather casual. His motivation seemed to be primarily utilitarian, to judge from the number of times he asked me if the course would improve his chances of professional security.

Kumar had majored in Geography when he took his Baccalaureate. Before becoming an English language teacher in a rural secondary school two years earlier, he had tried a variety of jobs, including accounting and clerical work. Thus, as for Sri, ELT had not been his first choice. But he displayed a philosophical and academic bent, and read more widely than the references I specified in my lectures on linguistics and sociolinguistics. He also intervened in lectures (much to the chagrin of the others in the class) to ask abstract questions on theoretical issues. He often visited me to debate issues ranging from religion and sociology to local politics. He was more ambitious than the others, and expressed an interest in using his postgraduate degree as a stepping-stone to join the university faculty.

Viji made no secret of her religious associations with a Pentecostal church, and often shared her faith with staff and students. She was also highly trained in professional and academic aspects of ELT, having read English language and literature for her B.A., and taught English in tertiary-level institutions throughout her career. So she was a seasoned professional who was also sensitive to the needs of her students. However, compared to the other two, she was socially and academically marginalized: as a Christian, from a traditionally Anglicized family, she fitted uneasily into the local political scene; as a female and a religious fundamentalist, she was also oddly placed within the academic culture. She was very much aware of these uncomfortable tensions, and confronted them directly. Having a tenured instructorship in the university, she was professionally secure, and so her motivation was not utilitarian. She wanted to take up the challenge of postgraduate research purely for reasons of personal achievement.

Many overlapping discursive fields could influence the communicative strategies and written products of these students. The range of discourses available, albeit in varying levels, in the local context are presented as polarities below. I will also demonstrate later how these dichotomized discourses are fused in different ways in the writing of the students.

Indigenous vs. Western forms of knowledge
The local epistemological constructs derive from a Saivite/Tamil world view, characterized by tradition-based, religiously-oriented, non-linear, intuitive, person-centered modes of thinking. By 'Western' discourses local subjects understand the conventions and values associated with a rationalistic, empirical, teleological, detached way of orientating to experience as it derives from a Judeo-Christian and Anglican cultural tradition.[7]

Oral vs. literate discourse conventions
The Tamil vernacular tradition is predominantly oral, even though it has a written tradition that dates back many centuries (Sivatamby 1979). The literate discourses that influence academic and center communities are relatively more impersonal, detached, decontextualized, abstract, rationalistic, teleological, restrained, and densely structured; oral discourses, by contrast, are personal, involved, contextualized, concrete, affective, circular, hyperbolic, and sparsely structured (Tannen 1982). It is often claimed that these differences influence the thought processes of the respective discourse communities.

Non-academic vs. academic discourses
A range of non-academic discourses influence the students. For Viji, it is charismatic Christianity. The reliance on divine revelation, the heightened emotionality and unhindered personal involvement with the supernatural are also present in Saivite bhakti traditions of worship (which Sri represents). The nationalistic tendency in local politics is another important non-academic discourse. It was originally borrowed from the Western Marxist tradition, which has a penchant for abstract, detached forms of approaching society and experience, in contrast to the indigenous oral experiential modes. These religious and political discourses, which call for absolute personal commitment, conflict in many ways with academic discourses, which value rationalism, balance, and objectivity.

The research process

An important concern of this narrative is to situate the writing process within the total context of knowledge construction. How do students' processes of research, reading, and information-gathering influence the written product? In choosing their subjects and beginning to study them systematically, the three scholars displayed different attitudes towards research. The different positions they adopted in relation to the discourses also suggest the strategies they used in order to convince the university of their academic credentials.

Kumar had high aspirations. He decided many months ahead that he would critique either Chomsky or Labov for his dissertation. He began by reading any book by Chomsky he could lay his hands on, and meeting me at least twice a week to discuss his new findings. He seemed to enjoy reading the books, despite the technical difficulties they presented. He was focusing on the Cartesian strain in Chomsky from a material point of view. When I advised him that such a debate had already been conducted, and that in order to make a sensible contribution he would have to cover a massive range of literature on this subject, he switched his interests to Labov. Kumar felt that his background in statistics could help him show the limitations in Labov's sampling methods and analytical approaches. Here he had difficulty relating the inquiry to the concerns of ELT. Clearly, Kumar was looking for a way of placing himself in a position of authority in the academic discourse by tapping his areas of specialized knowledge, when he was not sufficiently integrated into the disciplinary community of ELT to understand its separate scholarly developments.

In his enthusiasm to over-intellectualize his research, Kumar did not give sufficient attention to the need for focused and disciplined reading. The books he chose were not directly relevant to his research on pedagogical problems, and his material was not recent enough or specific enough for his project. These problems delayed his decision on the subject he was going to write about, thereby limiting the time available for the writing process. On the day the dissertation was due, Kumar surprised everybody with a thesis entitled 'Vicious Circle (in teaching and learning ESL)'. He described how the teaching of English in local secondary schools had become so overwhelmed by problems that it could no longer claim to develop communicative competence among students. His primary references on Chomsky and Labov failed to usefully inform the subject he had chosen.

Sri's approach was at the other extreme, in that he adopted a pragmatic, detached, workman-like approach to his research. He chose his subject by asking the faculty an eminently practical question: which language skill was under-researched in local schools? Their reply led him to focus on writing. Then, finding out the one significant reading that would orientate him to writing instruction, he armed himself with Raimes's (1991) state-of-the-art essay. He initially wanted to observe a representative number of schools in the region, but as the time for submitting his thesis drew near he chose a more convenient alternative strategy, which was to report the teaching conditions in his own school. His chosen topic was 'A study of teaching English writing as a second language skill in — College: A case study'. It was clear that the main source of authority he was drawing on for was first-hand knowledge, since nobody knew as much as he did about his teaching context. He constructed his argument around the words and behavior of his fellow teachers and school students. His pride in personal knowledge (rather than objective verifiability) as the proof of truth suggested influences from the vernacular intellectual tradition.

If Kumar's reading had been too broad and philosophical, Sri's was too narrow. Sri had not read a sufficiently diverse body of texts on composition scholarship, so he had to draw on pedagogical manuals for maxims on good writing, and rules of thumb on how to teach writing. He displayed similar limitations to Kumar, by adopting a linear process to research his subject (hoping to gather all the relevant data and information before starting to write), then failing to sustain his writing, and being obliged to write the final document without time for proper reflection, checking, and redrafting.

Viji wanted to choose a topic that was important to her, under the broad title 'English Language Teaching by Missionaries in Jaffna'. She wanted to show how effective and successful the pedagogy of the missionaries had been. The fact that she had studied in a missionary school herself gave her personal experience and other useful information to develop her thesis. Her choice of subject suggested a different motivation from Sri's expediency or Kumar's scholarly pretension.

Whereas Sri and Kumar undertook research primarily as an individualistic activity, Viji engaged her teachers and colleagues in dialog about her project. Her collaborative approach enabled her to become aware of the controversies inherent in her topic within the context of the local nationalistic fervor. This helped her to realize that she had to adopt a more sober and detached attitude towards the missionary experience. Her consultations also helped her to define her subject more narrowly. After it had been pointed out to her that there were missionaries of many nationalities in Jaffna— American, Belgian, British, Dutch, Italian, Portuguese—she decided to focus on the American missionary, who had an extensive history of work in Sri Lanka, which continues into the present. She further restricted her subject to the British colonial period, when the activities of the American mission were at a peak. Her final title was 'Approaches of the American Mission in Teaching the English Language during the British Period in Jaffna'. This carefully qualified title shows the distance she had traveled in detaching herself from her religious sympathies to adopt a disciplined attitude towards her subject.

Viji's delimitation of her subject early in the research process helped her to undertake the study in a constructive manner. She didn't widen her reading unnecessarily, or read without a research plan. Her focused approach to research influenced her to look for specific texts that answered the particular questions she had formulated. However, tracking down material relevant to her thesis involved some effort, since although the missionary teaching experience in Jaffna was much discussed, it had rarely been studied or documented. Viji was therefore forced to visit little-known libraries in churches, rural missionary schools, and the private collections of priests, to gather the handful of material that would go some way towards answering her questions. Although it was frustrating to find so few documents on the subject, this experience led her to read those she could gather more closely.

Unlike Sri and Kumar, who considered research to be a two-stage process of first gathering information and then writing it, Viji was forced to adopt a recursive process. As she began working on her introduction and initial chapters she realized that there were gaps in her data that she would have to fill in from additional sources. The new material she found forced her to revise her previous assumptions, and made her rewrite her drafts. Although this was a risky and strenuous process, it meant that her research was more cogently argued and insightful. The balance between personal interest, new information, and interpretative challenge in her research enabled her to produce a provocative thesis backed by original material.

The writing process

The scholars displayed different attitudes towards the writing process, suggesting that they were influenced by different traditions of text construction. Sri and Kumar adopted writing processes that differed from the literate academic conventions which value the detached, planned, elaborate, meticulous process of multiple drafting, revising, and editing. Both submitted what appeared to be their first and only draft as the dissertation. Having finally composed his thoughts, Kumar had delayed writing his thesis until some days before the deadline. The low priority he gave to drafting was clear from the many marks he made in ink and correction fluid while hurriedly editing the typescript. He said that some of his chapters had been typed out just as the words and ideas came to him, and boasted that 'I only needed a couple of hours to write the dissertation—once I got my ideas flowing. Can you believe that I did most of this work last night?' He was proud of what he considered to be the spontaneity and immediacy of his text.

Sri had begun the outline for his thesis well in advance. He wrote a draft script in pencil, then edited it for spelling, word choice, and syntactic fluency, before giving me the draft to skim through a couple of days before the deadline. The fact that he incorporated few of the changes suggested by his advisers made it clear that for Sri, as for Kumar, revision was of no consequence.[8] Sri's argument was that 'It is the ideas that are important. Aspects such as the expression, mechanics, or typographical errors shouldn't make a difference. If readers understand what we are saying, that should be the main thing.' These views, and certain assumptions he made regarding the writing process, were also shared by Kumar. They saw writing as a linear activity which begins with the organization of ideas and is followed sequentially by the composition of paragraphs and chapters; content was considered to be more important than form (which influenced the devaluing of problems in mechanics and presentation); to a large extent, writing was considered to be the solitary act of the composer; giving special attention to the text for its own sake was considered to be unnecessary.

Viji, by contrast, displayed rather more care in undertaking the composing process. Her first rough outline showed that she had given some thought to planning at both the global level (breaking down the subject; identifying relevant materials) and the local level (making tentative chapter divisions and sections). She also maintained well-organized notes on the reading she was doing. Not only did she write two drafts by pen before having the final draft typed, she also made it a point to have them read by her colleagues and supervisors. As well as going through the process of negotiating her ideas and revising her writing, she also solicited the help of a colleague in the editing process. Her acknowledgments reveal her attitude to composing: 'I am grateful to Dr — for his encouragement and *criticism*. I thank Mr — who untiringly went through the writing with a pair of eyes that hardly misses any *mistakes*' (emphasis mine). The result was that her writing process displayed more planning, collaboration, and care for textuality than the work presented by Sri and Kumar. As she continued to narrow down her subject, reinterpret her limited primary sources, and reorganize the content of the chapters, her writing process became quite recursive and generative. This may have resulted in part from the fact that Viji belonged to the Anglo-Christian literate community—which is not to say that she failed to accommodate the oral tradition's predilection for personal involvement. When, during the final revision, she was advised to mention the criticisms nationalist educators had made on the role of missionary education, she refused. She considered that to have written something she did not believe in, simply because it was part of the convention, would have been an academic charade. Such resistance may also be influenced by her religious discourse, which demanded whole-hearted commitment to her beliefs. To this extent, it could be said that she had to wrestle with competing discursive traditions while she was composing her text.

Written product

In the light of the processes the scholars followed to read, research, and write, we will now consider how their texts differed in realization.

Sri's dissertation, one of the longest of the texts received, ran to 63 pages. Its structure was somewhat circular, and relaxed. The introductory chapter and the second chapter, 'Different approaches to teaching writing', contain a compendium of statements from composition textbooks on the nature of writing, the skills that contribute to good writing, and the processes involved in composing. Although the next chapter, 'Study Made in — College', is reserved for the analysis of data, it is in fact a narrative, recounting the writer's experiences in the school. The fourth and final chapter, 'Conclusions', is subdivided into suggestions and recommendations, and contains prescriptive statements on what constitutes good writing. These recommendations are culled from manuals, and do not seem to emerge from the writer's personal data or study. In short, after starting from the general statements on writing, and proceeding briefly to teaching of writing in classrooms, the text returns to generalizations on writing. The effect appears to be to dazzle the reader with the slow and repeated accumulation of details, sources, and facts.

Although Sri includes many citations, he makes little attempt to arbitrate between the different claims made by the different books, or to problematize any of the claims. He simply records the categories and constructs which could be usefully extricated from each book. Perhaps his deference to the authority of the texts is a reflection of his relative unfamiliarity with the ELT community, and with the disciplinary constructs required for a critical vantage-point on its scholarship. This may also be due to the influence of the indigenous intellectual culture, which gives such high status to texts that attempts to question, critique, or even take interpretive liberties are likely to be discouraged. The reader is expected to stay close to the original text, using convenient summative statements, quotations, and aphorisms of writers in order to capture the message of the book. [9]

Sri does not usually bother to acknowledge the publications from which he borrows his lists of rules on writing. The final chapter, for example, has 17 points on ways to improve capitalization and punctuation, seemingly from diverse sources. Although a bibliography is provided at the end, the texts here are not related to the discussion, nor are they documented in the body of the dissertation. Sri maintained that all his ideas were generated through interaction with other people's texts, and that there would be no point in attributing some references and not the others. He claimed that it was knowledge as a collective body of ideas that mattered, rather than the individual acknowledgment of the producers of knowledge (i.e. the authors). We must remember that in the oral tradition of many periphery communities, knowledge only matters to the extent that it contributes to the community's stock of information. The literate academic community of the center, by contrast, is more likely to interpret the free borrowing of other people's words by periphery students as plagiarism.[10]

Sri's work does not present a sustained and coherent argument. The opening pages of the dissertation, for example, do not situate his research within the ongoing disciplinary conversation, nor does he make a claim for the polemical significance of his research. After making some personal assertions and describing classroom experiences, he cites the 'data' in the appendix. These consist of two questionnaires he distributed to students, and the transcript of an interview with a colleague on how she perceived the challenges encountered in teaching writing. However, the body of the dissertation fails to grapple with the data or relate them to his argument. In the third chapter, where he comes closest to discussing his data, he employs the personal voice to narrate how he and his colleagues teach in their school. Although this can be considered a form of classroom observation or ethnography, Sri makes little effort to objectify the experience. This is one of the few places where the writer speaks directly:

> Whenever I ask to write a composition on one of the given topics, only the very same students write, but even then, they too never speak or utter sentences in English. From my observations they feel shy, hesitation in pronouncing words in English. [They feel] others might laugh at me, etc. This creates problem in the language classrooms. Only some students volunteer to read a passage or answers written by them. There are some students who perform well, who have a good family background... Making meaning in the actual context is also a problem to many students. At least I could conclude, from the interviews, questionnaires, and observations most of the students (I am not ashamed to say even the teachers, including myself) need much attention not only in the field of writing English but also in the fields of listening, speaking and reading, in order to acquire or learn and master the language. (pp. 38–9)

There is a relaxed, conversational tone to the writing, with little effort made to document the observations or to authenticate their veracity. In keeping with the tone, Sri is also quite comfortable with using a version of English that, even in Sri Lankan terms, would be considered 'non-standard'. In the final sentence there is a surprising personal interjection, which reads like a reflexive comment on the researcher's own proficiency on the issues he is studying. The reference to other skills (i.e. listening, speaking, reading) in a research paper focused on writing also seems to be a deviation. But such is Sri's discursive preference that he feels comfortable about commenting on many things in his teaching experience as he goes along. The dissertation thus provides a 'thick description' that is valuable for the wealth of information contained. There is also a frankness of tone and personal involvement in the dissertation that is unusual in a genre well known for hedging devices and detachment.

Sri concludes by offering a series of prescriptive statements on how writing should be taught, in the form of a list of dos and don'ts for teachers:

> Some teachers translate the passages from English to Tamil, but translation does not teach writing, lectures do not teach writing. They display the teacher's opinion about writing. Therefore, writing and more writing, and then more writing, teaches writing; in other words practice, practice and still more practice. (p. 41)

The tone of high involvement and personal authority is striking here. The repeated words create a rhythm and emphasis that are unusual for this genre.

We must keep in mind that in the vernacular and oral discourse the authority of the scholar is often determined by the certainty and force with which claims are made. Despite the endearing effect of sincere communication, Sri's writing displays diverse discursive influences which reflect the local intellectual traditions, and are in tension within the text. In addition to particular oral and expressive communicative conventions, they include the use of extended narration and reflexive commentary, and the detached citation of copious references.

Kumar also submitted a lengthy dissertation, amounting to 63 pages. However, compared to Sri's narrative, Kumar's paper is very polemical. He makes a good justification in the opening chapter for the need for his research. He invokes the general feeling among educationists that ESL is a failure in the local schools, then offers to explore the reasons why students rarely develop communicative competence, even after several years of schooling. In order to develop his thesis he launches a sweeping attack on inept teachers, insensitive educational officials, the lack of facilities, and poor resources. The causes of the problem are identified in the second chapter and elaborated in the fourth chapter, whose title, 'Vicious Circle', is the motif Kumar employs to accuse the local ELT enterprise of being trapped in a paralytic vortex of inefficiency and failure. In this, at times, he appears to be pushing his thesis too far, and overstating his argument.

In the final chapter, 'The Failures of Improvements (Why and How)', Kumar fails to provide any solutions to the problems he raises, saying that this is the domain of language planners and policy-makers. Instead, he explains that the scope of his study is to empirically explore the problem, and not to guess solutions impressionistically. However, this detachment may also be explained as a stereotyping of the typical stance of academic objectivity. It is possible that he is 'hypercorrecting' the tendency in traditional and oral discourses to confirm received wisdom, and adopt a position of personal involvement in knowledge construction. Unlike Sri, therefore, Kumar is distancing himself from his writing.

Kumar displays the trappings of academic research throughout his dissertation. His methodology section in the third chapter is one of the most impressive among the dissertations received. He refers to undertaking interviews, questionnaire surveys, and classroom observation, in addition to library research, and justifies his research design as follows:

> [The] sizes of the samples may differ according to the nature of the studies but the size of the sample selected by me is sufficient in a study of quality related to the normal observed pattern widely seen in our society. In this case, the important consideration is the representative sample, which was carefully done within my reach (p. 25).

The statistical jargon serves to create a dispassionate prose and formal tone. It is clear that Kumar has mastered the relevant scholarly conventions in order to construct a formidable academic persona for himself. One might even form the impression that he is actually parodying academic discourse.

Kumar includes an impressive bibliography at the end. Compared to Sri, who manages to muster little theoretical literature, Kumar has cited scholarly texts on applied linguistics, sociolinguistics, and theoretical linguistics, and he claims that 'Many books were used in my readings, and the knowledge has been applied.' He goes on to say 'Some of the books are ...' followed by a list of only six books. Although the list does include *Communicating Naturally in a Second Language* by Rivers, *Linguistic Controversies* by Crystal, and *Language and Society* by Downes, the body of his dissertation fails to show how and where these texts have informed his writing. There is also a failure to engage closely with the content of these texts. Unlike Sri, who was far too dependent on the texts for his ideas, Kumar brought a critical mind to his reading that is only a shade too cavalier in making snap arguments against them. Although there is little doubt that Kumar has read these books, they seem to be included in the dissertation mainly in order to boost his authority. This stereotypical use of citations and references suggests what matters most to Kumar is the symbolic value of the academic conventions and codes. As an outsider to the academic community, now trying to enter it for professional advancement, he displayed a cynicism towards academe by considering that these trappings would enable him to become an insider. The parodying of academic style might, then, have oppositional implications.

What gives strength to this impression of parody is that, despite the statistical language in the methodology section, we see little specificity in the discussion of the data: '*All* the persons interviewed ... and the other persons [to] whom I have given the needed information were *all* very co-operative and pleased in this matter... They *all* agreed that the learning was essential for their children, but showed no urgent needs for the learning in the early years of the school' (p. 27; emphasis mine). This use of unqualified and hyperbolic language shows that the statistical precision promised is not fulfilled in the discussion of the data. In discussions such as the above (and in the extreme terms in which he builds his deterministic thesis) Kumar displays the vernacular forcefulness that comes from hyperbolic rhetoric. In Kumar's writing, therefore, as in Sri's text, we find unreconciled tensions: the abstract and technical discourse of the academic community jostles against a mixture of casual, and at times strident writing influenced by local and oral conventions.

Viji's is the briefest of the dissertations received, running to only 32 pages. The discussion is sustained and reader interest preserved by the controversial thesis she develops. In a social context where some 45 years of decolonization have led to the denigration of the missionary education, her intention is to give it more complexity. Thanks to her timely work in narrowing down the subject and undertaking the research in a disciplined manner, her writing is very focused. She adopts both a chronological and polemical progression.

After orientating readers to the colonial period, she introduces the main terms of the debate concerning the missionary educational enterprise in the introductory chapter. She also makes effective use of this chapter to create a niche for her work in the scholarly conversation: she cites a variety of local educationists, linguists, and social theorists of the post-colonial period who have criticized the missionary educational enterprise, to show why a re-examination is necessary to arrive at a more balanced assessment. She also argues that since the missionaries did not leave adequate records of their teaching mission (as they were preoccupied with evangelization), there is a need to reconstruct this dimension of their work. The political and academic significance of her thesis is made to stand out, since the text is situated in the relevant discursive contexts.

At the end of Chapter 1 Viji outlines the content of the following three chapters, displaying her conscious organization of the material.[11] She also provides reader-friendly signposts as she moves between the different sections of the work. In Chapter 2, 'A Brief History of the Foundations', she discusses the historical events that laid a foundation for the teaching of English in the local community. This provides the educational background for the times. In Chapter 3 she deals with the aims and objectives of the missionary teaching program, and in the next chapter deals directly with the pedagogy of English language teaching, analyzing the materials, testing, and teaching approaches employed. The final chapter, on the implications of what she has recorded, appraises the effectiveness of the missionary approach while spelling out the exemplary features of their pedagogy for present-day teachers. So there is a clear linear progression in the writing. The greater control she has over textualization, by comparison with the other writers, displays her meta-textual awareness, derived from her membership of the Anglo-Christian literate community.

Viji's references differ interestingly from those found in the other two theses. She does not include any theoretical or pedagogical publications, but lists local historical and educational writings—half of them articles or unpublished manuscripts—that discuss the colonial educational policies and practices. This means that all her citations are those that are directly used in her work. Since these texts are inadequate to answer all her questions, she has to read behind the lines in order to make valid inferences. Her writing shows that she is careful not to exaggerate in order to suit her perspectives, and that she is prepared to struggle with the texts to make reasonable interpretations. In addition, since there have been remarkable developments in language teaching in the post-colonial period, she has had to contextualize the policies of the missionaries in contemporary scholarship, and to interrogate their practices in the light of current knowledge. Although Viji does not cite pedagogical literature, it is clear that she is drawing from her insider status in the professional community, and employing this knowledge actively to interpret the teaching practices of missionary teachers. Moreover, the tension between her faith and profession, personal religious ideology, and nationalist political ideology, endow her with a critical interpretive bent. These remarkable exegetical skills may derive from her Christian discursive background of everyday biblical hermeneutics.

Although her writing here displays a qualified use of language, in some sections Viji also employs a more personal form of expression. She begins her thesis with the following acknowledgment: 'I thank my Lord and Master Jesus Christ for enabling me to complete this study with very limited sources at my disposal.' Although this language is permissible in this rather more personal section of the dissertation, it is eschewed in the body of the text, indicating a recognition of the appropriate genres of discourse to be employed in the different sections of the dissertation. She is able to find an acceptable way of expressing her religious identity in the pages of an academic work in the next page, which presents her Abstract, suggesting a scholarly tone and a more detached prose:

> This is an attempt at tracing the approaches of the American Mission in teaching the English Language during the British period in Jaffna. From most of the findings the course has been a successful one. In fact, it could be pointed out that at a certain period of time the cry for 'English and more English' came from the natives themselves ...

Here, the impersonal syntactic structures, the hedging devices, and the qualifications, all suggest a switch to more research-oriented discourse in the body of the dissertation. Viji is also able to detach herself sufficiently from her religious biases to acknowledge how education was sometimes used for the utilitarian reason of evangelization. This is a politically-astute concession, in recognition of the dominant nationalistic sentiments in the local community. Making concessions of this nature is a good rhetorical strategy in order to win audience acceptance for her thesis.[12] Viji's relative closeness to literate Anglicized discourse conventions helps her to be detached from her writing when she considers it appropriate.

The creative fusing of divergent discourses in textually-appropriate ways can also be seen in her use of citations:

> 'Ye shall be witnesses unto me unto the utmost part of the earth' (Holy Bible Acts 1:8)—the final command of the Master to the disciples of Jesus Christ has been fulfilled through the centuries ultimately paving the way for a band of missionaries from the American Board to reach the shores of Jaffna in 1813. Although the supreme goal of the missionaries was to evangelize, they found themselves being compelled 'to seek the aids of learning' (Plan: 1823) in order to prepare the ground for sowing the seed of the Gospel (p. 1).

It is interesting that the quotation from the Bible which was cited in her initial drafts as a proud announcement of the educational endeavors of the missionaries is cited here dispassionately to indicate the rationale for their educational activities. The citation that follows is from the proposal by a school board for starting one of the first missionary educational institutions. This bureaucratic text is at tension with the previous biblical quotation, suggesting the hybrid discourses embodied in the dissertation.

Although Viji's text displays some discursive tensions (like the other two dissertations), her conflicts are quite constructive as they show the writer attempting to reconcile the religious and academic discourses to develop her unique perspective. While taking the academic conventions seriously, the writer also finds space for her own desired discourses to emerge through the text. She wrestles with competing discourses and textualities to construct a hybrid or multivocal text that is still coherent. Thus she produces a text that not only contributes to new knowledge to the field, but is also rhetorically creative and original.

Strategies of negotiating discourses

Our task is to understand the strategies the three writers choose in order to negotiate the conflicting discursive influences, achieve coherence in their writing, and realize their desired mode of voice and subjectivity. Their motives for choosing quite distinct approaches are understandable. Their texts, although rhetorically different, may be considered effective by different communities (i.e. the vernacular or the academic, for example) in the light of their own communicative traditions. However, the perspective adopted here is to evaluate the effectiveness of these texts as dissertations addressed to the academic community, and as a consequence my narration above is considerably shaped by this rhetorical context and purpose.

Viji's dissertation earned her an 'A', and was judged to be the best by the team of faculty members who evaluated the assignment. The other writers each received a 'C'. I will therefore proceed to account for the effectiveness of the strategies Viji adopted.

At a local level, Viji uses certain composing strategies that have been proven to be effective by the 'process' school of research. Her approach is collaborative and calculated; she makes meticulous plans for the text at local and global levels before beginning her first draft; her composing process is dynamic in being goal-oriented, recursive, and generative; she values revision and multiple drafting; she adopts a clear sense of audience awareness, and relates well to the contexts and purposes of writing. However, these composing strategies, by themselves, are inadequate to explain the eventual shape of her text. There are larger discursive, ideological, and social reasons why she is able to use these strategies as she does. Perhaps the other two writers did not adopt the same strategies because they value alternate discursive traditions and rhetorical effects.

It is clear that these writers, drawn from multiple-discourse communities, show remarkable agency in negotiating the discursive conflicts they face. Their backgrounds motivated each of them to adopt an oppositional stance towards the academic discourse. But we can make finer distinctions on the types of agency and oppositionality they display. Kumar has a cynical attitude to the academic discourse, and employs it in a half-satirical and parodying manner by outwardly conforming to its conventions. As a result, he produces a text that is stereotypically academic. This is rhetorically unsatisfactory, since his text is too abstract and formulaic, and reveals few signs of his personal creative intervention as a writer. The text can only be described as stodgy, affected, mechanical, and vague. Kumar's oppositional strategy is incautious, since his parody could easily be mistaken for a lack of proficiency in the discourse that prevents him from employing it creatively and critically. Rather than making him an insider to the academic discourse community, his stereotypical use of this discourse would then position him as unskilled, incompetent, and marginal to the community.

Sri's strategy is diametrically opposed to Kumar's, though equally ineffective, for both rhetorical and ideological reasons. Drawing on his closeness to the indigenous discourse traditions, he employs a strategy which rejects a wide range of academic conventions. But writers cannot simply turn their backs on the communicative norms operating in a specific context for a particular audience. In addressing an academic audience, he should have taken account of the existing conventions of that genre of communication and worked through them in order to introduce his alternative conventions, messages, and ideologies. A failure to employ existing conventions puts any writer in danger of losing their intended audience, and of their text being judged as incoherent and irrelevant. Sri is badly advised in adopting a 'strategy of avoidance' to challenge the ideologies and conventions of the academy since, like Kumar, the academic community is quite likely to see him in a negative light, and marginalize him. In sum, Sri's strategy can only be seen as a one-sided, uninformed form of opposition that is not sufficiently engaged or contextualized to be effective.

Viji's approach to negotiating discourse conventions for critical expression is altogether more successful. She negotiates with the conventions of the academic community for the strategic expression of her own messages. Since she finds ways of interjecting her religious ethos in a relevant way into the academic discourse, her text gains a creative and critical edge. She attempts to find a space and voice for herself in the range of conflicting discourses, in order to encode the messages she prefers, while taking the academic discourse seriously, and contributes her own considered values in putting together an independent text. It is understandable that the text takes a multivocal, hybrid shape. While being rhetorically effective, the writing also makes an original contribution to knowledge construction in the field of applied linguistics. In other words, Viji appropriates the dominant conventions for her own purposes. Her strategy of discursive appropriation has the potential to interrogate center/academic discourses, reconstruct their conventions, and infuse them with alternate discourses for critical expression. It also suits what were earlier defined as constructive, strategic forms of *resistance*, distinct from mere *opposition* (here exemplified by Sri and Kumar).

Viji brings certain advantages and strengths to her writing experience. Her meta-discursive awareness enables her to have greater control over her text construction. To some extent this might result from her status as a marginalized female member of a literacy-dominant Anglicized community which has the capacity to detach itself in communication and adopt a reflexive stance. Her marginalized status in the local community may have given her a keen sensitivity to the tensions she faces. It should also be said that Viji's insider status in the ELT disciplinary community is an obvious advantage, since her familiarity with the dominant knowledge constructs enables her to negotiate her message strategically. She is also sufficiently committed to her own values and convictions to engage closely with the dominant discourses of the academic context, and so present her message in a contextually appropriate manner. The fact that Viji's motivation in writing her thesis, unlike that of the other two students, was non-utilitarian, may have enabled her to take more risks in her writing, and to find ways of reconciling the discursive tensions more satisfactorily. The other two students display less personal awareness of such tensions, perhaps because of their relatively more secure subjectivities, as males who identify closely with the dominant political ideologies. These two writers also failed to engage with the competing discourses, since they adopted extreme strategies of total conformity or avoidance. By comparison with Viji's hybrid text, their own theses employed relatively univocal discourses—i.e. too personal and narrative in Sri's case, and too detached and scholarly in Kumar's. Perhaps the reason they are less prepared to take risks in their writing is that their motive in undertaking this writing project is narrowly professional. While it would be wrong to explain the strategies used by these writers in a reductive or deterministic manner, it is none the less important to keep these social motivations in mind.

Much instruction in academic discourse, even by schools oriented along post-structuralist and critical perspectives (Bizzell 1982, Rose 1989), has been conceived in binary terms, i.e. moving from one discourse to the other, from the native to the alien, and from the familiar to the strange. The metaphor most often employed is that of 'crossing' discourse boundaries. But periphery students already inhabit a range of hybrid discourses, so categorizing them as being native to only a single discourse could be a stereotype of well-intentioned but uninformed teachers. The 'crossing' model also attempts to induct students into the 'new' discourses without adequately considering the ideological and social costs they will have to pay in taking on the new set of discourses without any influences from their own preferred discourses. But teaching them strategies to negotiate the discourses in their own terms, and constructing multivocal texts, is bound to be ideologically more desirable. The metaphor we need to employ is one of 'appropriating', or perhaps 'merging' discourses. My narrative shows that non-native students can go beyond the reproductive and deterministic influences of the English language and its discourses to display a measure of agency as they critically negotiate discourses in the light of their preferred ideologies and rhetorical traditions.

Periphery students already come to classrooms with a range of center-based academic and other discourses (in addition to their indigenous variants), so what they need is not another product-oriented introduction to them, but ways of employing them creatively and critically. As Kramsch (1993) points out, much of the 'communicative' instruction on academic or cultural discourses has taken place in a product-oriented manner, i.e. by introducing the forms and features of these discourses, rather than exploring what to do with them during communication. The contribution of my narrative is to situate writing in the ideological and social context, in order to consider the strategies students adopt to negotiate conflicting discourses in their struggle for voice. Proceeding along these lines, we can understand a range of issues that will help us to conduct learner strategy training for writers: Which strategies are students comfortable with? Which strategies work well for negotating their discursive conflicts? To what extent do students have a critical awareness of the discursive strategies they employ? What are the ideological and social implications of the strategies they use? The product-oriented approach, which treats literacy as the acquisition of decontextualized skills, misses much of the above type of information; even process schools, which conceive of writing as cognitive, fail to understand the complexities of writing as a social activity. Silva's (1993) comprehensive survey of the studies on second language writing shows the paucity of socially-situated research on the strategies of text construction. The overwhelming bias is towards product-oriented studies on linguistic and textual structures, or towards process-oriented studies on the cognitive modes of composing.

Conclusion

This narrative illustrates how ESL students experience a range of discourses that offer the possibility of negotiating for creative expression. The competing discourses they confront do not necessarily impair communication; they should be considered as elements that can enable effective expression. If students have the necessary critical awareness, independence, and boldness to take these conflicting discourses by the horns, and negotiate for expression, they can channel them for constructive purposes. Since students from multicultural, multilingual communities generally confront conflicting discourses in practicing literacy, a useful pedagogical strategy is to motivate them to engage with discourses as they encode and decode texts, to make them conscious of discursive tensions, and realize the positive potential of negotiating for expression. In other words, belonging simultaneously to different discourse communities, or being native to a marginalized discourse, does not necessarily imply that there is a 'problem'. Indeed, this situation can be a resource for critical expression.

Notes

1 This is a complicated connection that will take considerable space to develop. See Canagarajah 1996 for a perspective. Swales 1990 also considers the ways in which 'native English' scholars have an advantage in academic writing and research publishing.

2 See especially Gabriel Okara (1964, 1990), Chinua Achebe (1975), Parthasarathy (1976), Richard Rodriguez (1981), and Ngugi wa Thiong'o (1986, 1990).

3 The origins of the content-focused approach may appear less obvious. Although Raimes attributes its development to Mohan and his associates in the ESL context, this also has prior development in FL circles as a version of the process paradigm. The basis of the content approach on a 'common cognitive/academic component manifested in discourse across cultures' (Mohan and Lo 1985: 516) and its pedagogy of helping students with 'the language of the thinking processes and the structure or shape of content' (Mohan 1986: 18) make clear its cognitivist orientation—even though it also borrows somewhat from developments in English for Academic Purposes (EAP) and Writing Across the Curriculum (WAC). The difference is that while the early process scholars focused on thinking strategies (Zamel 1982, 1983, Raimes 1985, 1987), Mohan and his associates focus additionally on thought content. However, McCrimmon's (1984) notion of 'writing as a way of knowing' had already developed an emphasis on content within the FL process paradigm during the early 1970s.

4 We must note here that there are alternative perspectives on cognition, such as the 'social cognition' school of Vygotsky, which would argue that the socio-cultural context is not only a mediating factor but intrinsic to thinking.

5 This schema also has implications for reading pedagogies. Some of the traditional reading approaches have been product-oriented, in focusing on letter–sound correspondence and on vocabulary development that is reminiscent of the form-focused approaches in writing. The 'psycholinguistic guessing game' approach to reading thereafter emphasized the cognitive processes behind decoding texts. Scholars in this tradition have adopted a close empirical orientation to the mental strategies displayed

by readers. In recent times, top-down approaches influenced by ESP and EAP have focused on the content and discipline-specific background information students need in order to decipher texts. Such approaches may situate the text in the social context of readers, writers, and rhetorical conventions (as in the content/reader-focused writing approaches).

6 Having followed course work on subjects ranging from descriptive linguistics to sociolinguistics and educational psychology, the writers treated below were to submit a research report on a subject relevant to ELT pedagogical concerns. Although they had a full year to research and write their project, in reality they only focused on this component during the two months after completing the tests for their course work. Since they had already gained some experience by producing a final year research essay within their undergraduate studies, they chose to consult the faculty only on an optional basis. My observations derive from teaching in this program, and serving as a consultant for their writing projects.

7 To realize that the discursive boundaries are not always clear cut, we must note that Saivism also contains a rationalistic strand that engages in detached intellectual inquiry—which gained heightened significance after its encounter with colonial Christian educationists (Perinbanayagam 1988).

8 These attitudes throw some useful ethnographic light on Silva's (1993) finding from a survey of L2 research literature that non-native students did little re-reading of their drafts and/or attempted additional drafts of revision. We have to consider how such attitudes to textuality may be influenced by the oral traditions these students come from.

9 When Silva generalizes that 'L2 writers had more difficulty in interpreting the background reading text and made less reference to the background text in their introductions' (1993: 666), we must situate this finding in the social context to understand how Sri's weak positioning in the discourse community contributes to this problem.

10 Recently, a very sophisticated defense has been made for the textual borrowing of non-Western student groups (Pennycook 1996). However, Howard (1995) points out that there is a 'positive plagiarism' that welds the borrowing into a new whole, and a 'negative plagiarism' that borders on pastiche. Sri needs more expertise to practice the former.

11 While Silva (1993) characterizes L2 research consensus that students are weak in global and local planning (which is confirmed in the case of the other two scholars), Viji is exceptional. This shows why we must attend to individual differences among L2 students based on their unique hybrid discursive backgrounds.

12 This contradicts what Silva characterizes as typical of L2 writers whose 'orientation of readers was deemed less appropriate and acceptable' (1993: 668). Here again, a consideration of the differing discursive backgrounds of L2 students should help to qualify such generalizations.

8 The politics and pedagogy of appropriating discourses

Then all the nations of birds lifted together
the huge net of the shadows of this earth
in multitudinous dialects, twittering tongues,
stitching and crossing it.

Walcott, *The Season of Phantasmal Peace*

If language learning is ideological, as I have demonstrated in the chapters above, the solution is not to run away from politics, but to negotiate with the agencies of power for personal and collective empowerment. If ELT is implicated in larger social processes and cultural practices, the corrective is not to eliminate that connection in favor of autonomy or 'purity', but to seek a holistic pedagogy that will enable learners to engage with those domains for a richer educational experience. We are ready now to pull together the hints students themselves provide to fashion pedagogical approaches that reconcile the conflicts they face in acquiring and using English in the periphery. My aim here is to demonstrate the ideological complexity of the communicative and learning strategies they display.

The case for appropriating discourses

We must first grasp the nature of the challenge confronting learners from periphery backgrounds. As we saw in Chapter 4, students are indeed motivated to learn English. They acknowledge the need for the standard dialects of English, mainstream communicative conventions, and literacy practices for instrumental purposes in educational and vocational domains. They realize that English is a coveted linguistic capital in the contemporary world that can provide them with access to many economic and social rewards. We have therefore witnessed students and communities displaying a surprising level of opposition to the anti-English policies of their own nationalistic regime. As we saw in Chapter 3, they adopt surreptitious forms of learning and using English. This is largely motivated by their desire for pluralistic identities and hybrid discourses in their linguistic and social life. However, the lived culture of the students reveals cultural and ideological conflicts in using and learning English. Much of the opposition is in fact generated by the textbooks, curriculum, pedagogies, and discourse conventions recommended by center agencies. For example, the dominant academic discourses and literacy practices represent the identities of Viji, Sri, and Kumar in ways that are uncomfortable to them, especially in light of the alternate discourses they desire. Use of 'standard' English in classroom discourse creates conflicts in interpersonal relationships and community solidarity. The discourses in the curriculum and teaching material (as in *AKL*) clash with the discourses students themselves value. I have interpreted this situation as a tension students face between the threats of ideological domination experienced at an intuitive level and the promises of a socio-economic necessity acknowledged at a more conscious level. In other words, even though they vaguely sense the impositions on their value system, identity, and community solidarity, periphery students do not ignore the fact that they need the English language and literacy to vie for social status and economic prospects. This predicament helps us understand keenly the nature of the conflict facing periphery students in ELT. Any pedagogy designed for these students will have to take account of their desire to master the language, their fears of ideological/linguistic hegemony, and suggest a way of acquiring English with a satisfactory reconciliation of the conflicts posed.

What is demanded is a 'third way' that avoids the traditional extremes of rejecting English outright for its linguistic imperialism or accepting it wholesale for its benefits. The communicative and learning strategies of periphery students—however tentative, spontaneous, and untheorized—suggest ways of overcoming this impasse. We have seen in previous chapters how they gesture towards an appropriation of the discourses, codes, and grammar of English in terms of their own traditions and needs. The Tamilized English and hybrid academic texts are attempts periphery subjects themselves make towards a suitable alternative for their communicative and ideological conflicts in using English.

Consider how Viji negotiates a range of conflicting discourses to develop a formidable text that speaks uniquely and originally on the subject she chooses to explore for her thesis. She wrestles with the established conventions and codes of academic discourse to construct a hybrid text that is infused with her own desired discourses. In this way, she provides a representation of her identity, thought, and values that are more satisfactory and empowering for her. What is strategic is that in engaging with the conventions of the academic community, she ensures that she does not lose her audience. Keeping the channels of communication open, she then challenges them with her own ideologies. Thus she is able to make a powerful advocacy of her own point of view and knowledge. If she had ignored the established discourse, she would have lost her audience and kept her critical knowledge only to herself.

This discursive appropriation takes place not only at the level of textual structure, communicative conventions, idea development, tone, and style, but also involves grammar. Although Viji largely sticks to the system of standard English in her writing, she *uses* the grammar to represent an ethos of her own choosing. The changes in grammar are more radical in the writing of Sri as he uses English to represent rhetorical and discursive values from the local oral tradition. Notice his prose: 'Some teachers translate the passages from English to Tamil, but translation doesn't teach writing, lectures do not teach writing. They display the teacher's opinion about writing. Therefore, writing and more writing, and then more writing, teaches writing; in other words practice, practice and still more practice.' Center readers will consider the syntax and idiom peculiar. There are other examples in Sri's writing that might be even considered 'non-educated Sri Lankan English' (Kandiah 1984) according to local norms. More radical forms of grammatical appropriation are the dynamic processes of code alternation, mixing, and switching displayed by students in classroom discourse (see Chapter 6). These utterances are rarely described for their system and are considered 'freak' forms of usage. However, through these discursive strategies students are linguistically negotiating values, identities, and group relationships that are of complex socio-political relevance. Note that in these classroom interactions students and teachers can use something approximating standard English in contexts defined as formal or official; they switch to mixed codes only when they feel it is rhetorically suitable. What all this implies is that students are building a repertoire of grammars and discourses in English that they will use strategically in each context.

We must not fail to note here that English is getting pluralized in the hands of these students. The standard grammars and established discourses are being infused with diverse alternate grammars and conventions from periphery languages. There are two important processes of significance here: the empowerment of minority communities and the democratization of English. Both interests are interrelated. While the center-based rules and values underlying English could alienate minority students, it is a more pluralized English that can accommodate their needs, desires, and values. English should become pluralized to accommodate the discourses of other cultures and facilitate fairer representation of periphery subjects. Periphery communities are therefore compelled by virtue of their marginalized status and location to reform English. Note also that through this process of appropriation the students are taking ideological resistance into the very heart of English. Rather than keeping competing discourses outside English, they are infusing them into the very structure of the language to reconfigure its ideological character.

This option answers the dilemma facing the students quite effectively. The question confronting the students is not *whether* English should be learned, but *how*. They will neither refuse to learn English nor acquire it unconditionally in the terms dictated by the center. They will appropriate the language in their own terms, according to their needs, values, and aspirations. Whereas the uncritical use of English leads to accommodation or domination, and avoidance of English leads to marginalization or ghettoization, critical negotiation leads to their empowerment. In choosing this option the students are simply tapping a tradition of discursive and linguistic appropriation going as far back as the earliest colonial encounters. As demonstrated in the third chapter, local subjects have been developing such hybrid discourses as a strategy of opposition even outside the classroom. This discursive tradition reaches a high point in the life and work of the Saiva reformist Arumuga Navalar. One might say that processes of mediation and appropriation always take place when cultures come into contact—even in pre-colonial times. Therefore the students have ample precedents for the discursive strategy they adopt.

Periphery subjects must then acquire English in their own terms, while maintaining proficiency in their native languages and discourses. They have to negotiate with English to gain positive identities, critical expression, and ideological clarity. Rather than slavishly parroting the language and accepting the typical values it embodies with the unfavorable representations it provides, periphery students will become insiders and use the language in their own terms according to their own aspirations, needs, and values. They will reposition themselves in English language and discourse to use these not as slaves, but as agents; to use English not mechanically and diffidently, but creatively and critically.

Relating to language debates

It is important to understand how the position carved out by the students relates to the thinking propounded by scholars on the place of English in the periphery communities. In fact, periphery scholars have themselves held conflicting perspectives on these questions. While giving a sympathetic hearing to the alternate perspectives, this discussion will also help us understand the wisdom of the position adopted by the students.

Among the most radical is what we might call the 'nationalist' position, which proposes that periphery communities should have no truck with English. The most sensational proponent of this line of thinking is the Kenyan protest fiction writer Ngugi wa Thiong'o (1986, 1990). Consistent with his view, he has announced in his *Decolonizing the Mind* (1986) that he would abandon English for written expression after that book and use his native Kikuyu. The main points of this position can be outlined as follows.

- It is difficult, if not impossible, to articulate the native sensibility and ideologies through this alien language.

- The repressive and alien ideologies identified with English are so inextricably a part of it that one cannot use the language without being dominated by (and spreading) those discourses.
- Though periphery communities have decolonized themselves in political terms, in continuing to use English they are subjecting themselves and their communities to an insidious form of mental colonialism.
- It is important to stem the tide of English developing at the cost of vernacular traditions and languages by committing oneself single-mindedly to rejuvenating indigenous art forms, oral tradition, and aesthetic values. Periphery subjects who use English are enriching the alien language at the cost of the local communicative resources.

This position displays such extreme suspicion with English language and Western discourses that it encourages people to be wary of having any contact with them. It is important to be alert to the insidious forms in which language can be hegemonical. It is also necessary for periphery subjects to commit themselves to developing the local languages and discourses which are largely marginalized in geopolitical terms. However, there are many reasons why this oppositional strategy may be ill conceived:

- Treating English as incapable of representing any other ideology or discourse other than that associated with center communities is an overdetermined perspective. This view is akin to the reproduction schools in its philosophical determinism.
- A 'separatist' response could in fact ghettoize minority communities, preventing them from mutually enriching interaction with other societies.
- Marginalized communities do have a lot to gain by learning other languages and discourses and their underlying knowledge systems. The competence they acquire in multiple discourses empowers them to interact confidently in different contexts of communication and culture. (The ethnographic evidence from previous chapters confirms the desire of periphery students to master the language for their advantage.)
- Such communities are also throwing away the means of networking with the other colonized communities in the post-colonial world. A lingua franca such as English can enable periphery communities to interact with each other and learn from each other— if it be, for the subversive end of resisting English.
- Refusing to engage with English may not defeat its hegemony; this response might only let its power go unchallenged. Therefore this is not a solution to the ideological challenges, but an escape from it.

Opposed to this position is that of the 'universalists'—represented by those like the Nigerian novelist Chinua Achebe (1975) and the Sri Lankan poet Yasmine Gooneratne (1971). They believe that English is expansive, malleable, and neutral enough to accommodate diverse sensibilities. Therefore the writers representing this position believe that their culture will inevitably get reflected in their use of English. They gain confidence from the philosophical tradition that views language as a value-free, autonomous instrument that can be used for whatever purpose one desires. They would also subscribe to the view of human subjects as transcendental, with a mind that can perceive and express without linguistic or cultural mediation. In her poem 'This Language, This Woman' (which she frames as a debate with the nationalists), Gooneratne (*ibid.*) goes on to argue that English has lost its imperialistic connections after decolonization—'no more an Empress's daughter' and the 'distorting old connection done', English 'wanders here alone and unbefriended,/herself at last, and nothing else to offer'. Gooneratne considers the language fit to be her muse, as it is 'supple' and 'generous'.

It is significant that these thinkers believe in the power of human subjects to manage authentic expression and the creative possibilities available in any language. But their position is somewhat naive. Consider the following problems in their thinking:

- Even after the decolonization of the 1960s, imperialism associated with Britain and other Western nations is still being continued through the English language. The role of the United States should also not be forgotten.
- Language cannot willy-nilly separate itself from history, ideology, and social institutions to become pure and autonomous.
- Language is an active ideological agent that constrains our consciousness, and its mediation in human perception and expression cannot be avoided.
- Language also has implications in social terms for interpersonal relations, group dynamics, and the distribution of symbolic and material rewards.

The ethnography reported above demonstrates the conflicts students face for their values, community solidarity, and identity in using English. They are also painfully aware of the implications English has for their social status and economic standing. It is ironic that the periphery subjects who sing the praises of English are those who have mastered the language and enjoy its rewards.

Among those who represent the more balanced, 'third way' is Nigerian poet and novelist Gabriel Okara. He opts for negotiating with English for expression of indigenous values, with full awareness of its potential for ideological domination. Refusing to be complacent, like the universalists, Okara also avoids being defeatist, like the nationalists. Not subscribing to a rigid linguistic or ideological determinism as Ngugi does, Okara assumes that a language can represent multiple discourses. Similarly, he assumes the relative autonomy of the speaking subject to engineer ideological changes even if one cannot totally free oneself from the ideologies inscribed in one's language. I have already made a case for such a balanced philosophical standpoint in the opening chapter.

Okara explains this process of linguistic reconstruction as

> a continuing quest, through experimentation, for a mode of employing the English language, which we have appropriated, to give full expression to our culture and our point of view, to our message, without our seeing ourselves, or others seeing us, as through a distorting mirror... If, therefore, an African wishes to use English as an effective medium of literary expression, he has to emulsify it with the patterns, modes and idioms of African speech until it becomes so attenuated that it bears little resemblance to the original. (1990: 16–17)

Okara is aware that vernacularizing English is not something completed in one shot—that it is a 'continuing quest', a process marked by different stages of approximation and experimentation. Okara himself in his *The Voice* (1964) and other 'third world' creative writers, such as Raja Rao in *Kanthapura* (1938), have provided examples of such appropriated English discourses influenced by their own local oral traditions in their writing. They show how written English can be used with varying degrees of indigenization to ensure intelligibility with the pan-English readership, while not sacrificing local values and conventions. The periphery poets from whom I draw my inscriptions for many of the chapters are in fact exponents of this communicative tradition. Notable among them is the Nobel Prize-winning Derek Walcott, who uses a range of center-based and Creole dialects in his writing. In the inscription for this chapter, he envisions a world which would respect a plurality of voices and dialects. It is good to realize that the untheorized reconciliations the students fashion for their linguistic and discursive conflicts are being actively experimented by other periphery thinkers.

Relating to standardization arguments

The option articulated above has relevance to the narrowly grammatical dimension of the debates in ELT as well. What is the place of 'standard' English (as defined by Anglo-American or center-based communities) in the periphery? There is ongoing debate on this question.

The British grammarian Quirk (1990) still continues to champion the orthodoxy that appropriated Englishes are a threat to a universal standard, as they spring from deviations and errors from the 'norm'. Periphery dialects are considered interlanguages that reflect an ossified or stunted development while moving towards the target grammatical system. Teaching periphery Englishes, for these scholars, is to institutionalize imperfect language systems, eventually leading to the unintelligibility of the diverse variants spoken by the different communities. Braj Kachru (1986, 1991) has done much to show that these dialects reflect the sociolinguistic rules, communicative conventions, and cultural traditions of the local people that suit best their communicative purposes. Arguing that such linguistic nativization is a sociolinguistic fact in language contact situations, Kachru proposes that they should be considered independent *Englishes* in their own right rather than being given secondary or inferior status. However, Kachru's challenge does not go far enough, since he is not fully alert to the ideological implications of periphery Englishes. In his attempt to systematize the periphery variants, he has to standardize the language himself, leaving out many eccentric, hybrid forms of local Englishes as too unsystematic. In this, the Kachruvian paradigm follows the logic of the prescriptive and elitist tendencies of the center linguists. Parakrama (1995) has recently exposed how the legitimized periphery Englishes are themselves ideological constructs in valorizing the educated versions of local English, while the so-called 'non-educated' versions of periphery Englishes display more dynamic forms of resistance and communicative potential.

Meanwhile, other center linguists have attempted to reconcile the claims of standard and non-standard Englishes. David Crystal (1997) in his *English as a Global Language* argues for a 'World Standard Spoken English' as a universal common dialect motivated by reasons of efficiency, while local dialects and vernaculars are maintained for in-group communication. He acknowledges that WSSE will largely be influenced by American English. Crystal is apparently not troubled by the linguistic inequalities set up by his proposal, the hegemony of the center Englishes through the 'standard', and the ways in which WSSE can provide ideological and economic advantages to center communities.

Widdowson has recently attempted to move beyond the either/or terms of the debate to argue that both standard English and emergent periphery Englishes 'have their proper place in the scheme of things and both are of crucial concern in English language education' (1993: 329). Quite radically, he is prepared to provide a place for periphery Englishes in ELT pedagogy. Invoking 'sociolinguistic understanding of different conditions of appropriacy' (*loc. cit.*), he acknowledges that while nativized Englishes have a place for intra-community purposes in periphery societies, standard dialects have a place in institutional and formal communication in inter-community relations. He sensibly argues that to deny standard dialects to periphery students is to deny them access to gate-keeping contexts of institutional communication. In other places he is prepared to acknowledge that nativized Englishes serve purposes of personal identity and communal solidarity, just as 'standard English' provides them access to institutional power. In fact, developing a sensitivity to the contextual appropriacy of different codes in diverse situations is itself of educational value.

While Widdowson is ready to provide a place for both variants in the process of schooling, assigning standard English as the *ends* of learning and nativized variants as the *means* towards that end (1993: 326) is to reify the latter's secondary position. (In fact, he refers to 'standard' and 'non-standard' English without any irony.) Similarly, his proposal for how the power of center dialects can be challenged by other Englishes is based on a questionable strategy. The way to do this, for him, is to show that the communal and personal functions served by periphery Englishes are no less important than the institutional functions of 'standard' dialects. However, making students feel good about their own dialect is insufficient to challenge the power of the dominant codes. The dominance of 'standard' dialects is sustained by economic and political realities—which domains need to be interrogated if we are to contest or reconfigure the hierarchy of codes.

More importantly, though Widdowson is correct to say that offering periphery students competence in standard dialects is a way of empowering them, he is limited in thinking that 'standard English' has to be learned and used without modifications and should be canonized for universal official purposes. Following the position articulated above for discourse genres, periphery students may appropriate standard dialects too to serve their values and interests. If 'standard English' is to be an international language, then the natural process of hybridization, diversification, and development cannot be controlled. If language is not to remain the abstract system of grammar but socially functional in actual contexts, periphery students will use standard dialects too with varying levels of indigenization. However, there will be natural processes of self-regulation and intelligibility developed endo-normatively as appropriate for different situations of use and changing historical contexts. 'Standard' does not have to be developed and enforced for mutual intelligibility by teachers or institutions. The term 'standard' must then be used more flexibly—each variant, even registers and sociolects (i.e. legalese, journalese, and diverse disciplinary discourses) will have standards of different levels of generality for the respective communities. There will be multiple systems of English with their own norms and rules of usage. 'Standards' become pragmatic systems developed in the process of linguistic interaction by each speech community to conduct effective communication. This dynamic conception of linguistic systematization assures us that appropriation by periphery communities can take place without sacrificing intelligibility of communication with other speech communities. This also flattens the status of traditional standard dialects.

My position, then, is that while we must recognize the contextual ap-propriacy of different Englishes and teach students as many variants as possible (including more formal, public, and institutionalized variants—some of which are presently 'owned' by the center-based communities), it is equally important to teach students that any dialect has to be personally and communally appropriated to varying degrees in order to be meaningful and relevant for its users. This would lead to the pluralization of standards and democratization of access to English.

Theorizing appropriation

Although students display their strategies of linguistic appropriation in largely non-reflective ways, the wider ramifications of this option need to be theorized with the help of periphery scholars who have given this matter some thought. The processes of negotiating multiple discourses and languages have a special resonance for post-colonial thinkers. Scholars such as Said and Bhabha celebrate the hybridity of discourses and cultures that characterize the post-colonial subject. This plurality and hybridity are considered the hallmark of the post-colonial condition. Caught between the colonizing influence of the West (which has left indelible traces on their cultural life) and the equally resilient indigenous traditions, the challenge for periphery subjects is to forbid such conflicting cultural sensibilities to disintegrate them. A more constructive attitude is to accept this hybridity and negotiate with the competing values and discourses to one's advantage. Rather than running away from heterogeneity in favor of uniformity, it is important for periphery subjects to embrace this rich inherent hybridity that enables them to arbitrate between different cultures, communities, and discourses.

Said, in his *Culture and Imperialism*, sees both this hybridity and the suppression of it as paradoxically the work of Western colonialism: 'Imperialism consolidated the mixture of cultures and identities on a global scale. But its worst and most paradoxical gift was to allow people to believe that they were only, mainly, exclusively, white, or black, or Western, or Oriental' (1993: 336). The radical potential of post-colonial subjects lies therefore in resisting the pressure by colonizing forces (whether of the East or the West) to box them into one-dimensional (often negative) subject positions. Affirming the agency of subjects, Said has faith in their ability to reconstruct their cultures and identities to their advantage: 'Yet just as human beings make their own history, they also make their cultures and ethnic identities' (1993: 336). To stick stubbornly to one's indigenous discourses or to surrender unconditionally to English are positions of accommodation to the imperialist dynamics that offer post-colonial subjects only negative or stereotypical identities or absorb them into center's cultural logic.

It is for this reason that Said sees much power in the marginal position of the exile, transient, immigrant, and minority. For him, such people have the potential to resist the forces of uniformity and hegemony:

> Yet it is no exaggeration to say that liberation as an intellectual mission, born in the resistance and opposition to the confinements and ravages of imperialism, has shifted from the settled, established, and domesticated dynamics of culture to its unhoused, decentered, and exilic energies whose incarnation today is the migrant, and whose consciousness is that of the intellectual and artist in exile, the political figure between domains, between forms, between homes, and between languages.
> (1993: 332)

What post-colonial subjects display is the critical detachment they are able to adopt towards the cultures and communities they inhabit. The position of the hybrid subject situated in the margins of discourses and cultures is therefore creative and radical. Probing the dynamics of one culture from the spectacles afforded by the other, they are able to resist the tendency to be uncritically absorbed into a single cultural or discursive system.

Said is careful, however, to note that such discursive negotiation cannot be achieved by staying detached from one's roots and non-committally playing with plural discourses and identities in the fashion of much 'ludic' post-structuralism. To be a cultural hybrid is not to be race-less or non-ethnic. Nor does it mean that one can stand free of ideological commitments. He insists that 'the "strong" or "perfect" person achieves independence and detachment by *working through* attachments, not by rejecting them. Exile is predicated on the existence of, love for, and a real body with one's native place' (1993: 336; emphasis in original). It is important therefore for post-colonial subjects to take a clear stand for local interests and traditions as they move fluidly between multifarious discourses and cultures. Being sympathetically grounded in one's primary community is not inimical to multicultural status; on the contrary, it deepens the meaning and significance of one's cosmopolitan provenance.

The implications of negotiating competing discourses for identity formation and empowerment have been further theorized by feminist thinkers and minority-women scholars. Faced with the dominant discourses which are hegemonical, they have found it important not to run away from them. After all there is no life as a subject without inhabiting available discourses. The alternative for marginalized groups is to reposition themselves in such discourses. They challenge the negative subject positions offered by dominant discourses by appropriating them and infusing them with their own values to serve their interests and aspirations. Shifting their position from objects of this discourse to become agents, they use the discourse critically and creatively. Although the available discourses may not always be favorable to one's interests, still one must use these discourses as the starting-point to discover oneself through the very process of resisting these discourses. Subjecthood therefore involves working through, working along, working against available discourses with a clear grounding in one's values to construct favorable subject positions further (Alcoff 1988).

The appropriation of hegemonical discourses for the development of an independent 'voice' has been theorized by bell hooks (1989) in relation to the African-American community's problems in the dominant discourses. The way to do this for her is to 'talk back'. It is by resisting the dominant discourses that one creates a space for one's voice within that discourse. In order to talk back, however, one must understand and engage with the rules of dominant discourses. This is in fact a process of bringing vernacular values to critically inform and reconfigure mainstream discourses. While ensuring communication with the mainstream by using the conventions and linguistic rules valued by them, one attempts to challenge, reform, and expand their rhetoric by bringing in the vernacular discourses. Therefore, in her book *Talking Back*, she employs a novel discourse that infuses many of the features of vernacular discourse within the structure of academic text conventions. She accommodates everyday anecdotes, vernacular expressions, and idioms of Black street speech into her theoretical writing in a superb negotiation of languages and styles.

hooks also explores the 'ambivalence' Black students experience in being motivated to succeed in the academy and the mainstream and yet feeling guilty about the alienation from the folk ways of thinking and speaking this involves. She is, however, of the view that one does not have to follow Rodriguez's (1981) path of deserting the community for academic success in order to resolve this conflict. One can be both academically successful and rooted in one's own community. She therefore sets a daring new agenda for minority students—i.e. to use their ambivalence as resource. She argues, 'Learning to listen to different voices, hearing different speech challenges the notion that we must all assimilate—share a single, similar talk—in educational institutions ... Even in the face of powerful structures of domination, it remains possible for each of us to define and determine alternative standards, to decide on the nature and extent of compromise' (hooks 1989: 79, 81). In other words, the ambivalence minority students face between competing discourses and identities should be seen as the means for their empowerment. Not only would they maintain proficiency in their own vernacular discourses to display their competence in multiple codes, but they would use the dominant discourses from the perspective of their vernacular standpoint to creatively modify the codes. hooks thus deviates from the 'monolingualists' within the African-American community who either propose the use of Black Vernacular English for all contexts as a form of opposition (i.e. Smitherman 1981a, b, 1984, Grubb 1986) or insist on Standard English as the norm in order to cope with the mainstream (Baugh 1983).

This perspective on appropriating hegemonizing discourses for the formation of identity and voice should not be understood as a need for marginalized subjects only. Foucault and other post-structuralist scholars have theorized this strategy as a general condition for thought. In 'The Discourse on Language' (1972) Foucault dramatizes the conflict facing subjects for thought as one between instinct and institution. On the one hand, we desire to speak instinctively without conforming to any conventions or constraints whatsoever. This is the ultimate form of free expression mythically envisioned by many. But this is an illusory freedom as there is no speaking without conventions, symbols, or codes to represent our thought. At the other extreme are the institutionalized discourses which offer to represent us in the preconstructed conventions. But this is to be silenced as we can channel our messages only according to the ideologies and rules permitted by these discourses. Since we cannot conduct thought by conforming to institutionalized discourses, or by abandoning them completely in favor of personal originality, it is by traversing these polarities that we find space for ourselves. To capture Foucault's dialectic, Spellmeyer invokes etymology: 'The very word "discourse", in its root sense a "running back and forth", implies the need for such a doubleness' (1989: 722). By probing the margins of discourses we can adopt a critical detachment from the conventions, develop a reflexive awareness of the discourses we think by, and reformulate the rules of these discourses to conduct relatively independent thought. For Foucault this is the manner in which new knowledge paradigms have been always constructed in history.

Bakhtin (1981) identifies the need for appropriation in the very micro-structures of heteroglossic language. While language-as-system is abstract and mechanical, in actual contexts of communication texts and words display a rich polyvalence. They embody multiple values deriving from their history of use. Bakhtin's principle of dialogism envisions that we have to always negotiate this linguistic tension for speech. We have to struggle with the prior denotations, historical connotations, and genre conventions embodied in language to create meaning. Needless to say, certain meanings in language are enforced by dominant ideologies and institutions. But we must work against the dominant meanings in order to communicate meaningfully. Therefore, meaning-making is intrinsically oppositional. The polyvalence of language, with all its unpredictable and unmanageable potential for communication, is thus the source of resistance for Bakhtin. Since there is potential for multiple meaning-making in language, it is difficult for any institution to enforce its own desired meanings and thought. The hybridity of language enables subjects to represent alternate meanings denied by dominant institutions, if they can negotiate the inherent tensions strategically.

Towards a pedagogy of appropriation

It is important now to consider how the instinctive, untutored, and untheorized modes of appropriation students and teachers display in the classroom can be developed to form appropriate pedagogical alternatives for the periphery. The strategies students display while negotiating texts, discourses, and codes in the classroom provide useful hints for the development of a critical pedagogy that addresses the specific challenges they confront in learning English.

Consider once again the learning and thinking strategies displayed by students in the different pedagogical tasks discussed. Students move in and out of dialects, languages, discourses, contexts, and communities in classroom activities as they appropriate English for their purposes. The glosses in the margins of *AKL* show them relating the text to their own social and cultural frames. In classroom discourse, they alternate L1 and L2 as they negotiate their relationships, roles, values, and knowledge content in strategic ways. In the safe houses, they interpret instructional material and curricula according to their community and home-based knowledge. In writing activities they move between competing rhetorical and discursive traditions to find coherence for their thought and expression. Since much of this activity is pedagogically disallowed—as the orthodoxy perceives any movement outside the target language and prescribed texts as a corrupting influence on carefully controlled language acquisition—teachers and students have to practice it surreptitiously.

The cognitive and educational advantages of this practice of shuttling between codes and conventions should be appreciated. In relating textual discourses to their own cultural contexts, even as they consider the contexts imposed by the texts, students are demythologizing the hidden values and curricula. They are also developing a keener sensitivity to the differences between their own and the text's discourses. Similarly, in moving between L1 and L2, they are developing a meta-linguistic awareness of the conflicting values and grammars behind these languages. Engaging with, rather than ignoring, the multiple discourses that clamor for attention as they compose texts, students are also developing a meta-discursive awareness. The competing values, conventions, and resources represented by these discourses are explored deeply in the process. Apart from the complex cognitive awareness developed through this activity, the very proficiency in negotiating multiple codes and discourses is of educational value.

This pedagogical approach then involves a reflexivity on the discourses and strategies students bring with them, as well as those established by dominant institutions. This reflexivity could also develop a critical awareness of the processes and practices involved in educational activity. Since knowledge and the methods employed to gain it are value-ridden, to critically reflect on the hidden values, agendas, and interests embodied in the learning activity is empowering for students. Furthermore, learners should be encouraged to become reflexive about their classroom relations since knowledge is socially constructed. Eventually, learners must be encouraged to become reflexive about themselves—i.e. how their values, community membership, historical background, and subject-positions motivate them to negotiate language and knowledge in particular ways. The end result of this pedagogy is a critical awareness of the rationale, rules, and consequences of the competing discourses in the classroom and outside. It is such a pedagogy that would enable students to appropriate the dominant codes and discourses according to their needs and interests.

The value of such reflexive styles of learning for education in the post-colonial world are realized by many educational theorists today. Pratt's notion of the school as a contact zone envisions classrooms as 'social spaces where cultures meet, clash, and grapple with each other, often in contexts of highly asymmetrical relations of power, such as colonialism, slavery, or their aftermaths as they are lived out in many parts of the world today' (1991: 34). Contemporary classrooms constitute students (and teachers) from diverse socio-cultural backgrounds who must not only negotiate their own differing knowledge systems but increasingly deal with texts and curricula from different discursive traditions. Pratt takes care to note that such meeting of cultures and discourses takes place under asymmetrical relations as the discourses of the dominant groups are privileged and often institutionalized by the school. However, interaction in the contact zone gives birth to hybrid forms of knowledge, texts, and codes which may resist homogeneity and domination. She shows how these texts and languages may display complex skills of mediating alien cultures, appropriating hegemonic discourses, and negotiating foreign languages for the communicative purposes of marginalized communities. The act of seeing one's own culture through the eyes of another cultural group is itself a sobering experience, enabling one to detach him or herself from one's own discourses, gain reflexive understanding, and develop a more critical attitude towards things. The tension of inter-cultural clashes can also bring forth new knowledge—generating new paradigms for understanding nature and society. Others, such as Giroux and his associates, are envisioning a 'border pedagogy' (Giroux 1992, Giroux and MacLaren 1994) which similarly recommends reflexive strategies suitable for 'students to write, speak and listen in a language in which meaning becomes multi-accentual and dispersed and resists permanent closure' (Giroux 1992: 29). This mode of learning develops the competence necessary to cope with the hybrid cultural context of the post-modern world.

More importantly, post-colonial scholars of English consider many of the above strategies as useful pedagogical alternatives in a context of linguistic hegemony. Although they are mostly theorizing the teaching of literature in the periphery, their correctives compare interestingly with the learning strategies displayed by my language students. Viswanathan (1993) invokes the classical Tamil exegetical tradition of code-mixed writing (i.e. Sanskrit and Tamil) to argue that this indigenous strategy of *manipravalava* writing suggests ways in which students can creatively negotiate the cultural baggage of the 'alien' texts. She sees this as a way of appropriating the English texts into the cultural and linguistic frames brought by the students and thus interpreting them according to their own values. Spivak (1993) also sees liberatory potential in the use of code-mixed interactions and texts in English classes to enable students to invoke competing epistemologies and alternate readings. de Souza (1994) elaborates Caribbean writer Wilson Harris's (1992) strategy of 're-visioning'—a self-reflexive reading strategy that relates the text to one's personal life and holds alternate interpretations parallel with the established ones—as a pedagogy of resisting colonial interpretive schema and subjectivities. Rajan (1993) sees such pedagogies of appropriation as holding great potential for taking the sting out of the hidden curricula of

English texts and, in fact, serving to create better awareness of indigenous traditions. In the light of such scholarly developments, we can appreciate the wisdom behind the spontaneously-practiced learning styles of my students.

Developing appropriate methods

We must note that this pedagogy goes beyond the communicative teaching methods which are often celebrated in ELT as suitable for orientating students to culture and discourse (Holliday 1994). Communicative pedagogy inducts students into the foreign culture in a non-reflexive manner, often insensitive to the ideological implications of this induction. Claire Kramsch (1993) argues that in teaching a foreign language it is limiting both to teach the 'foreign' culture behind the language or to employ the students' indigenous culture. Even building bridges across cultures is futile as it is impossible ever to go 'native' in the foreign culture. The students' primary culture will always mediate their awareness of the new culture. Kramsch argues that letting students negotiate the borders of each culture as they confront the foreign language is educationally more valuable. She states, 'We can teach the boundary, we cannot teach the bridge. We can *talk about* and try to *understand* the differences between the values celebrated [in contrasting cultures]. We cannot teach directly how to resolve the conflict between the two' (1993: 228, emphasis in original). Therefore, rather than finding methods that are culturally comfortable to the local students and teachers, it is important to develop strategies that encourage them to explore inter-cultural differences. The pedagogy Kramsch advocates 'requires a gradual move from communicative to cross-cultural activities, from discourse to meta-discourse and aesthetic reflection' (1993: 231). She envisions her pedagogical practice as almost 'aesthetic' in nature as it encourages students and teachers to engage in a highly interpretive, imaginative, and impressionistic exploration of differing cultural sensibilities. The reflexivity advocated can be developed by quite playful activities, and does not have to be intellectually threatening.

As we move towards developing teaching methods and materials to practice such a pedagogy it is important to consider how existing textbooks can be used for negotiating cultures. This can be a creative enterprise where teachers take communicative activities a few steps beyond what are prescribed in textbooks to enable students to move in and out of cultures. While the activities of communicative pedagogies attempt to accommodate students into the foreign culture, we will subvert or reverse the process to make students develop a meta-cultural awareness by critically interrogating the communicative rules prescribed. An example can be provided from how some teachers in the University of Jaffna subvert the expectations of *AKL* in creative and productive ways. As we discussed in Chapter 4, the textbook presents situations, interactions, and communicative rules of Anglo-

American communities as the ones foreign students have to master in order to communicate appropriately in English. Apart from posing the threat of cultural hegemony, these values and practices are irrelevant for local students in their own communities. What some teachers have done, however, is to use the situations and dialogs as a springboard for critical reflection. So in the lesson on the 'Talkative Lady'—who misses her bus because her conversational style was not focused—teachers would provide a series of discussion questions (not anticipated by the authors of the textbook) to encourage students to explore from different perspectives:

- Why did the lady miss the bus? Why does the situation appear comical (for the writers of the textbook)? What are the authors teaching about proper ways of talking?
- How does this compare with typical ways of talking in our society? Do speakers have similar ways of digressing and deviating from the 'point' in conversations? Why do we do that? What cultural factors influence us to behave so in our conversations?
- How does the direct conversation style of the Westerners (as represented in the book) appear to you? Why would it be perceived pejoratively in our community?
- How would our indirect conversational style appear to Westerners? Why would our conversational norms appear comical to them?
- To what extent should we maintain our own communicative norms in order to assert our identity and values? To what extent should we accommodate to the conversational styles of 'native' English speakers when we interact with them?

The idea here is to problematize the cultural messages of the textbook so that students will attain a critical understanding of the competing communicative practices. For this purpose, the cultural conflicts that develop in classrooms should not be ignored or resolved but exposed, so that students can explore them critically. The point behind these exercises is not to find a correct answer; it is to enable students to move in and out of cultures since the very process of doing so develops sociolinguistic competence of a higher level than envisioned by communicative pedagogies.

The above demonstration also suggests how poorly-funded institutions in the periphery can still use for critical learning purposes the (often) unsuitable textbooks supplied by center cultural agencies. Such teaching materials can be exploited to develop meta-discursive awareness. Teachers don't have to refuse to use the American book or use only locally-produced material. In fact, in an underdeveloped educational institution teachers often do not enjoy such an alternative. They have to make do with the available texts. More positively, the cultural capital of the mainstream communities does provide certain valuable analytical skills, intellectual resources, and social values for marginalized students. From this perspective, the colonial curriculum based on situations from Western culture and readings from canonical Western literature can still be tapped for the resources they offer for periphery students—as long as they are also demythologized for their hidden ideologies.[1]

On the other hand, it is very important to use readings from minority writers and even oral or folk texts from the students' own communities. Such a practice will demonstrate to them that their own cultural capital is valued by the school. This will provide them confidence to tap their own linguistic and discursive resources and further develop them. Note how the students on their own initiative bring in texts from the vernacular into the English classroom. The glosses and safe houses show texts from Tamil movies, traditional proverbs, and contemporary resistance songs being employed in the pedagogical activities of the students. But even here, minority students must be encouraged to critically analyze their own discourses, to realize their strengths and limitations, and discover their relevance to mainstream discourses and social contexts.

In a pedagogy that encourages students to cross cultural and discursive borders, we must integrate popular culture and serious literature, play with rigor, art with scholarship, imagination with intellect. In fact, we see in the graffiti and underlife discourses reported above how students themselves bring sources of popular culture (i.e. cinema, liberation songs, popular lyrics) from outside the classroom to inform their learning. There is a playfulness as they imaginatively reconstruct the situations and characters in fascinating new ways. Cartoons, caricature, and painting complement their learning in the safe houses. We should be mindful of the criticism made against critical pedagogues, that they give too much importance to rationalistic learning approaches as being congenial for student empowerment (Atkinson 1997). Often these supposedly critical thinking strategies are borrowed from Western cultural traditions. Such teaching approaches also ignore the cultural and pedagogical traditions of non-Western communities which display a greater tendency to integrate passion, affect, intuition, and aesthetics into their non-formal pedagogies.

An advantage of ethnographically orientating to the learning strategies adopted by the students and developing pedagogies bottom-up is that we are able to interrogate the orthodoxies in critical pedagogy itself. Not everything that passes for a critical pedagogy (CP) automatically qualifies as providing methods and strategies suitable for periphery classrooms. We must realize that CP is itself motivated by social practice and brings with it the assumptions and influences of the communities where it is defined. But certain brands of CP define teaching in terms that are universally applicable to all student groups, irrespective of the cultural, social, and material differences characterizing the learning situation. For example, activities prescribed in ESL textbooks as ways of encouraging critical thinking are modeled on Eurocentric thought processes. Ramanathan and Kaplan (1996) show that syllogistic, Aristotelian, or Toulminian forms of argumentation are employed in ESL composition textbooks with the assumption that they are conducive to developing critical thinking among any student group. Schenke and Pennycook (1995) discuss how writers of certain textbooks assume that these are more progressive than the others by virtue of their learner-centered approach. We have considered in the chapters above how students use certain product-oriented methods as strategies of opposition to the ideological domination resulting from certain learner-centered approaches. Teachers like Rani effectively integrate product-oriented activities into a pedagogy that engages students in developing critical discursive awareness.

Still another axiom of CP is that talk indicates, encourages, or constitutes critical learning. The ability to articulate one's personal views is taken to mean that the student is developing a critical perspective in opposition to the teachers, authorities, and institutionalized discourses. With this in mind, most classrooms are organized in a student-driven, hyperactive, supravoluble fashion, where students have much scope for conversation, discussion, and interaction.[2] Another assumption taken for granted by many critical pedagogues is that a confrontational approach is conducive to critical thinking. bell hooks (1989) has made a powerful argument that challenging the limited values and biased assumptions students bring into the classroom leads to deeper social awareness and changes in values. Although confrontation may be unpleasant, blunt, and painful, such an approach may expose and eventually reduce many hidden prejudices and suppressed tensions in the classroom (also Miller 1994). However, there are many important reasons why students may shy away from confrontation and discussion. Some may even be motivated by oppositional reasons.

To show the limitation of these assumptions I wish to take up for more extended consideration the phenomenon of classroom underlife in the chapters above. The safe houses show that there may be learning processes of considerable critical potential that may be passive, silent, and non-confrontational in the public domain. In the glosses students inscribe in textbooks, in the secretive exchange of codes and discourses, and in the underlife, we see how practices of critique, resistance, and even discursive appropriation may take place away from the public site. To understand their place we must recognize that negotiating discourses in the classroom involves negotiating power as well. It is unwise for critical pedagogues to imagine that students have the freedom to transcend the institutionalized forms of power in the classroom to engage in creative linguistic experimentation and text production. Through the grading system, the evaluation practices, teacher authority, and curricular agendas, the educational institution poses a threat to the discursive experimentation and creativity of students. Therefore students often seek the safe houses to cope with the structures of in-stitutionalized power. Safe houses enable students to experiment with language and make efforts towards discursive resistance without penalization. The safe house is not there merely to provide relief from the rigors of the course, as assumed by Pratt (1991).[3]

My ethnography shows many significant pedagogical uses of this site for oppositional learning:

- This site enables students to express subtle forms of opposition to classroom ideologies without jeopardizing their chances of academic success by openly resisting the institution.
- It is a site that nurtures collaboration among students for interaction, play, and alternate curricular agendas as a response to the boredom, alienation, and threats of schooling.
- It is a site that encourages pride in students' own cultural and discursive traditions and provides a safe site to celebrate and nurture them.
- It is a subversive site of alternative community, based on values that differ from the classroom and institutional culture.
- It is an educationally productive site that enables students to engage with classroom proceedings even as they remain somewhat detached from institutional agendas and authorities.

Other educational research confirms that, paradoxically, classroom underlife is not dysfunctional, but pedagogically valuable (W. Anderson *et al.* 1990, Brooke 1987, Canagarajah 1997b, Giroux 1992: 33). It is possible that the need and uses of safe houses by students are motivated by the cultural and historical background of their communities. Scott (1985) and Adas (1992) argue that the powerless in periphery communities have displayed subtle and indirect forms of opposition from pre-colonial times. These are after all 'the weapons of the weak' (to evoke the title of Scott's book) who may not always find overt forms of resistance practical, desirable, or effective. Goffman (1961) and Kochman (1981) show how marginalized communities in the center may display such surreptitious forms of opposition that are ideologically productive.

While the students who were portrayed in the preceding chapters identify institutional gaps and niches in the school to develop safe houses by themselves, teachers can consider other ways to nurture such sites in their classrooms. Small group discussions, peer reviews/interactions, collaborative writing, and paired assignments are simple ways in which students can be provided scope for experimentation and independence. Collaborative projects, guided fieldwork, and research activities (in libraries, dormitories, or off campus) enable students to construct safe houses outside classrooms. We must also become sensitive to what is typically regarded as disruptive behavior during class time—such as the ubiquitous whispers, secret notes, and digressive comments in classroom underlife—for what they show about incipient oppositional discourses and critical learning strategies of the students.

We need to also find ways of bringing the surreptitious and unacknowledged uses of L1 into the open. We learn from empirical studies on classroom practices that overly teacher-fronted pedagogies often deny possibilities for students to employ their vernacular and local discourses to inform their learning.[4] It is clear, however, that a collaborative learning environment offers sufficient flexibility for students to use their preferred linguistic forms.

Some useful strategies emerge from the creative ways students themselves use L1 in their learning process without teacher initiative or support. Students collaborate in the learning process by using their own languages to negotiate the lesson content in peer group or one-to-one interactions (as in example 12 in Chapter 6). Teachers can creatively set up situations where students may use L1 to assist their learning process even when teachers are not proficient in the vernaculars of their students or when they stick to the official policy of English-only in the more formal learning situations. Following are some of the strategies that encourage L1 usage:

- Setting up small groups for tasks and discussion with students from the similar language groups.
- Pairing more proficient students with less proficient students of the same language group for peer tutoring provides opportunities for peer translation of text or teacher instruction.
- Encouraging the use of bilingual dictionaries and provision of native language reference books will enable students to deal with L1 written material and negotiate bilingual literacy.
- Maintaining journals will help to provide students with ways to use their own languages or mixed codes for expressing themselves imaginatively.

In order to understand and exploit safe houses for pedagogical purposes, teachers have to become ethnographers who are prepared to unravel the hidden cultures of their classrooms and students. This need compels teachers to creatively devise ways to participate in the different learning sites and interactions in their classrooms. It is not difficult to adopt suitable research orientations and pedagogical practices to gain access to the insurgent discourses and literacies in our classrooms and campuses. Apart from the institutional boundaries and cultural borders we have to cross to discern the many discourses practiced by our students in our classrooms, we have also to transcend ideological barriers to see atypical forms of behavior as loaded with meaning and significance. To consider safe house or oppositional behavior as not educationally disruptive but pedagogically engaging requires ideological shifts in teachers' perspectives. Teachers are therefore compelled to critically examine their own location in the matrix of dominant and subordinate discourses in the society and the academy.

In fact, the role of the teacher in critical pedagogy has undergone justifiable questioning. The typical position teachers adopt, as ideologically informed agents who have the requisite knowledge and skills to lead students to empowerment, ignores the cultural capital students themselves bring with them. In the instinctive forms of everyday opposition in the chapters above, we find that students already come with oppositional perspectives and values that constitute a critical attitude to schooling. It is condescending to think that students have to be led by the nose to express opposition. It is also dangerous—and self defeating—that students should depend on authority figures to orchestrate their oppositional behavior (Ellsworth 1989). This attitude, furthermore, is unhealthy for teachers who may feel unmotivated to cultivate the openness to learn from students' alternate strategies and perspectives which can further 'educate' them on the challenges and possibilities of critical teaching (Giroux 1992: 34–5). We must insist, then, that teachers too must become border-crossers and practice a pedagogy that negotiates competing discourses and cultures. It might even become necessary for teachers to be researchers (at least in informal ways) to learn from their students and constantly rethink their pedagogical practice.[5] Such undertakings as teacher-led classroom research and classroom ethnography play a useful function in developing such a practice.

As we see above, the learning experience of students creatively complicates the prescriptions of pedagogues—critical or otherwise. It is perhaps such misleading and narrow axioms behind the practice of CP that have led to the embarrassing predicament of students resisting pedagogies of resistance (Auerbach *et al.* 1996, Delpit 1995). An easy way to explain this is to say that students are blinded by reactionary ideologies to appreciate the aims and processes of CP. But resistance to CP has to be treated seriously if teachers are to learn more about the values and attitudes of students. Such resistance may suggest ways in which CP can be defined and practiced more effectively in terms of the backgrounds, needs, and aspirations of the student communities. It is certainly important to ground pedagogies of resistance in the everyday life of student groups if the teaching is to hold relevance to them.

While it is important to respect students in their actual discursive and cultural contexts, we must not go away with the impression that teachers must remain passive in the classroom or romanticize student culture. We must guard against essentializing all student groups as coming with adequate conscientization and ideological clarity. In previous chapters we found how students are sometimes influenced by questionable discourses and accommodationist learning strategies. The sensationalism, sexism, and pornography we found in the students' graffiti in Chapter 4 need to be interrogated—whether they are borrowed from local or Western media. The contradictory strands in their culture, straddling a valorization of contemporary Marxist/nationalist discourses on the one hand and traditional Hindu religious discourses on the other need to be unraveled. The pitfalls of adopting a product-oriented and examination-motivated learning strategy also needs to be exposed (even if it may contain some oppositional value). Students must also be encouraged to bring their resistant learning strategies into the public forums from the safety of the safe houses if they are to initiate more constructive changes in education and society. In undertaking such a task we must recognize the effects of domination in shaping the thinking, values, and behavior of colonized communities. There is pressure on minority communities to accept the world view of the dominant groups. Giroux reminds us that 'subordinate cultures are situated and recreated within relations of domination and resistance, and they bear the marks of both' (1983: 229). Hence the ambiguities in student culture.

The paradoxical responsibility as it emerges from this consideration is that while teachers appreciate the socio-cultural specificity of their student groups by listening attentively to their different voices and traditions, they will also interrogate the limitations of students' discourses to lead them to the effective practice of appropriated discourses. It is through such a critical awareness of the capabilities and limitations of their students, matched by their own balance between humility and confrontation, that teachers can acquire what Grossberg (1994) calls 'earned authority' in the classroom. In such a context, the teacher–student relationship has to be negotiated anew according to the culture of the different student groups. Teachers need to aim for a proper balance between criticism and respect, leadership and solidarity. Opening up the domain of pedagogy for negotiation, so that students can hold equal responsibility for negotiating the necessary pedagogy for their purposes, also democratizes the language classroom. As has been pointed out by Allwright (1984), both teachers and students should be considered 'managers of learning'. In fact, such classroom practice makes the learning experience more 'participatory' (Auerbach 1994) as teachers and students actively negotiate the curriculum and pedagogy.

ELT methods, as they are currently defined and practiced, stifle such reflexivity and negotiation as they enforce a partisan set of values, thought processes, and learning strategies as the norm. The emergent post-method movement, however, liberates learners and teachers from the totalizing control of methods and encourages them to develop the reflexive approach I have articulated above in order to construct pedagogies suitable to their respective contexts. In this reflexive and negotiated process of pedagogy there is scope for developing a context-sensitive and culture-specific approach to language teaching. Such an orientation to pedagogy functions as a heuristic to develop appropriate practices from bottom up. These learning strategies would also straddle the different skills (i.e. speaking, writing, listening, reading) that are traditionally compartmentalized in language teaching. We have to note also that this approach deals with the thorny problem of center/periphery inequalities in pedagogical transfer. This pedagogy can potentially enable periphery learning communities to conduct language learning in terms that are relevant and effective to their socio-cultural context and needs. It thus challenges the bases of center expertise. In the absence of preconstructed methods, teachers are thrust completely into local classrooms to discover relevant pedagogical approaches in negotiation with their students. Rather than looking at the classrooms through the spectacles offered by ready-made methods, they open themselves more fully to the realities of their educational context. Periphery teachers would become authorities in their own way—as nobody else (least of all, center practitioners) can understand better the linguistic needs and learning styles of local students. Such an approach will de-center the terms of expertise, as each periphery community will develop its own strategies of negotiating discourses according to its needs, aspirations, and educational traditions.

Such a pedagogical attitude checks the prescriptivism and essentialism that has been considered to harm certain models of critical pedagogy. CP has been exalted into a recipe for educational success. The principles and concepts influencing CP have been turned into a list of golden rules or maxims which have prescriptive value for most teachers (Simon 1992). Perhaps unwittingly, even otherwise guarded critical pedagogues have fallen into the trap of reducing their thinking into slogans and labels for the convenience of busy practitioners (Giroux 1992).[6] Defining critical pedagogy into a list of dos and dont's irrespective of the different learning contexts, and institutionalizing it, takes the edge out of this well-meant approach. It may even reify the very evils local communities might be attempting to overcome. It is important not to take CP as a settled body of practices, but to problematize its assumptions and strategies. It is in this manner that we can maintain the critical edge of CP and ensure its ability to speak relevantly to different pedagogical situations. Therefore we must reconceive critical pedagogy as a dynamic heuristic—a set of provocative questions or challenging concerns that need to be answered in ongoing engagement with the material and discursive background of the different learning groups.

Conclusion

It is important to understand the extent to which classroom resistance may play a significant role in larger transformations in the social sphere. To say that signs of critical thinking, writing, or reading mean that such students are assured of political and material empowerment is to exaggerate matters. To think that such signs are indications of imminent political transformation and social reconstruction is to simplify such processes. Although the school has an obvious connection in the reproduction of power structures, material and ideological realities have a life of relative autonomy that needs to be tackled in its own right. We must also remember, as it was exemplified in the chapters above, that there are a range of attitudes and motivations characterizing student resistance: some are individualistic and adventurous, others are collective and organized; some are instinctive and vague, others are reflective and informed; some result in accommodation, others are extremist and idealistic. Therefore oppositional acts need be interrogated carefully for their potential in relation to the social context. It is also important to understand that accommodation and resistance are an ongoing dynamic that characterizes social relations for marginalized communities. The view of pedagogical politics as a zero-sum game—where victory is all or nothing—is another exaggeration by certain versions of CP that has to be revised (MacLaren 1994). We therefore have to explore cautiously how pedagogy can be located in the ongoing struggles of communities for empowerment.

But it is an important theme of this book that the classroom is a significant site in the reconfiguration of larger social structures and processes. Too often scholars in language planning have conducted their theorizing at macro-social levels, ignoring the everyday processes of linguistic appropriation and resistance that take place in such local sites as the classroom. In fact, the classroom is not a microcosm of society, but society itself—involving the relationships, values, and conflicts experienced in collective life. The linguistic struggles and communicative practices displayed in the classroom give remarkably sharp insights into the problems and prospects facing periphery communities today. They enable us to plan linguistic and social relations bottom-up, revealing emergent patterns of discourses and community. Appropriating English while maintaining their vernaculars makes periphery subjects linguistically competent for the culturally hybrid post-modern world they confront. The maintenance of polyvocality with a clear awareness of their own socio-ideological location empowers them to withstand the totalitarian tendencies—of local nationalist regimes and Western multinational agencies—enforced through uniformity of thought and communication. The simplest gestures of code-switching and linguistic appropriation in the pedagogical safe houses suggest the strategic ways by which discourses may be negotiated, intimating the resilient ability of human subjects to creatively fashion a voice for themselves from amidst the deafening channels of domination.

Notes

1 Paulo Freire (1970), in his literacy courses for peasants in Brazil, has similarly incorporated texts from both mainstream and marginalized communities to conscientize learners and develop critical literacy skills. Kramsch (1993) too demonstrates how existing communicative textbooks can be used for reflexive pedagogies.

2 Schenke (1991) points out that even silence may constitute a mode of opposition to the existing pedagogical practice. Student silence can be motivated by histories of violence, racism, and domination that may be evoked by instructional codes and texts. These silences can be productive if they can be sensitively tapped and students are made to interrogate the sources of these inhibitions.

3 Pratt is among the first to define safe houses in ELT circles. For her these are 'social and intellectual spaces where groups can constitute themselves as horizontal, homogeneous, sovereign communities with high degrees of trust, shared understandings, and temporary protection from legacies of oppression' (1991: 40). However, her understanding is somewhat misleading as she considers safe houses only as a therapeutic, soothing, passive environment. My research here and elsewhere shows that the site can be of oppositional pedagogical value (Canagarajah 1997b).

4 Pease-Alvarez and Winsler (1994) insightfully point out that the task-based, student-centered, whole-language pedagogy employed by the monolingual teacher in the school they observed contained sufficient latitude for students to accommodate their vernacular in the learning process. This insight is ironically confirmed by Jo Arthur's 1995 study in Botswana primary schools where the teachers' employment of a teacher-fronted pedagogy helped impose English-only practices. Similarly, Heller in her research on French language-minority schools in Ontario (Canada) shows how the Initiation–Response–Feedback structure of teacher-centered classroom talk provides avenues for the legitimization of standard French as the official language (Heller 1995).

5 Grossberg (1994) goes further to develop this perspective into 'a pedagogy of articulation and risk' since listening to students and learning from them challenges the traditional authority of the teacher. Giroux too argues that teachers learn from students in his border-crossing pedagogy (1992: 34–5).

6 Giroux (1992) encapsulates what he calls 'Border Pedagogy' into three principles (in Chapter 2 of his *Border Crossings*); later, calling this a 'Post-modern Pedagogy' he sums it up in nine points (in Chapter 3); again, defining a 'Post-colonial Pedagogy' he provides seven principles (in Chapter 5). Much of this activity of labeling and formalizing results from a rush to institutionalize CP as an acceptable body of scholarship.

Bibliography

Achebe, C. 1975. *Morning Yet on Creation Day*. London: Heinemann.

Adas, M. 1992. 'From avoidance to confrontation: Peasant protest in precolonial and colonial Southeast Asia' in N. Dirks (ed.). *Colonialism and Culture*. Ann Arbor: University of Michigan Press.

Alcoff, L. 1988. 'Cultural feminism vs. poststructuralism: The identity crisis in feminist theory'. *Signs* 13: 418–34.

Allwright, R. L. 1984. 'The importance of interaction in classroom language learning'. *Applied Linguistics* 5: 156–71.

Althusser, L. 1969. *For Marx*. Trans. Ben Brewster. London: Allen Lane.

Althusser, L. 1971. 'Ideology and ideological state apparatuses (Notes towards an investigation)' in *Lenin, Philosophy and other Essays*. London: New Left Books.

Anderson, G. 1989. 'Critical ethnography in education: Origins, current status, and new directions'. *Review of Educational Research* 59: 249–70.

Anderson, W., C. Best, A. Black, J. Hurst, B. Miller, and S. Miller. 1990. 'Cross-curricular ablex: A collaborative report on ways with academic words'. *College Composition and Communication* 41: 11–36.

Anyon, J. 1980. 'Social class and the hidden curriculum of work'. *Journal of Education* 162: 67–92.

Appadurai, A. 1994. 'Disjuncture and difference in the global cultural economy' in P. Williams and L. Chrisman (eds.). *Colonial Discourse and Post-Colonial Theory*. New York: Columbia University Press.

Apple, M. 1971. 'The hidden curriculum and the nature of conflict'. *Interchange* 2: 27–40.

Apple, M. 1986. *Teachers and Texts: A Political Economy of Class and Gender Relations in Education*. New York: Routledge and Kagan Paul.

Aronowitz, S. and H. Giroux. 1985. *Education under Siege: The Conservative, Liberal and Radical Debate over Schooling*. South Hadley, Mass.: Bergin and Harvey.

Aronowitz, S. and H. Giroux. 1993. *Education Still under Siege: The Conservative, Liberal and Radical Debate over Schooling*. South Hadley, Mass.: Bergin and Harvey.

Arthur, J. 1995. 'Policies, practices and pedagogy: A case study of language in Botswana primary schools'. Unpublished doctoral dissertation. Lancaster University.

Arumuga, N. 1872. *Yaalpaana samaya nilai* [Religion in Jaffna]. Reprinted, Jaffna: Navalar Sabai, 1951.

Arunachalam, Sir Ponnambalam. (undated) *The Speeches and Writings of Sir Ponnambalam Arunachalam*. Vol. 1. Colombo: Cave.

Asad, T. (ed.). 1973. *Anthropology and the Colonial Encounter*. London: Ithaca Press.

Atkinson, D. 1997. 'A critical approach to critical thinking in TESOL'. *TESOL Quarterly* 31/1: 71-94.

Auerbach, E. R. 1993. 'Reexamining English only in the ESL classroom'. *TESOL Quarterly* 27: 9–32.

Auerbach, E. R. 1994. 'Participatory action research'. *TESOL Quarterly* 28: 693–7.

Auerbach, E. R. with B. Barahona, J. Midy, F. Vaquerano, A. Zambrano, and J. Arnaud. 1996. *Adult ESL Literacy from the Community to the Community: A Guidebook for Participatory Literacy Training*. Mahwah, NJ: Lawrence Erlbaum.

Bakhtin, M. M. 1981. *The Dialogic Imagination*. Austin: University of Texas Press.

Barber, B. 1995. *Jihad vs McWorld: How the Planet is Both Falling Apart and Coming Together—and What This Means for Democracy*. New York: Times Books.

Baugh, J. 1983. *Black Street Speech*. Austin: University of Texas Press.

Beach, R. and L. Bridwell. 1984. 'Learning through writing: A rationale for writing across the curriculum' in A. D. Pellegini and T. D. Yawey (eds.). *The Development of Oral and Written Language in Social Contexts*. Norwood, NJ: Ablex.

Beardsmore, H. B. 1993. 'European models of bilingual education: Practice, theory, and development'. *Journal of Multilingual and Multicultural Development* 14: 103–20.

Bereiter, C. and S. Engelmann. 1966. *Teaching Disadvantaged Children in the Pre-school*. Englewood Cliffs, NJ: Prentice-Hall.

Bernstein, B. 1971a. *Class, Codes and Control* 1. London: Routledge and Kegan Paul.

Bernstein, B. 1971b. 'On the classification and framing of educational knowledge' in M. Young (ed.). *Knowledge and Control*. London: Collier Macmillan.

Bernstein, B. 1977. *Class, Codes and Control* 3. London: Routledge and Kegan Paul.

Bernstein, B. 1981. 'Codes, modalities, and the process of cultural reproduction: A model'. *Language in Society* 10: 327–63.

Bhabha, H. K. 1991. 'The post-colonial critic'. *Arena* 96: 61–3.

Bizzell, P. 1982. 'Cognition, convention and certainty: What we need to know about writing'. *PRE/TEXT* 3: 213–43.

Blanc, M. and J. F. Hamers. 1982. 'Social networks and multilingual behaviour: The Atlantic provinces project'. Paper given at the 4th Sociolinguistics Symposium, University of Sheffield.

Blommaert, J. 1992. 'Codeswitching and the exclusivity of social identities: Some data from Campus Kiswahili' in C. Eastman (ed.). *Codeswitching*. Clevedon: Multilingual Matters.

Bourdieu, P. 1977. 'The economics of linguistic exchanges'. *Social Science Information* 16: 645–68.

Bourdieu, P. 1979. 'Symbolic power'. *Critique of Anthropology* 4: 77–85.

Bourdieu, P. 1984. *Distinction: A Social Critique of the Judgement of Taste*. Trans. R. Nice. Cambridge, Mass.: Harvard University Press.

Bourdieu, P. and J-P. Passeron. 1977. *Reproduction in Education, Society and Culture*. London: Sage.

Bowers, R. 1980. 'The background of students from the Indian subcontinent'. *ELT Documents 109: Study Modes and Academic Development of Overseas Students*. London: The British Council.

Bowles, S. and H. Gintis. 1977. *Schooling in Capitalist America*. New York: Basic Books.

Brooke, R. 1987. 'Underlife and writing instruction'. *College Composition and Communication* 38: 141–53.

Brown, D. H. 1991. 'TESOL at twenty-five: What are the issues?' *TESOL Quarterly* 25: 245–60.

Butler, J. 1990. *Gender Trouble*. New York: Routledge.

Camilleri, A. 1996. 'Language values and identities: Codeswitching in secondary classrooms in Malta'. *Linguistics and Education* 8: 85–104.

Canagarajah, A. S. 1987. *Contrastive Rhetoric: A Critique and a Proposal*. (Monograph B 171) Duisburgh: Linguistic Agency, University of Duisburgh.

Canagarajah, A. S. 1992. 'Research report: an ethnography of argumentative discourse in a Saiva Tamil village'. Mimeo. Research and higher degrees committee, University of Jaffna, Sri Lanka.

Canagarajah, A. S. 1993a. 'Up the garden path: Second language writing approaches, local knowledge, and pluralism'. *TESOL Quarterly* 27: 301–6.

Canagarajah, A. S. 1993b. 'Critical ethnography of a Sri Lankan classroom: Ambiguities in opposition to reproduction through ESOL'. *TESOL Quarterly* 27: 601–26.

Canagarajah, A. S. 1993c. 'American textbooks and Tamil students: A clash of discourses in the ESL classroom'. *Language, Culture and Curriculum* 6: 143–56.

Canagarajah, A. S. 1994. 'Competing discourses in Sri Lankan English poetry'. *World Englishes* 13: 361–76.

Canagarajah, A. S. 1995a. 'Use of English borrowings by Tamil fish vendors: manipulating the context'. *Multilingua* 14: 5–24.

Canagarajah, A. S. 1995b. 'The political economy of code choice in a revolutionary society: Tamil/English bilingualism in Jaffna'. *Language in Society* 24: 187–212.

Canagarajah, A. S. 1995c. 'Functions of code switching in the ESL classroom: Socialising bilingualism in Jaffna'. *Journal of Multilingual and Multicultural Development* 16: 173–96.

Canagarajah, A. S. 1995d. 'Task-based method appropriated: Center methods in periphery communities'. Paper presented at TESOL, Long Beach.

Canagarajah, A. S. 1995e. Review of *Linguistic Imperialism. Language in Society*: 24: 590–95.

Canagarajah, A. S. 1996. 'Non-discursive requirements in academic publishing, material resources of periphery scholars, and the politics of knowledge production'. *Written Communication* 13: 435–72.

Canagarajah, A. S. 1997a. 'Teaching and researching the thesis/dissertation in ESP'. Panel presentation (with D. Atkinson, D. Belcher, A. Hirvela, and T. Dudley-Evans). TESOL, Orlando.

Canagarajah, A. S. 1997b. 'Safe houses in the Contact Zone: Coping Strategies of African American Students in the Academy'. *College Composition and Communication* 48:173–96.

Canagarajah, A. S. and M. S. Iyer. 1993. 'Social inequality and the distribution of English proficiency among Jaffna university students'. Paper presented to the Jaffna Science Association, University of Jaffna, Sri Lanka.

Canagaratne, A. J. 1982. 'WASP ideology: the kernel of the American Kernel Lessons'. *Lanka Guardian* 5: 15–18.

Casey, D. J. 1968. 'The effectiveness of teaching English as a foreign language to some Finnish secondary schools'. Unpublished report. University of Helsinki.

Chamot, A. U. and J. M. O'Malley. 1994. *The CALLA Handbook: Implementing the Cognitive Academic Language Learning Approach*. Reading, Mass.: Addison-Wesley.

Chappell, V. C. 1992. *Seventeenth Century Natural Scientists*. New York: Garland.

Chelliah, J. V. 1922. *A Century of English Education*. Vaddukoddai: Jaffna College.

Chick, K. 1996. 'Safe-talk: Collusion in apartheid education' in H. Coleman (ed.). *Society and the Classroom: Social Explanation for Behavior in the Language Class*. Cambridge: Cambridge University Press.

Connor, U. 1996. *Contrastive Rhetoric: Cross Cultural Aspects of Second Language Writing*. Cambridge: Cambridge University Press.

Coomarasamy, A. K. 1946. *The Religious Basis of the Forms of Indian Society*. New York: Noonday.

Coomarasamy, A. K. 1957. *The Dance of Shiva*. New York: Noonday.

Coward, R. and J. Ellis. 1977. *Language and Materialism: Developments in Semiology and the Theory of the Subject*. London: Routledge and Kegan Paul.

Crystal, D. 1997. *English as a Global Language*. Cambridge: Cambridge University Press.

Cumming, A. 1994. 'Alternatives in TESOL research: descriptive, interpretive, and ideological orientations'. *TESOL Quarterly* 28/4: 673–704.

Cummins, J. 1991. 'Interdependence of first and second language proficiency in bilingual children' in E. Bialystok (ed.). *Language Processing in Bilingual Children*. Cambridge: Cambridge University Press.

de George, R. and F. de George (eds.). 1972. *The Structuralists: From Marx to Lévi-Strauss*. New York: Doubleday Anchor.

de Lauretis, T. 1986. *Feminist Studies/Critical Studies*. Bloomington: Indiana University Press.

de Souza, L. M. 1994. 'Post colonial literature and a pedagogy of re-visioning: the contribution of Wilson Harris'. *Claritas* 1: 55–61.

Delpit, L. 1990. 'Dilemmas of a progressive Black educator'. Paper presented in the Conference on College Composition and Communication, Chicago.

Delpit, L. 1995. *Other People's Children: Cultural Conflict in the Classroom*. New York: New Press.

Denzin, N. 1970. *The Research Act*. Chicago: Aldine.

Derrida, J. 1972. 'Structure, sign and play in the discourse of the human sciences' in R. Macksey and E. Donato (eds.). *The Structuralist Controversy: The Languages of Criticism and the Sciences of Man*. Baltimore: Johns Hopkins University Press.

Derrida, J. 1981a. *Dissemination*. Trans. B. Johnson. London: Athlone Press.

Derrida, J. 1981b. *Positions*. Trans. A. Bass. Chicago: University of Chicago Press.

Derrida, J. 1982. *Margins of Philosophy*. Trans. A. Bass. Chicago: University of Chicago Press.

Doughty, C. 1991. 'Instruction does make a difference: The effect of instruction on the acquisition of relativization in English as a second language'. *Studies in Second Language Acquisition* 13: 401–8.

Dreeben, R. 1968. *On What is Learned in Schools*. Reading, Mass.: Addison Wesley.

Dudley-Evans, T. and J. Swales. 1980. 'Study modes of students from the Middle East'. *ELT Documents 109: Study Modes and Academic Development of Overseas Students*. London: The British Council.

Duranti, A. 1992. 'Language in context and language as context: The Samoan respect vocabulary' in A. Duranti and C. Goodwin (eds.). *Rethinking Context: Language as an Interactive Phenomenon*. Cambridge: Cambridge University Press.

Eastman, C. M. 1992. 'Codeswitching as an urban language-contract phenomenon' in C. M. Eastman (ed.) *Codeswitching*. Clevedon: Multilingual Matters.

Ellsworth, E. 1989. 'Why doesn't this feel empowering? Working through the repressive myths of critical pedagogy'. *Harvard Educational Review* 59: 297–324.

Emeneau, M. B. 1955. 'India and linguistics'. *Journal of the American Oriental Society* 75: 143–53.

Emig, J. 1977. 'Writing as a mode of learning.' *College Composition and Communication* 28: 122–8.

Faigley, L. 1986. 'Competing theories of process: A critique and proposal'. *College English* 48: 527–42.

Fairclough, N. 1989. *Language and Power*. London: Longman.

Faltis, C. and S. Hudelson. 1994. 'Learning English as an additional language in K-12 schools'. *TESOL Quarterly*, 28/3: 457–68.

Ferguson, R., M. Gever, T. Minh-ha, and C. West (eds.). 1990. *Out There: Marginalization and Contemporary Cultures*. Cambridge, Mass.: MIT Press.

Fernando, S. 1994. 'Taking stock of university ELT and planning for the nineties' in M. Gunasekera *et al.* (eds.). *Compendium of University ELT Papers: 1987-1991*. Colombo: ELT units of Sri Lankan universities.

Fetterley, J. 1978. *The Resisting Reader: A Feminist Approach to American Fiction*. Bloomington: Indian University Press.

Feyarabend, P. 1975. *Against Method*. London: Verso.

Fishman, J. A. 1967. 'Bilingualism with and without diglossia: diglossia with and without bilingualism'. *Journal of Social Issues* 32: 29–38.

Flinders, D. J. and E. W. Eisner. 1994. 'Educational criticism as a form of qualitative inquiry'. *Research in the Teaching of English* 28: 341–57.

Flower, L. and J. R. Hayes. 1981. 'A cognitive process theory of writing'. *College Composition and Communication* 32: 365–87.

Foucault, M. 1972. 'The discourse on language' in *The Archeology of Knowledge*. Trans. A. M. Sheridan Smith. New York: Pantheon.

Foucault, M. 1980. *Power/Knowledge: Selected Interviews and other Writings 1972–77*. New York: Pantheon.

Fowler, R. 1985. 'Power' in T. A. Tuan van Dijk (ed.). *Handbook of Discourse Analysis*. Vol. 4. London: Academic Press.

Fowler, R., B. Hodge, G. Kress, and A. Trew (eds.). 1979. *Language and Control*. London: Routledge and Kegan Paul.

Fowler, R. and G. Kress. 1979. 'Critical Linguistics' in Fowler *et al. Language and Control*. London: Routledge and Kegan Paul.

Frank, A. G. 1969. *Latin America: Underdevelopment or Revolution*. New York: Monthly Review Press.

Freire, P. 1970. *Pedagogy of the Oppressed*. New York: Herder.

Freire, P. 1985. *The Politics of Education*. South Hadley, Mass.: Bergin and Garvey.

Fulwiler, T. 1982. 'Writing: An act of cognition' in C. W. Griffin (ed.). *Teaching Writing in All Disciplines*. San Francisco: Jossey-Bass.

Gadamer, H. 1981. *Reason in the Age of Sciences*. Trans. F. Laurence. Cambridge, Mass.: MIT Press.

Gal, S. 1989. 'Language and political economy'. *Annual Review of Anthropology* 18: 345–67.

Galtung, J. 1971. 'A structural theory of imperialism'. *Journal of Peace Research* 8: 81–117.

Galtung, J. 1980. *The True Worlds: A Transnational Perspective*. New York: Free Press.

Gardner, R. C. and W. E. Lambert. 1972. *Attitudes and Motivation in Second Language Learning*. Rowley, Mass.: Newbury House.

Gass, S. 1982. 'From theory to practice' in M. Hines and W. Rutherford (eds.). *On TESOL '81*. Washington DC: TESOL.

Geertz, C. 1983. *Local Knowledge: Further Essays in Interpretive Anthropology*. New York: Basic Books.

Giddens, A. 1990. *The Consequences of Modernity*. Stanford: Stanford University Press.

Giles, H. (ed.). 1984. 'The dynamics of speech accommodation'. *International Journal of the Sociology of Language* 46.

Giroux, H. A. 1979. 'Writing and critical thinking in the social studies'. *Curriculum Inquiry:* 291–310.

Giroux, H. A. 1983. *Theory and Resistance in Education: A Pedagogy for the Opposition*. South Hadley: Bergin.

Giroux, H. A. 1992. *Border Crossings: Cultural Workers and the Politics of Education*. New York: Routledge.

Giroux, H. A. and R. Simon. 1984. 'Curriculum study and cultural politics'. *Journal of Education* 166: 211–36.

Giroux, H. A. and P. McLaren. (eds.). 1994. *Between Borders: Pedagogy and the Politics of Cultural Studies*. New York: Routledge.

Goffman, E. 1961. *Asylums: Essays on the Social Situation of Mental Patients and Other Inmates*. New York: Anchor.

Goodwin, C. and A. Duranti. 1992. 'Rethinking context: an introduction' in A. Duranti and C. Goodwin. *Rethinking Context: Language as an Interactive Phenomenon*. Cambridge: Cambridge University Press.

Gooneratne, Y. 1971. *Bird Word Motif*. Colombo: Tisara.

Goonetilleke, D. C. R. A. 1983. 'Language planning in Sri Lanka'. *Navasilu* 5: 13–18.

Grosjean, F. 1989. 'Neurolinguists, beware! The bilingual is not two monolinguals in one person'. *Brain and Language* 36: 3–15.

Grossberg, L. 1994. 'Introduction: Bringin' it All Back Home—Pedagogy and Cultural Studies' in H. Giroux and P. McLaren (eds.). *Between Borders: Pedagogy and the Politics of Cultural Studies*. New York: Routledge.

Grubb, H. J. 1986. 'The Black parole and whitespeak: Black English from an Orwellian perspective'. *Race and Class* 27: 67–80.

Gunesekera, M., M. Jayewardene, L. Gunawardene, S. Fernando, S. Ilangakoon, and S. Sivasuriya (eds). 1994. *Compendium of University ELT Papers: 1987–91.* Colombo: ELT units of Sri Lankan universities.

Gysels, M. 1992. 'French in urban Lubumbashi Swahili: codeswitching, borrowing, or both' in C. Eastman (ed.). *Codeswitching.* Clevedon: Multilingual Matters.

Hairston, M. 1982. 'The winds of change: Thomas Kuhn and the revolution in the teaching of writing'. *College Composition and Communication* 33: 76–88.

Halverson, J. 1966. 'Prologomena to the study of Ceylon English'. *University of Ceylon Review* 24: 61–75.

Hamers, J. F. and M. Blanc. 1989. *Bilinguality and Bilingualism.* Cambridge: Cambridge University Press.

Hampson, N. 1968. *A Cultural History of the Enlightenment.* New York: Pantheon.

Hanson-Smith, E. 1984. 'A plan for the improvement of English instruction in Sri Lanka'. *Navasilu* 6: 26–30.

Haraway, D. 1989. *Primate Visions: Gender, Race, and Nature in the World of Modern Science.* New York: Routledge.

Harding, S. 1986. *The Science Question in Feminism.* Ithaca: Cornell University Press.

Harding, S. 1991. *Whose Science? Whose Knowledge? Thinking from Women's Lives.* Ithaca: Cornell University Press.

Harland, R. 1987. *Superstructuralism: The Philosophy of Structuralism and Post-Structuralism.* London: Methuen.

Harlow, B. 1987. *Resistance Literature.* New York: Methuen.

Harris, J. 1989. 'The idea of community in the study of writing'. *College Composition and Communication* 40: 11–22.

Harris, W. 1992. 'The radical imagination' in A. Raich and M. Williams (eds.). *The Radical Imagination: Lectures and Talks by Wilson Harris.* Liège: University of Liège Press.

Hassan, I. 1987. *The Post-modern Turn: Essays in Post-modern Theory and Culture.* Columbus: Ohio University Press.

Hawkey, R. and C. Nokornchai. 1980. 'Thai students studying' in *ELT Documents 109: Study Modes and Academic Development of Overseas Students.* London: The British Council.

Heath, S. B. 1983. *Ways With Words.* Cambridge: Cambridge University Press.

Heller, M. 1992. 'The politics of codeswitching and language choice' in C. Eastman (ed.). *Codeswitching.* Clevedon: Multilingual Matters.

Heller, M. 1995. 'Language choice, social institutions and symbolic domination'. *Language in Society* 24: 373–405.

Hess, D. J. 1995. *Science and Technology in a Multicultural World.* New York: Columbia University Press.

Hodge, R. and G. Kress. 1988. *Social Semiotics.* Ithaca: Cornell University Press.

Holborow, M. 1993. Review of *Linguistic Imperialism. ELT Journal* 47: 358–60.

Holliday, A. 1994. *Appropriate Methodology and Social Context.* Cambridge: Cambridge University Press.

hooks, b. 1989. *Talking Back: Thinking Feminist, Thinking Black.* Boston: South End Press.

hooks, b. 1990. 'Choosing the margin as a space for radical openness'. *Yearning: Race, Gender and Cultural Politics.* Boston: South End.

hooks, b. 1994. 'Eros, eroticism, and the pedagogical process' in H. Giroux and P. McLaren (eds.). *Between Borders: Pedagogy and the Politics of Cultural Studies.* New York: Routledge.

Hornberger, N. 1994. 'Ethnography'. *TESOL Quarterly* 28: 688–90.

Howard, R. M. 1995. 'Plagiarisms, authorships, and the academic death penalty'. *College English* 57: 788–806.

Huff, T. 1993. *The Rise of Early Modern Science: Islam, China, and the West*. Cambridge: Cambridge University Press.

Hutcheon, L. 1988. *The Poetics of Post-modernism*. London: Routledge and Kegan Paul.

Hutcheon, L. 1989. *The Politics of Post-modernism*. London: Routledge and Kegan Paul.

Hymes, D. (ed.). 1969. *Reinventing Anthropology*. New York: Pantheon.

Jameson, F. 1990. *Post-modernism or the Cultural Logic of Late Capitalism*. Durham: Duke University Press.

Jeyasuriya, J. E. (undated). 'The indigenous religious traditions in education' in *Educational Policies and Progress during British Rule in Ceylon*. Colombo: Associated Educational Publishers.

Kachru, B. B. 1986. *The Alchemy of English: the Spread, Functions and Models of Non-Native Englishes*. Oxford: Pergamon.

Kachru, B. B. 1991. 'Liberation linguistics and the Quirk concerns'. *English Today* 25: 3-13.

Kachru, Y. 1994. 'Monolingual bias in SLA research'. *TESOL Quarterly*, 28/4: 795–800.

Kandiah, T. 1984. '"Kaduva": Power and the English language weapon in Sri Lanka' in P. Colin-Thome and A. Halpe (eds.). *Honouring E. F. C. Ludowyk*. Colombo: Tisaro Prakasayo.

Kaplan, R. B. 1966. 'Cultural thought patterns in intercultural education'. *Language Learning* 16: 1–20.

Kochman, T. 1981. *Black and White Styles in Conflict*. Chicago: University of Chicago Press.

Kolb, D. 1986. *The Critique of Pure Modernity*. Chicago: University of Chicago Press.

Kramsch, C. 1993. *Context and Culture in Language Teaching*. Oxford: Oxford University Press.

Kress, G. and A. Trew. 1978. 'Ideological transformation of discourse: or how the *Sunday Times* got its message across'. *Journal of Pragmatics* 2 : 311–29.

Kress, G. 1983. 'Linguistic processes and the mediation of "reality": the politics of newspaper language'. *International Journal of the Sociology of Language* 40: 43–57.

Kress, G. 1985. 'Ideological structures in discourse' in T. A. Tuan van Dijk (ed.). *Handbook of Discourse Analysis*. Vol. 4. London: Academic Press.

Kuhn, T. S. 1962. *The Structure of Scientific Revolutions*. Chicago: University of Chicago Press.

Kumaravadivelu, B. 1994. 'The postmethod condition: (E)merging strategies for second/foreign language teaching'. *TESOL Quarterly* 28: 27–48.

Labov, W. 1972. *Language in the Inner City: Studies in the Black English Vernacular*. Philadelphia: University of Pennsylvania Press.

Labov, W. 1984 . 'Field methods of the project on linguistic change and variation' in J. Baugh and J. Sherzer (eds.). *Language in Use*. Englewood Cliffs: Prentice Hall.

Lane, M. (ed.). 1970. *Introduction to Structuralism*. New York: Doubleday Anchor.

Larsen, N. 1990. *Modernism and Hegemony*. Minneapolis: University of Minnesota Press.

Lather, P. 1991. *Getting Smart: Feminist Research and Pedagogy with/in the Post-modern*. New York: Routledge.

Law, J. D. 1993. *The Rhetoric of Empiricism: Language and Perception from Locke to I. A. Richards*. Ithaca: Cornell University Press.

Leki, I. 1995. 'Coping strategies of ESL students in writing tasks across the curriculum'. *TESOL Quarterly* 29: 235–60.

Levin, L. 1972. *Comparative Studies in Foreign Language Teaching*. Stockholm: Almqvist and Wiksell.

Lindholm, J. 1980. 'A note on the nobility of women in popular Tamil fiction' in S. Wadley (ed.). *The Powers of Tamil Women*. New York: Syracuse University.

Lindstrom, L. 1992. 'Context contests: debatable truth statements on Tanna (Vanuatu)' in A. Duranti and C. Goodwin (eds.). *Rethinking Context: Language as an Interactive Phenomenon*. Cambridge: Cambridge University Press.

Long, M. H. and G. Crookes. 1992. 'Three approaches to task-based syllabus design'. *TESOL Quarterly* 26: 27–56.

Loomba, A. 1994. 'Overworlding the "Third World"' in P. Williams and L. L. Chrisman (eds.). *Colonial Discourse and Post-Colonial Theory: A Reader*. New York: Columbia University Press.

Lucas, T. and A. Katz. 1994. 'Reframing the debate: The roles of native languages in English-only programs for language minority students'. *TESOL Quarterly* 28: 537–62.

Lunn, E. 1982. *Marxism and Modernism*. Berkeley: University of California Press.

Lyotard, J-F. 1984. *The Post-modern Condition: a Report on Knowledge*. Minneapolis: University of Minnesota Press.

MacDonell, D. 1986. *Theories of Discourse: an Introduction*. Oxford: Blackwell.

Maley. A. 1986. 'Xanadu – "A miracle of rare device" ' in J. M. Valdes (ed.). *Culture Bound*. Cambridge: Cambridge University Press.

Marcus, G. and M. M. J. Fischer. 1986. *Anthropology as Cultural Critique: an Experimental Moment in the Human Sciences*. Chicago: University of Chicago Press.

Martin-Jones, M. and M. Heller. 1996. 'Introduction to the special issues on education in multilingual settings: Discourse, identities, and power: Part 1: Constructing legitimacy'. *Linguistics and Education* 8: 3–16.

Martin-Jones, M. and M. Saxena. 1996. 'Turn-taking, power asymmetries, and the positioning of bilingual participants in classroom discourse'. *Linguistics and Education* 8: 105–30.

McCrimmon, J. M. 1984. 'Writing as a way of knowing' in R. L. Graves (ed.). *Rhetoric and Composition*. Upper Montclair, N. J.: Boynton/Cook.

McLaren, P. 1994. 'Multiculturalism and the post-modern critique: Toward a pedagogy of resistance and transformation' in H. Giroux and P. McLaren (eds.). *Between Borders: Pedagogy and the Politics of Cultural Studies*. New York: Routledge.

Mehan, H. 1985. 'The structure of classroom discourse' in T. A. van Dijk (ed.). *Handbook of Discourse Analysis*. Vol. 3. London: Academic Press.

Mendis, G. C. (ed.). 1956. *The Colebrook–Cameron Papers* Vols. 1–2. London: Oxford University Press.

Merrit, M. 1982. 'Repeats and reformulations in primary classrooms as windows on the nature of talk engagement'. *Discourse Processes* 5: 127–45.

Merrit, M., A. Cleghorn, J. Abagi, and G. Bunyi. 1992. 'Socialising multilingualism: Determinants of codeswitching in Kenyan primary classrooms' in C. Eastman (ed.). *Codeswitching*. Clevedon: Multilingual Matters.

Miller, R. 1994. 'Fault lines in the contact zone'. *College English* 56: 389–408.

Miller, T. and L. Emel. 1988. 'Modern methodology or cultural imperialism'. Paper presented at TESOL, Chicago.

Mills, P. 1987. *Women, Nature, and Psyche*. New Haven: Yale University Press.

Milroy, L. 1987. *Observing and Analysing Natural Language*. Oxford: Blackwell.

Minh-ha, T. 1989. *Women, Native, Other*. Bloomington: Indiana University Press.

Mishra, V. and B. Hodge. 1991. 'What is post-colonialism?' *Textual Practice* 5/3: 399–414.

Mohan, B. 1986. *Language and Content*. Reading, Mass.: Addison-Wesley.

Mohan, B. and W. Lo. 1985. 'Academic writing and Chinese students: Transfer and developmental factors'. *TESOL Quarterly* 19: 515–34.

Mohanty, C. 1988. 'Under Western eyes: Feminist scholarship and colonial discourses'. *Feminist Review* 30: 65–88.

Mohanty, C. 1990. 'On race and voice: challenge for liberal education in the 1990s'. *Cultural Critique* Winter 1989/90: 179–208.

Morris, T. 1991. *The Despairing Developer: Diary of an Aid Worker in the Middle East.* London: Tauris.

Muchiri, M., G. Nshindi, G. Mulamba, and B. Deoscorous. 1995. 'Importing composition: Teaching and researching academic writing beyond North America'. *College Composition and Communication* 46: 175–98.

Murphy, R. 1986. *Culture and Social Anthropology: An Overture.* Englewood Cliffs: Prentice Hall.

Myers-Scotton, C. 1990. 'Élite closure as boundary maintenance: The case of Africa' in B. Weinstein (ed.). *Language Policy and Political Development.* Norwood, N. J.: Ablex.

Myers-Scotton, C. 1992. 'Comparing codeswitching and borrowing' in C. Eastman (ed.). *Codeswitching.* Clevedon: Multilingual Matters.

Nandy, A. (ed.). 1988. *Science, Hegemony, and Violence.* Delhi: Oxford University Press.

Nunan, D. 1990. 'Action research in the language classroom' in J.C. Richards and D. Nunan (eds.). *Second Language Teacher Education.* Cambridge: Cambridge University Press.

Nunan, D. 1991. 'Ignorance or bliss? The current state of research in second language classrooms' in P. Drury and R. Wijesinha (eds.). *Aspects of Teaching and Learning English as a Second Language.* Maharagama, Sri Lanka: National Institute of Education.

Okara, G. 1964. *The Voice.* London: Heinemann.

Okara, G. 1990. 'Towards an evolution of the African language for African literature'. *Kunapipi* 12: 11–18.

O'Neill, R., T. Yeadon, and E. T. Cornelius. 1978. *American Kernel Lessons: Intermediate.* New York: Longman.

Osterloh, K. 1986. 'Intercultural differences and communicative approaches to foreign language teaching in the Third World' in J. M. Valdes (ed.). *Culture Bound.* Cambridge: Cambridge University Press.

Oxford, R. 1990. *Language Learning Strategies: What Every Teacher Should Know.* New York: Newbury House.

Pandit, I. 1986. *Hindi English Code Switching: Mixed Hindi English.* Delhi: Datta Book Centre.

Parakrama, A. 1995. *De-hegemonizing Language Standards.* Basingstoke: Macmillan.

Parker, O. D. and Educational Services Staff AMIDEAST. 1986. 'Cultural clues to the Middle-Eastern Student' in J. M. Valdes (ed.). *Culture Bound.* Cambridge: Cambridge University Press.

Parthasarathy, R. 1976. *Rough Passage.* Delhi: Oxford University Press.

Passe, H. 1943. 'The English language in Ceylon'. *University of Ceylon Review* 1: 50–65.

Pease-Alvarez, L. and A. Winsler. 1994. 'Cuando el maestro no habla español: Children's bilingual language practices in the classroom'. *TESOL Quarterly* 28: 507–36.

Peirce, B. 1989. 'Towards a pedagogy of possibility in teaching of English internationally'. *TESOL Quarterly* 23: 401–20.

Peirce, B. 1995. 'Social identity, investment, and language learning'. *TESOL Quarterly* 29: 9–32.

Pennington, M. 1995. 'The teacher change cycle'. *TESOL Quarterly* 29: 705–32.

Pennycook, A. 1989. 'The concept of "method", interested knowledge, and the politics of language teaching'. *TESOL Quarterly* 23: 589–618.

Pennycook, A. 1994a. *The Cultural Politics of English as an International Language.* London: Longman.

Pennycook, A. 1994b. 'Critical pedagogical approaches to research'. *TESOL Quarterly* 28: 690–3.

Pennycook, A. 1996. 'Borrowing others' words: Text, ownership, memory, and plagiarism'. *TESOL Quarterly* 30: 201–30.

Perinbanayagam, R. S. 1988. 'The social foundation of educational and economic activity in Jafna, Sri Lanka' in M. Chitralega *et al.* (eds.). *Kailasapathy Commemoration Volume.* Jaffna: Catholic Press.

Phillipson, R. 1992. *Linguistic Imperialism*. Oxford: Oxford University Press.
Poplack, S., S. Wheeler, and A. Westwood. 1987. 'Distinguishing language contact pheonmena: Evidence from Finnish–English bilingualism' in P. Lilius and M. Saari (eds.). *The Nordic Languages and Modern Linguistics* 6. Helsinki: University of Helsinki Press.
Prabhu, N. S. 1990. 'There is no best method–Why?' *TESOL Quarterly* 24: 161–76.
Pratt, M. 1991. 'Arts of the contact zone'. *Profession* 91. New York: MLA.
Purves, A. (ed.). 1988. *Writing across Languages and Cultures: Issues in Contrastive Rhetoric*. Newbury Park, Cal.: Sage.
Pushparajan, M. 1985. 'Piiniks' in R. Cheran., A. Jesurajah, I. Padmanaba, and P. Natarasan (eds.). *maraNattuL vaaLvoom: 31 kavijarkaLin 82 arasiyal kavitaikaL* ['Let's live amidst death: A collection of 82 political poems in Tamil by 31 poets']. Jaffna: Tamiliyal.

Quirk, R. 1990. 'Language varieties and standard language'. *English Today* 21: 3–10.

Raheem, R., N. Abeysekera, M. Fernando, and N. Yildiz. 1987. *Proceedings of the Conference on ELT in Universities 1986*. Colombo: ELT units of Sri Lankan universities.
Raimes, A. 1985. 'What unskilled ESL students do as they write: A classroom study of composing'. *TESOL Quarterly* 19: 229–58.
Raimes, A. 1987. 'Language proficiency, writing ability, and composing strategies: A study of ESL college student writers'. *Language Learning* 37: 439–68.
Raimes, A. 1991. 'Out of the woods: Emerging traditions in the teaching of writing'. *TESOL Quarterly* 25: 407–30.
Rajan, R. 1993. 'Fixing English: Nation, language, subject' in R. S. Rajan (ed.). *The Lie of the Land: English Literary Studies in India*. Oxford: Oxford University Press.
Ramanathan, V. and R. Kaplan. 1996. 'Some problematic "channels" in the teaching of critical thinking: Some implications for L2 student-writers'. Paper presented at the AAAL Annual Meeting, Chicago.
Rao, R. 1938. *Kanthapura*. Delhi: Oxford University Press.
Resnik, M. 1993. 'ESL and language planning in Puerto Rico'. *TESOL Quarterly* 27: 259–73.
Ricento, T. 1994. Review of *Linguistic Imperialism*. *TESOL Quarterly* 28: 421–7.
Richards, J. and T. Rogers. 1986. *Approaches and Methods in Language Teaching: A Description and Analysis*. Cambridge: Cambridge University Press.
Rodriguez, R. 1981. *Hunger of Memory: The Education of Richard Rodriguez*. Boston: Godine.
Romaine, S. 1989. *Bilingualism*. Oxford: Blackwell.
Rose, M. 1989. *Lives on the Boundary*. New York: Penguin.
Ruthven, K. 1984. *Feminist Literary Studies: An Introduction*. Cambridge: Cambridge University Press.
Ryan, M. 1989. *Politics and Culture: Working Hypothesis for a Post-Revolutionary Society*. Baltimore: Johns Hopkins University Press.

Sabel, C. 1982. *Work and Politics: the Division of Labor in Industry*. New York: Cambridge University Press.
Said, E. 1979. *Orientalism*. New York: Random House.
Said, E. 1993. *Culture and Imperialism*. New York: Alfred Knopf.
Said, E. 1995. 'East isn't east: the impending end of the age of orientalism'. *Times Literary Supplement* 3 February No. 4792: 3–5.
Sampson, G. 1984. 'Exporting language teaching methods from Canada to China'. *TESL Canada Journal* 1: 19–31.
Saussure, F. de. 1959. *Course in General Linguistics*. Trans. Wade Baskin. New York: The Philosophical Library.
Savignon, S. 1991. 'Communicative language teaching: State of the art'. *TESOL Quarterly* 25: 261–77.

Schalk, P. 1990. 'The concept of martyrdom in Tamil discourse'. *Lanka* 5: 1–35.

Schegloff, E. 1992. 'In another context' in A. Duranti and C. Goodwin (eds.). *Rethinking Context: Language as an Interactive Phenomenon*. Cambridge: Cambridge University Press.

Schenke, A. 1991. 'The "will to reciprocity" and the work of memory: Fictioning speaking out of silence in ESL and feminist pedagogy'. *Resources for Feminist Research* 20: 47–55.

Schenke, A. and A. Pennycook. 1995. 'Questioning empowerment: Is learner-centered pedagogy enough?' Paper presented in the TESOL convention, Long Beach.

Scheurich, J. J. and M. D. Young. 1997. 'Colouring epistemologies: Are our research epistemologies racially biased?' *Educational Researcher* 26/4: 4–17.

Schimitt, E. 1996. 'House approves measure on official U.S. language'. *New York Times*, 2 September: Part A, 10.

Scott, J. C. 1985. *Weapons of the Weak: Everyday Forms of Peasant Resistance*. New Haven: Yale University Press.

Scotton, C. 1983. 'The negotiation of identities in conversation: A theory of markedness and code choice'. *International Journal of the Sociology of Language* 44: 116–36.

Selinker, L. 1972. 'Interlanguage'. *International Review of Applied Linguistics* 10: 209–31.

Sessional Paper. Sessional Paper 1867. Sessional Paper 8.

Sheen, R. 1994. 'A critical analysis of the advocacy of the task-based syllabus'. *TESOL Quarterly* 28: 127–53.

Shih, M. 1986. 'Content-based approaches to teaching academic writing'. *TESOL Quarterly* 20: 617–48.

Shor, I. (ed.). 1987. *Freire for the Classroom: a Sourcebook for Liberatory Teaching*. Portsmouth: Heinemann.

Showalter, E. (ed.). 1989. *Speaking of Gender*. New York: Routledge.

Silva, T. 1993. 'Toward an understanding of the distinct nature of L2 writing: The ESL research and its implications'. *TESOL Quarterly* 27: 657–78.

Simon, R. 1987. 'Empowerment as a pedagogy of possibility'. *Language Arts* 64: 370–83.

Simon, R. 1992. *Teaching against the Grain: Essays towards a Pedagogy of Possibility*. Boston, Mass.: Bergin and Garvey.

Sirisena, U. D. I. 1969. 'Editorial introduction' in *Education in Ceylon: Part 1*. Colombo: Ministry of Education and Cultural Affairs.

Sivatamby, K. 1979. 'English and the Tamil Writer'. *Navasilu* 3: 53–60.

Sivatamby, K. 1990. 'The ideology of Saiva–Tamil integrality: Its sociohistorical significance in the study of Yalppanam Tamil society'. *Lanka* 5: 176–82.

Skutnabb-Kangas, T. 1994. 'Linguistic human rights and minority education'. *TESOL Quarterly* 28: 625–8.

Slavin, R. S., S. Sharan, R. Kagan, C. Hertz-Lazarowitz, and R. Schmuck. (eds.). 1985. *Learning to Cooperate, Cooperation to Learn*. New York: Plenum.

Smith, P., Jr. 1970. 'A comparison of the cognitive and audio-lingual approaches to foreign language instruction' in *The Pennsylvania Foreign Language Project*. Philadelphia: Center for Curriculum Development.

Smith, P. 1988. *Discerning the Subject*. Minneapolis: University of Minnesota Press.

Smitherman, G. (ed.). 1981a. *Black English and the Education of Black Children and Youth*. Detroit: Wayne State University Center for Black Studies Press.

Smitherman, G. 1981b. 'What go round come round: King in perspective'. *Harvard Educational Review* 57: 40–56.

Smitherman, G. 1984. 'Black language as power' in C. Kramrae, M. Schulz, and W. M. O'Barr (eds.). *Language as Power*. Beverly Hills: Sage.

Smolicz, J. 1980. 'Core values and cultural identity'. *Ethnic and Racial Studies* 4: 75–90.

Somasegaram, S. W. 1969. 'The Hindu tradition' in U. D. I. Sirisena (ed.). *Education in Ceylon: Part 3*. Colombo: Ministry of Education and Cultural Affairs.

Spack, R. 1988. 'Initiating ESL students into the academic discourse community'. *TESOL Quarterly* 22: 29–51.

Spellmeyer, K. 1989. 'Foucault and the freshman writer: considering the self in discourse'. *College English* 51: 715–29.

Spivak, G. 1990. *The Post-Colonial Critic*. New York: Routledge.

Spivak, G. 1993. 'The burden of English studies' in R. S. Rajan (ed.). *The Lie of the Land: English Literary Studies in India*. Oxford: Oxford University Press.

Sridhar, S. 1994. 'A reality check for SLA theories'. *TESOL Quarterly* 28: 800–5.

Stanford Working Group. 1993. *Federal Education Programs for Limited-English Proficient Students: A Blue Print for the Second Generation*. Palo Alto, CA: Stanford University.

Strutt, E. 1913. *A Missionary Mosaic from Ceylon*. London: Charles Kelley.

Stubbs, M. 1976. *Language, Schools and Classrooms*. London: Methuen.

Suseendirarajah, S. 1992. 'English in our Tamil society: A sociolinguistic appraisal'. Mimeo. Academic Forum, University of Jaffna, Sri Lanka.

Swales, J. 1980. 'The educational environment and its relevance to ESP programme design' in *Projects in Materials Design. ELT Documents Special*. London: The British Council.

Swigart, L. 1992. 'Two codes or one? The insider's view and the description of codeswitching in Dakar' in C. Eastman (ed.). *Codeswitching*. Clevedon: Multilingual Matters: 83–102.

Tannen, D. 1982. *Spoken and Written Language: Exploring Orality and Literacy*. Norwood, NJ: Ablex.

Tawney, R. 1964. *Religion and the Rise of Capitalism: an Historical Study*. London: Murray.

Taylor, H. 1989. *Standard English, Black English, and Bidialectalism: A Controversy*. New York: Peter Lang.

Tennant, J. 1850. *Christianity in Ceylon*. London: John Murray.

Terdiman, R. 1985. *Discourse/Counter-Discourse*. Ithaca: Cornell University Press.

TESL-L Digest. 1995a. 'Re: L1 in class'. 17 November.

TESL-L Digest. 1995b. 'Re: L1 in the classroom'. 19 November.

Trew, A. 1979. 'Theory and ideology at work' in Fowler *et al.* (eds.). *Language and Control*. London: Routledge and Kegan Paul.

Tuman, M. 1988. 'Class, codes, and composition: Basil Bernstein and the critique of pedagogy'. *College Composition and Communication* 39/1: 42–51.

van Dijk, T. A. 1985. *Handbook of Discourse Analysis*. 4 Vols. London: Academic Press.

Vandrick, S. 1995. 'Privileged ESL university students'. *TESOL Quarterly* 29: 375–80.

Vignarajah, S. 1994. *Approaches of the American Mission in Teaching the English Language during the British Period in Jaffna*. Unpublished diploma thesis. English Language Teaching Centre, University of Jaffna, Sri Lanka.

Viswanathan, G. 1993. 'English in a literate society' in R. S. Rajan (ed.). *The Lie of the Land: English Literary Studies in India*. Oxford: Oxford University Press.

von Elek, T. and M. Oskasson. 1973. *Teaching Foreign Language Grammar to Adults: A Comparative Study*. Stockholm: Almqvist and Wiksell.

wa Thiong'o, N. 1986. *Decolonizing the Mind: the Politics of Language in African Literature*. London: Currey, Heinemann.

wa Thiong'o, N. 1990. 'Return of the native tongue'. *Times Literary Supplement*, September 14–20: 972, 985.

Wallace, M. 1990. *Invisibility Blues*. London: Verso.

Wallerstein, I. 1974. *The Modern World-System, 1: Capitalist Agriculture and the Origins of the European World-Economy in the Sixteenth Century*. New York: Academic Press.

Wallerstein, I. 1991. *Geopolitics and Geoculture*. Cambridge: Cambridge University Press.

Walsh, C. 1991. *Pedagogy and the Struggle for Voice: Issues for Language, Power and Schooling for Puerto Ricans*. Toronto: OISE Press.

Watson-Gegeo, K. 'Ethnography in ESL: defining the essentials'. *TESOL Quarterly* 22: 575–92.

Wickramasuriya, S. 1976. 'Strangers in their own land: The radical protest against English education in colonial Ceylon'. *Navasilu* 1: 15–31.

Wickramasuriya, S. 1981. 'James de Alwis and Second Language Teaching in Sri Lanka'. *Navasilu* 4: 11–29.

Widdowson, H. G. 1984. *Explorations in Applied Linguistics* 2. Oxford: Oxford University Press.

Widdowson, H. G. 1987. 'The roles of teacher and learner'. *English Language Teaching Journal*, 41/2: 83–8.

Widdowson, H. G. 1993. 'Proper words in proper places'. *ELT Journal* 47/4: 317–29.

Widdowson, H. G. 1994. 'The ownership of English'. *TESOL Quarterly* 28/2: 377–88.

Widdowson, H. G. 1996. 'Authenticity and autonomy in ELT'. *ELT Journal* 50/1: 67–8.

Wikkramasinha, L. 1965. *Luster Poems*. Kandy: Ariya.

Wilkins, R. 1971. 'Black nonsense'. *Crisis Vol 78*: 78.

Williams, P. and L. Chrisman. 1994. 'Colonial discourse and post-colonial theory: An introduction' in *Colonial Discourse and Post-Colonial Theory: A Reader*. New York: Columbia University Press.

Williams, R. 1977. *Marxism and Literature*. London: Oxford University Press.

Willis, P. 1977. *Learning to Labor: How Working Class Kids Get Working Class Jobs*. Manchester: Saxon House.

Willis, P. 1978. *Profane Culture*. London: Routledge.

Willis, P. 1983. 'Cultural production and theories of reproduction' in L. Barton and S. Walker (eds.). *Race, Class and Education*. London: Croom Helm.

Woolard, K. 1985. 'Language variation and cultural hegemony: toward an integration of sociolinguistic and social theory'. *American Ethnologist* 12: 738–48.

Zamel, V. 1982. 'Writing: The process of discovering meaning'. *TESOL Quarterly* 16: 195–209.

Zamel, V. 1983. 'The composing process of advanced ESL students: Six case studies'. *TESOL Quarterly* 17: 165–87.

Index

The index refers to the Introduction and Chapters 1 to 8.
References to chapter notes are indicated by '*n*'.

academic texts and discourses, appropriation 147–98
academic vs. non-academic discourses 154
action research 53–4
agendas 82–4
  hidden 80
ambivalences
  towards colonial English 58–60
  towards standard English 184
American Kernel Lessons: Intermediate (AKL) 85–8, 100–1
Anglicism and Orientalism 58–9, 63
appropriation
  of discourses 173–98
  of teaching methods 117–22
  of texts 147–71
Arumuga Navalar 66–7, 176
Asia Foundation 83–4, 85, 99*n*3, 111
assimilationist ideology 152

back-channeling cues 133, 134
BANA countries 43–4, 105
Batticotta Seminary 62–3, 66, 77*n*2
Bernstein, B. 105, 106, 107
'betrayal' of the vernacular 1–2
bilingualism
  in education 128–9, 144–5*n*2
  élite 72, 74–5
  passive 69
Black Vernacular English 184
border pedagogy 187, 198*n*5, *n*6
borrowings, from English 73, 77*n*5, 139, 140–1
British Council 40–1, 83
'broken English' 140
'busy work' syndrome 115

capitalism 18–19
caste 61, 62

center agencies and organizations 40–1, 81–2, 83–5, 99*n*3, *n*5
center Englishes 4
center/periphery 4, 7*n*2, 43
Chiac 75
Chomsky, N. 127–8
cinema, students' glosses from 89–90
class (social stratification), 61, 72
classes, size 110
classroom
  curriculum policy and practice 79–101
  underlife 92–3, 137–9, 191–2
classroom culture 81
classroom discourse 125–46
classroom facilities 109–10
classroom interaction 125–46
classroom management 131–4
classroom studies 51–2
codes
  choice 73–6
  linguistic stratification 72–3
  negotiation 73–6, 125–46
code-switching 75, 131–5, 139–44
'cognitive process' 122*n*2
collectionist pedagogies 44, 105–6
colonization 18–19, 60–7, 182
community studies 52
competence 127–8, 140–1
composition, teaching 148–53
conceptual concerns 120
content-focused approach 149, 151, 152, 169*n*3
contrastive linguistics hypothesis 127
coping strategies
  students' 88–93, 100*n*8
  teachers' 111–17, 123*n*8
critical ambivalences
  towards colonial English 58–60
  towards standard English 184

critical ethnography 47–55
critical pedagogy (CP) 9–37, 190–1, 194, 196
critical (post-colonial) thinking 2, 33–5, 190–1
cultural agencies of center 40–1, 81–2, 83–5, 99*n3*, *n5*
cultural capital 28
cultural hegemony 31–2
cultural reproduction models 27–8
culture 31–2, 44
    lived 93–4, 96
current-traditional paradigm 148
curricula 79–101
    hidden 14, 23, 85–8
'curse of Caliban' 100*n9*

decolonization 67–73
deductive method 108
democratization of English 175
descriptive ethnography 48
descriptive orientation 40
dialogical learning method 108–9
dialogism 185
diglossic Tamil 63, 69, 70
discourse *definition* 30
discourses, appropriation 147–98
dissertations, students' 158–65

economic reproduction models 27, 36*n6*
'educational criticism' 123*n7*
'educational shock' 99*n5*
élites 61, 67, 69, 72, 74–5
empirical approach 18
empowerment
    minority communities 175
    periphery teachers 120–1
    students 181
Englishes, center/periphery 4, 88, 179–81
Englishized Hindi 75
Englishized Tamil 70–1, 72
Enlightenment tradition 17–19, 20, 63
ESL writing pedagogy 148–53
ethnographic present 47–8
ethnographic realism 50
ethnography 47–55
'expanding circle' 4
'expressive process' 122*n2*

factionalism vs. globalization 76
films, students' glosses from 89–90
form-focused (product-oriented) approach 95–7, 105–7, 122*n3*, 148–53
fossilized items 128

Freire, Paolo 20, 35, 197*n1*

geopolitics 7*n2*, 40–6
Giroux, H. A. 36*n5*, 97–8, 122*n2*, 150, 151, 187, 198*n6*
'give back what they give' 1–2
globalization vs. nationalism 76
glosses, in student textbooks 88–93, 95, 97, 190, 191
Gooneratne, Yasmine 177–8
gossip 134
grammar-based approaches 111, 114
grounded theory 5
guru-shisya tradition 60, 108

hegemony 31–2, 71, 183–5
hidden curricula 14, 23, 85–8
hidden ideologies 97
hidden languages and discourses 143
Hindi, Englishized 75
historical perspective 57–77
Holliday, A. 5, 40, 43–6, 99*n1*, 105–6
hooks, bell 35, 183–4
hybridity 75, 182

identity formation 183–5
'ideological liberation' 100–1
ideological reproduction models 27
ideological state apparatus 27
ideological tensions 85–93
ideologies 30, 40
    hidden 97
    of language 36–7*n11*
imperialism 48, 182–3
    linguistic 40–3
indigenization 67
indigenous Englishes 4, 88, 179–81
indigenous vs. Western cultures 1, 154
inductive thought 18
industry, Western 18–19
informal learning approach 109
informant-researcher relationship 49–50
Initiation-Response-Feedback structure 137, 198*n4*
insider/outsider status 48, 54
instrumental ideology 150, 152
integrationist pedagogies 44, 105–6
integrative motivation 95, 99*n7*
intellectuals 35
interaction ideology 151, 152
interlanguage model 128
internationalism 76
'internationalist' community 71

interpersonal concerns 119
interpretive orientation 40
interviews, for research 49–50, 55n5

knowledge 16, 18, 19, 32–3

language 29–30, 36–7n11
  of critique 26
  of possibility 26
  socialization 139–43
'large-class culture' 110
learning
  CP and MP frameworks 15–17
  methods 108–10
  strategies 88–93
  styles 95–6
lesson content 134–7
'liberated zone' 67–8, 77n4
'library language' 82–3
linguicism 41
linguistic capital 28
linguistic genocide 127
linguistic imperialism 40–3
linguistic insecurity, teachers' 141
linguistic interdependence principle 128
linguistic stratification 72
literacies 147–71
literate vs. oral discourse conventions 154
lived culture 93–4, 96
location, politics of 35

macro-societal theoretical perspective 6,
  41–2
mainstream pedagogy (MP) 15–17
Maltese 145n6
Marxism 27, 28, 35
methods, teaching 103–23
micro-politics of post-structuralism 29–30
micro-social perspective 42–3
minorities, empowerment 175
missionaries 61–7, 77n2, 109, 156
modality splitting 131–4
'monolingual bias' 77n6, 128
monolingual fallacy 126–7
motivation, students' 94–5, 96, 99n7, 100n8,
  173–4

nationalism vs. globalization 76
nationalist vs. universalist position 176–8
native-speaker competence 127–8
native-speaker fallacy 126
native vs. non-native English communities 4

negotiation
  of codes 73–6, 125–46
  of discourses 165–8
  of pedagogies 110–15, 117–20
Ngugi wa Thiong'o 176–7

observer's paradox 88, 116
Okara, Gabriel 178–9
opposition
  students' 79–101
  teachers' 103–23
  to colonialism 62–7
  vs. resistance 98
oral vs. literate discourse conventions 154
Orientalism and Anglicism 58–9, 63
'outer circle' 4
outsider/insider status 48, 54

panopticon 58
participant action research 53–4
pedagogical paradigms 13–17
pedagogy 103–23
  critical (CP) 9–37, 190–1, 194, 196
  mainstream (MP) 15–17
  of appropriating discourses 173–98
  of articulation and risk 198n5
Pennington, M. 119–21, 123n9
Pennycook, A. 5, 58–60, 76–7, 97
periphery/center 4, 7n2, 43
periphery Englishes 4, 88, 179–81
periphery pedagogies 105–10
Phillipson, R. 5, 40–4, 46, 76–7, 87, 99n5
pidginized English 140
plagiarism 159, 170n10
pluralization of English 175
politics
  of appropriating discourses 173–98
  of location 35
positivistic philosophy 18
post-colonial attitudes towards English
  59–60, 71–2
post-colonial communities *definition* 4
post-colonial condition 182–3
post-colonial thinking 33–5
post-method condition 104
post-method movement 195
post-modern view of knowledge 32
post-structuralist perspectives 29–30
power 80
  of center dialects 180–1
  researcher/informant relationships 49,
  55n5
  'writing with' 151

procedural concerns 113, 119
process-oriented approach 105–7, 122*n1*, *n2*
product-oriented (form-focused) approach 95–7, 105–7, 122*n3*, 148–53
proficiency in English 69
Protestant work ethic 61, 62
protest movements 62–7
Puerto Ricans, attitudes to English 96–7

racism 100
reader-focused approach 149, 151, 152
reading, in students' research process 155–7
reflexivity 186–7
relative autonomy of school 28
religion 61, 64–7, 72, 108, 153, 154
reproduction orientation and theories 2, 22, 24–5, 27–9, 36*n6*
researcher-informant relationship 49–50, 55*n5*
research interviews 49–50, 55*n5*
research orientations 39–55
research process, in student writing 154–7
resistance, vs. opposition 98
resistance perspective 2
resistance theories 22–36
're-visioning' 187
rhetorical functions of code-switching 136, 140
rhetorical significance, of borrowings from English 140–1

safe houses 138–9, 186, 191–2, 198*n3*
Said, E. 182–3
Saivism 61–2, 89, 154, 170*n7*
Sanskrit 72
Saussure, F. de 29
science 18–19, 36*n4*
second language acquisition (SLA) theory 127–9
self-translation 74
Selinker, L. 128
sex, students' attitudes towards 90–1
silence, students' 197*n2*
Sinhala 67
'social cognition' 169*n4*
social reproduction 27–8
social stratification 61, 72
standard English 3, 86, 88, 110, 179–81
state agencies 81, 99*n1*
strategies
  coping 88–93, 110–17, 123*n8*
  learning 88–93
  negotiating discourses 165–8

teaching 193–4
  writing 154–68
stratification, social and linguistic 61, 72–3
structuralism 27, 28, 29, 36*n10*, 41–2
students
  coping strategies 88–93
  curriculum 80
  opposition 79–101
  silence 197*n2*
  writing 153–65
'students' lesson' 100*n9*
subjectivity 30–1

'talk back' 183–4
Tamil
  in classroom 131–42, 146*n7*
  code-mixed writing 187
  Englishized 70–1, 72
  Sanskritized 72
  after independence 67–73
  oral and written traditions 154
  prose 63
Tamil community 51–4
Tamilized English 76
task-based teaching 95, 111–15, 123*n6*
teacher change cycle 120–1
teachers
  coping strategies 110–17
  empowerment 120–1
  opposition 103–23
  teaching strategies 193–4
teaching methods 103–23
technology, Western 18–19
TESEP (tertiary, secondary, primary) countries 43–4
textbooks 84–8, 99*n5*, 111, 126
texts
  appropriation 147–71
  relation to discourses 30
  written by students 158–65
thinking, critical and post-colonial 2, 33–5
'third way' 174, 178–9
transformational generative paradigm 127–8
transplanted learners 129

underlife language 92–3, 137–9, 191–2
United States Information Agency 40–1
universalist vs. nationalist position 176–8

values
  in textbooks 87–8
  see also ideologies
vernacularism 1–3, 59, 66

vernacularization 143, 179
voice, gain and development 31, 183–5

Walcott, Derek 1, 179
Western organizations and agencies 40–1,
    81–2, 83–5
Western regimes, imperialist use of
    ethnography 48
Western vs. indigenous cultures and
    knowledge 1–2, 12–14, 154
'white man's burden' 18, 60–7
Widdowson, H. G. 180–90
Wolof 75
women
    forms of knowing 32
    modes of resistance 35
    teachers' coping strategies 123*n8*
work ethic 61, 62
World Standard Spoken English (WSSE) 180
world systems perspective 7*n2*
writer-focused approach 148–9, 150–1, 152
writing
    'as a way of knowing' 149, 169*n3*
    ethnographic, rules 50
    pedagogy 148–53
    students' strategies 154–68
    'with power' 151
Writing Across the Curriculum (WAC) school
    149
written product, students' 158–65